Between Justice and Politics

Between Justice and Politics

THE LIGUE DES DROITS
DE L'HOMME, 1898–1945

William D. Irvine

STANFORD UNIVERSITY PRESS
STANFORD, CALIFORNIA
2007

Stanford University Press
Stanford, California

Printed in the United States of America on acid-free, archival-quality paper

Library of Congress Cataloging-in-Publication Data
Irvine, William D., 1944 –
  Between justice and politics : the Ligue des droits de l'homme, 1898–1945 / William D. Irvine.
    p. cm.
  Includes bibliographical references and index.
  ISBN-13: 978-0-8047-5317-3 (cloth : alk. paper)
  ISBN-10: 0-8047-5317-2 (cloth : alk. paper)
  1. Ligue des droits de l'homme (Paris, France)--History. I. Title.
JC599. 8178 2007
323.0945'09041--dc22   2006026636

Typeset by Thompson Type in 11/14 Adobe Garamond

To Marion, Carl, and Ben

Contents

Acknowledgments

During the long gestation period of this book, a number of individuals have offered me their generous support and encouragement. My old friend Arno J. Mayer suggested the topic to me fifteen years ago in a café in Paris. It was, more than he probably realized, an inspired suggestion and for that, and much else over the last forty years, I am deeply grateful. Wendy Ellen Perry, Norman Ingram, and Cylvie Claveau, good friends all, generously shared with me their incomparable knowledge of the *Ligue des droits de l'homme*. Much of the "heavy lifting" for this book was done by two exceptionally talented research assistants: Diane Labrosse and Sean Kennedy. The staff of the *Bibliothèque de documentation internationale contemporaine* created a warm and inviting atmosphere where it was a pleasure to work. I would like to thank *Historical Reflections/Reflections Historiques* for permission to quote from my article, "Politics of Human Rights: A Dilemma for the Ligue des Droits de l'Homme." 20, 1 (Winter 1994) 5–28, and Berghahn Books for permission to quote from my chapter, "Women's Rights and the 'Rights of Man,'" in Kenneth Mouré and Martin S. Alexander (eds.), *Crisis and Renewal in France: 1918–1962* (New York, 2002). Much of the initial research for this project was made possible by a grant from the Social Sciences and Humanities Research Council of Canada (1995–97).

William Drummond Irvine
Toronto
July 2006

Between Justice and Politics

Introduction

The *Ligue des droits de l'homme* (League of the Rights of Man) was founded in Paris in June 1898. It took its title from the French Revolution's Declaration of the Rights of Man of August 1789. What prompted its foundation was the growing concern about the unjust and illegal conviction for treason of Captain Alfred Dreyfus. But the League long outlived the Dreyfus affair and became, in its first forty years, the largest and most influential civil liberties organization in the world. The closest North American equivalent was the American Civil Liberties Union (ACLU), founded in 1920 and modeled in part after the League. But the League was different from the ACLU in several ways. It was a much larger organization. The League had 8,000 members within two years of its foundation, 80,000 within ten years. At its peak in 1933, it had 180,000 members organized in nearly 2,500 sections. By comparison, thirty years after its foundation the ACLU had barely 9,000 members, 45,000 in 1960, and at its largest in the early 1970s, hardly more than the League, in a nation with a population one-seventh that of the United States, had enjoyed in the early 1930s.[1] Moreover, in the first half of the twentieth century, the League carried far more political clout than the ACLU ever would. In the 1988 presidential contest, George Bush Sr. would make much of the fact that his Democratic opponent, Michael Dukakis was "a card carrying member of the ACLU" and therefore on the extreme left of his party. French conservatives were no more charitably disposed to the League but rarely made an issue out of the League membership of their opponents because it would have been difficult to find, at least by the interwar years, a prominent left-wing politician who did not belong (or had not belonged) to the League.

Despite its prominent role in French political life in the first half of the twentieth century, the last history of the League, very much an insider account, dates from 1927.[2] Until recently, an important reason for the relative historical neglect of the League has been a paucity of archival sources. Although the various house organs of the League, both national and local, provide particularly rich documentation, its archives disappeared in 1940. Anticipating a German invasion of Paris, the League began to pack up its copious archives in June 1940 with the intent of shipping them to safety. Before it could do so, the invading Germans captured them. In 1941 these archives, along with several others, were shipped to Germany where, in 1945 they were, in turn, captured by the Soviet armies. Shipped to Moscow, they became part of a separate and entirely secret "western" section of the Soviet archives. Only in 1991, in the last weeks of the Soviet Union, was their existence finally revealed. There followed a decade of protracted negotiations between the French and Russian governments concerning the eventual repatriation of the archives. Agreement was reached in 2000, and in February 2001 the archives were returned to the *Bibliothèque de Documentation Internationale Contemporaine* in Nanterre. Cataloguing the archives was completed by 2002, at which point they were opened to scholars.

Even before the opening of the archives, the history of the League attracted the attention of a growing number of scholars in France and abroad. This reflects the fact that the League, albeit far smaller than it was in the early decades of the twentieth century, remains an active and vital part of French public life to this day. Moreover, French historians, many of them associated with today's League, tend to view the League as one of the few redeeming features of a Third French Republic that met an inglorious end in June 1940. As a result, much of the existing literature on the pre-1940 League has a "memorializing" quality; as the American historian, Wendy Perry, has noted, the League has become one of the classic *lieux des mémoires,* reverential signposts on the history of France.[3] The League was present at all the finest moments of France from 1898 until 1945. Courageous defenders of Dreyfus, tenacious advocates for victims of arbitrary justice during World War I, the "conscience of democracy" during the heyday of the Third Republic, central architects of the Popular Front to save France from the fascist menace in the 1930s, and finally, victims of a murderous Vichy regime—so goes the heroic version of the League. The subtitle of a recent biography of Victor Basch, fourth president of the League and one of the most admirable figures in French history, is entitled "From the Dreyfus Affair to the crimes of the Milice"—the Milice being the Vichy militia that cruelly murdered Basch and his wife in 1944.[4]

Recent writings on the League have not been, for all that, uncritical.[5] Scholars have paid close attention to the internal divisions within the League, to its relative insensitivity to "the other"[6] and above all to the speciousness of its claim to have been above politics. All acknowledge that the League had a substantial representation in parliament and that politicians played an important role in the directing circles of the League. But few choose to examine carefully who those League politicians were, perhaps because it would turn up some unexpected names: Gaston Doumergue, Marcel Déat, and Pierre Laval, to say nothing of virtually all the corrupt deputies and senators implicated in the notorious Stavisky affair. Passing mention is made of the intestine feuding within the League occasioned by the ministerial conduct of some of its high-profile ministers, Paul Painlevé in the 1920s and Edouard Herriot in the 1930s. These "affairs" seemed to involve ministerial conduct that conflicted with the League's principles. But rarely is there any discussion of the frequent deliberations of the League's Central Committee, which involved purely partisan and narrowly political issues with only the most tenuous connections to the defense of human rights: the wisdom of Socialist participation in post-1924 governments, the ratification of the interallied accords on war debts, and the merits of proposed changes to the electoral system. All acknowledge, and rather applaud, the League's efforts to obtain a more expansive definition of the rights of man. But few note that some of the partisans of this broader definition wanted the 1789 declaration scrapped altogether. The broader definition of the rights of man expanded the type of issues the League could address, but because of the openly political motives behind this expanded vision it also narrowed them. Causes that might have awkward political consequences such as women's suffrage, rights of religious congregations, and an unequivocal defense of the free press were discreetly off-limits to the League and its subsequent historians.

The League claimed to be "the conscience of democracy." The distinguished historian, Madeleine Rebérioux, also one of the most prominent leaders of the postwar League, has perceptively noted that in time the League became instead the "guardian" (*vigie*) of democracy, by which she means the defenders of a sclerotic parliamentary regime.[7] She does not mention that many members of the League, and not the least of them, were given to excoriating that very regime in terms that, with respect to form and sometimes to substance, resembled its fascist enemies. The divisions within the League caused by World War I gave rise to a powerful pacifist minority. The origins of that minority currently have been carefully explored; less so its behavior in the post-Hitler years. Rebérioux notes that those in the League who, after 1933, called for a firmer stance against Hitler "found themselves accused of wanting 'a war for the Jews'."[8] She neglects to mention that those charges came from within the ranks of League leaders, some of whom by the late 1930s shied neither from an overt defense of the Nazi regime nor from explicitly anti-Semitic slurs. Moreover, there is almost total silence on the role played by a number of prominent members of the League in defending the Vichy government and its policy of collaboration with Nazi Germany. One of the tragic ironies in its history is that at the very moment when Basch and his wife were being cruelly murdered by Vichy thugs, prominent members of the prewar League were openly defending the Vichy regime.

Rebérioux also raises the question of why, at a time when *la vie associative* was in its infancy, the League should have attracted such a large membership.[9] She offers no real answer to this pertinent question and chooses not to reflect on the possibilities that occurred to contemporary leaguers, that is, for many of its members the League was primarily one or more of the following: an inexpensive political club, the French equivalent of a Rotary club or civic improvement society, an inexpensive form of insurance, or a well-connected patronage network. Above all, no historians are prepared to recognize that there is something problematic about being both a defender of civil liberties and a committed member of the political Left.

This study does not pretend to be an exhaustive history of the League and the prominent role it played in almost all aspects of French society and politics in the first half of the twentieth century. It is, instead, a sustained critical essay probing one, and arguably *the*, central issue faced by the League: its attempt to balance its dedication to civil liberties and its commitment to left-wing politics. Precisely because the League was one of the more admirable institutions of Third Republic France it deserves to be approached with a degree of critical detachment, recognizing both its real strengths but also acknowledging its serious, and at times, fatal flaws.

ONE

Origins, Organization, and Structure

In 1894 a French army officer, Captain Alfred Dreyfus, was tried and convicted of espionage and sentenced to life imprisonment. The trial caused a brief public sensation and was soon forgotten except by a handful of relatives, intellectuals, and army officers who had growing reservations both about Dreyfus's guilt and about the conduct of his trial. Faced with the government's refusal to reopen the case, in January 1898 the famous novelist Emile Zola published *J'Accuse,* an open letter to the President of the Republic, appearing in the Radical newspaper *L'Aurore,* which bluntly and eloquently accused the army of having knowingly convicted an innocent man. The government promptly laid criminal charges against Zola.

On February 20, 1898, in the midst of the Zola trial, a group of upper-class Parisian intellectuals met at the home of Senator Ludovic Trarieux. The senator, who had just testified in Zola's defense, desperately wanted to found "a group, an association, a League [or] something" whose mission was to "safeguard individual rights, the liberty of citizens and their equality before the law."[1] There was in fact precedent for such a League. Ten years earlier, when the democratic republic had seemed menaced by the renegade General Boulanger, a group of militant republicans had founded a League of the Rights of Man to defend public liberties and the regime. As that League had dissolved itself on the defeat of Boulanger, Trarieux and his associates decided to readopt the name.[2]

Within a month of the initial meeting, the new League had attracted 269 members. By the time it held its first general assembly on June 4, there were 800 members; by the end of that year there were 4,580 members, 200 of whom attended the second general assembly in December. When Dreyfus was finally pardoned by the French government at the end of 1899, the League had 12,000 dues-paying adherents in seventy sections. The new League also displayed an indefatigable energy. The Central Committee elected in June 1898 met no fewer than twenty-three times in the next six months. When Trarieux wrote an open letter to the minister of war, General Cavaignac, demonstrating the blatant illegality of the 1894 trial, the League published 400,000 copies and distributed one to every local and municipal politician as well as to every schoolteacher, priest, pastor, or rabbi in the nation. When Dreyfus was granted a new trial in the summer of 1899, the League established a stenographic service dispatching a verbatim transcript of the court session to any newspaper that wanted it, ensuring that the story was on the streets of Paris within three hours. It also published a million copies of the complete transcript of the new trial. Throughout the affair, and until Dreyfus's final rehabilitation in 1906, the League churned out an endless stream of documentary evidence (comparisons, for example, of the handwriting on the *bordereaux* and that of Esterhazy) and scores of polemical pamphlets. It also held a large number of public rallies.[3] Its militant activity certainly disquieted the government of the day; in the spring of 1899 the police searched League headquarters, and its leaders were fined a symbolic sixteen francs for belonging to an illegal association.

From the beginning, leaders of the new League agreed that, unlike its predecessor, it would not be a single-issue organization and that the Dreyfus affair was the beginning but not the end of its campaign for justice. Its membership continued to expand dramatically. By the time Dreyfus had been completely rehabilitated in 1906, there were nearly 60,000 members in over 500 sections; by 1910 there were 80,000 members in over 800 sections. Owing to internal political conflict,[4] membership declined to just over 50,000 on the eve of World War I. By 1919, however, League membership had surpassed that of 1910; in 1926 it stood at 140,000 and reached it peak in 1932 with 180,000 members in some 2,400 sections. This made it, by French standards, a huge organization. Neither the Socialist party nor the Communist party had a comparable membership before 1936. In the early 1930s, the League may well have been larger than all of France's left-wing parties combined.[5] And it was certainly the largest organization of its kind in the world. A decade after its creation the League had 80,000 members; by contrast, thirty years after its formation, the comparable ACLU had a mere 9,000.

What kind of people joined the League? Men, mostly. Women were admitted to the League from its beginnings, although it took until 1925 for the League to change the wording of its statutes to make female membership sound like a right rather than a concession. Of the 204 people who served on the Central Committee from 1898 until 1940, only thirteen were women—rarely more than one or two out of forty in any given year. [6] Their role in the deliberations of the Central Committee was, with a few exceptions, minimal. The League took some pride in the fact that three of the members of its first Central Committee in 1898 were women, although one was the wife of the treasurer and the other two quickly ceased attending meetings. It is not possible to state with any certainty what percentage of the rank-and-file members of the League were women as this was one statistic the League did not (and probably could not) record. In the 1930s, the League introduced a half-price tariff for women members who were married to leaguers. In 1937, of 118,867 members who had paid their dues, 996 (or less than 1 percent) fell into that category.[7] These statistics would not show widows or unmarried women, of whom there were a higher than usual number in interwar France. Nor would they include married women who belonged to an association their husbands did not, although this group is unlikely to have been large. Of the 262 members of the section of Parthenay in the Deux-Sèvres, nine, or 3.8 percent, were women.[8] It seems unlikely, therefore, that women accounted for more than 5 percent of League members. Women were even more seriously underrepresented at the local leadership level. A woman, usually a schoolteacher, might be the secretary of a local section, rather less often the vice president, and only rarely the president. In 1923, of 995 known presidents of sections, five were women. By the end of the decade, nine of the 1,871 section presidents were women.[9]

Members of the Central Committee, the League's governing body, were drawn overwhelmingly from the Parisian academic world, the legal profession, and increasingly from the parliamentary elite. A third of those who served on the Central Committee in the 1920s were employed in higher education (the universities and the Lycées); a quarter were current or former senators or deputies, and about one-tenth were high-profile lawyers. Of the fifty-seven members on the 1931 Central Committee nineteen were teachers, three-quarters at the university level, and a further fifteen parliamentarians (twelve deputies, one senator, and two former deputies.) The rest were, in roughly equal proportions, journalists, *hommes de lettres,* lawyers, and trade-union executives. Members of the working class (as opposed to their trade-union representatives) were rare. Nor was there much turnover; resignations and deaths rather than electoral defeats determined most departures from the Central Committee.[10] The presence of so many deputies, as well as the almost total absence of peasants or workers (but not women), was a source of annual grumbling by representatives of the League's left-wing minority, for whom the Central Committee's composition provided a clue to its insufficient militancy. In fact, however, there was little, professionally or sociologically, that distinguished members of that minority from the rest of the Central Committee.

A sociological profile of the League's rank and file is a good deal more problematic and necessarily more impressionistic. Only in the case of a few sections have complete lists of the membership, including occupations, survived. Such lists are probably not representative of the League as a whole; the vagueness of many occupational descriptions and the inherent ambiguity of self-description render specious any attempt at sociological rigor. Of the nearly 600 members of the essentially rural section of the Mâcon, 17 percent described themselves as workers or artisans, 17 percent as small businessmen, and a further 17 percent as farmers (*cultivateurs* or *proprieteurs*). Nineteen percent described themselves as teachers and a further 22 percent as civil servants.[11] Another example, drawn from a very different environment and nearly thirty years later, was the section of Nancy. Of its 528 members, 305 identified themselves professionally. Thirty-eight percent defined themselves as workers, about two-thirds of whom worked in the local state-owned railway yards. A further 15 percent were "cadres"—foremen or supervisors, again more often than not in the rail yards. Fourteen percent were civil servants, and 15 percent were teachers at some level or other. The rest were either liberal professionals or independent business owners.[12] In the section of Parthenay, schoolteachers made up only 6 percent of the members but represented 60 percent of the teachers in the town.[13]

In the 1920s, roughly one-third of the presidents of all local sections described themselves as teachers or civil servants, a further third as small-business owners, and another third merely as local politicians (typically mayors, members of the municipal council, or members of the councils of the arrondissement or of the department). About 10 percent were members of the liberal professions.[14] At the level of departmental federations, by 1925 more than half of the presidents of departmental federations were either teachers or civil servants (36.2% and 14.9%, respectively). By 1929, the relevant figure was 57 percent (45 percent teachers and 12 percent civil servants). Liberal professions were better represented among the presidents of federations, at around one-fifth (as opposed to one-tenth at the section level.) Small business owners by contrast declined in importance, with 12 to 15 percent of the presidents compared to typically around 30 percent at the sectional level. Similarly, local politicians declined in importance compared to the sectional level; their numbers dropped from 12.8 percent in 1925 to 2.5 percent in 1929; by contrast deputies and senators, understandably, were more important at this level, representing 9 percent and 7.5 percent of the federation presidents in 1927 and 1928, respectively. A recent study of the League's leadership cadres, national and local, for the interwar years, has demonstrated that the liberal professions (law, medicine, and journalism, in that order) were dramatically overrepresented. So too, although less pronounced, were teachers and civil servants. Peasants and workers were significantly underrepresented.[15] Although sociologically heterogeneous, the League was the terrain, par excellence, of the lawyer, doctor, journalist, schoolteacher, or civil servant.

The relative underrepresentation of the more humble elements of French society in the leadership—both national and local—of the League, not very surprising in itself, was always a sore point. As if to compensate for the League's essentially middle-class composition, many leaguers made something of a fetish of the lower classes. The economic constraints on the working classes served as a standard argument for refusal to increase League dues. League president, Victor Basch, who could have a tin ear for the sensitivities of his audience, enraged everyone at the League's 1931 congress by sarcastically noting that the proposed (and rejected) increase in dues would cost the typical worker all of two aperitifs a year. Of course, he was also alert to the substantial degree of posturing that went on at such events. At the next congress a delegate, speaking on behalf of the peasantry, attacked him for his penchant for Latinate phrases, more or less incomprehensible to the poorer elements of French society. Because his antagonist was in fact a graduate of the Sorbonne, Basch could not resist reminding him that he was perhaps not ideally placed to speak for the more humble elements in the League.[16]

The League's many critics often charged that it was dominated by Protestants, Jews, and Freemasons. The claim was excessive, but all three groups incontestably played an active role in the League from its foundations. This should not be surprising, as these elements had played a critical role in cementing the foundations of the democratic republic in the 1870s and 1880s.[17] Certainly, Protestant ministers had been active in the early years of the League, and both Francis de Pressensé (president from 1904 until 1914) and his successor, Ferdinand Buisson (until 1926) were Protestants. So too were Mathias Morhardt, secretary general from 1901 until 1911, and Alfred Westfall, treasurer for most of the League's first thirty years. In 1926 Victor Basch, a Jew, became president and, in 1932, another Jew, Emile Kahn, became secretary general. Both Jews and Protestants were well represented on the Central Committee. Because the degree of religious devotion varied enormously among the League's leaders, it is next to impossible to establish exactly how many of its leaders were Jewish or Protestant. By the most elastic definition some 17 percent of the members of the Central Committee were Protestant; a further 12 percent were Jewish. Five percent were notionally Roman Catholic but married to Protestants or, in the case of an additional 3 percent, to Jews.[18]

The Freemasons were another story. As the League repeatedly pointed out, no president or secretary general of the League ever belonged to the Masons.[19] In fact, however, the milieu from which the League drew its members was deeply impregnated by Masonry. Masons played an active role in founding League sections,[20] and, as the right-wing press was fond of noting, officially blessed the League as its secular branch.[21] At the League's 1925 congress in La Rochelle, the president of the host federation announced that the local Masonic lodge had prepared an "intimate" reception for the Masons present and unhesitatingly declared that he expected that three-quarters of the delegates would be attending[22] Many of the Radical (although fewer of the Socialist) deputies and senators who belonged to the League were Masons. Eleven of the twenty-six parliamentarians who served on the Central Committee in the 1920s belonged to the Masons. Over the span of forty years, fully one-third of Central Committee members belonged to Masonic lodges.[23] Although most Masons were relatively marginal figures in the League, some played an important role. Camille Planche (deputy from the Allier) and René Château (deputy from the Charente-Maritime) were both presidents of the large League federations of their respective departments. Ernest Lafont (deputy from Paris); Eugène Frot (deputy from the Loiret), Marc Rucard (deputy from the Vosges), Maurice Viollette (senator from the Eure-et-Loire), all Masons, were high-profile members on the Central Committee.[24] The overlapping memberships between the two associations prove little beyond the fact that both appealed to defenders of the lay republic and, less nobly, membership in both was of incontestable utility to aspiring politicians.

Why would someone join the League? Given that so many Frenchmen did—there were probably as many League members in 1933 as there were members in all French political parties combined—the question is an important one. The League took some pride in its large and usually growing membership. Yet League leaders suffered few illusions as to the reasons for its healthy membership rolls. In 1927, shortly after becoming the League's president, Victor Basch, wryly observed that the 44,000 new members recruited in the previous eighteen months probably did not reflect a concomitant increase in concern for the defence of civil liberties.[25] A decade later he would remind his colleagues that it was misleading to suggest, as they so often did, that the League had 160,000 *militants;* what it had instead was 160,000 dues-paying members.[26] Basch knew only too well that many leaguers were in the organization for the material advantages membership might afford. Sceptics within the League sometimes suspected that the real reason for its large mem-

bership was because League dues were significantly lower than those of the political parties of the Left, making the League, for many, a "cheap" political
party.[27] Certainly any attempt to raise dues, even to take account of inflation,
involved a protracted struggle with the militants who invariably invoked the
penury of the proletariat, a predictable response that overlooked the fact that
the proletariat was seriously underrepresented in the League. Much of the activity of local sections involved, and at times was limited to, political activity
that a leaguer could carry on in his or her section at a fraction of the cost of
an often like-minded counterpart in a neighboring Socialist section.

What was supposed to set a leaguer apart from a Socialist militant was the
former's dedication to fighting cases of injustice. But the distinction between
left-wing politics and fighting injustice was not obvious to many of the
League's rank and file. In 1930, for example, the ten sections (with 622 members) in the department of the Mayenne reported having dealt with no individual cases of injustice in that year and having limited itself exclusively to
propaganda.[28] Moreover, the League's grass roots had a notoriously elastic definition of "injustice" as the thousands of resolutions made annually by the
local sections demonstrate. The section of Caen, for example, arguing that
among the rights of man was the right not to be injured in automobile accidents, passed a motion calling for improvements in municipal traffic regulation.[29] The section in Mâcon once gave equal weight to two resolutions: one
dealt with the question of separation of church and state; the other dealt with
postage rates for local newspapers.[30] As one member of the League wryly
noted, sections were not beyond voting motions calling for spelling reform.[31]
The causes were usually worthy but better suited for civic improvement associations than for the League of the Rights of Man. The League invariably attracted single-issue advocates; one individual, troubled by the widespread
practice of riding unlit bicycles at night, promised to join the section of
Villerupt (Meurthe-et-Moselle) if only it would address this pressing social
problem.[32] The leader of the League's section in Marseilles was obsessed with
bullfights and filled his local bulletin with so much copy on this topic that
exasperated members finally had to protest that this was the League of the
Rights of Man and not the Society for the Protection of Animals.[33] In 1928,
the section of Laôn badgered the Central Committee about rabbits from
nearby hunting preserves that were devouring crops. For once, most members of the Central Committee agreed that the depredations of rabbits were
outside the remit of the League. But Secretary General Henri Guernut, who
just happened to represent that constituency in parliament, countered that one

of the rights of man was surely the right to "harvest the fruits of one's labor."[34] This kind of activity risked trivializing the work of the League. In 1935, Léon Emery, a member of the Central Committee, caustically observed that the typical resolution of a local section involved a demand for the regulation of heavy truck traffic, which, he hinted, might explain why officials in the government did not always take the League's interventions very seriously.[35]

The basic unit of the League was the local section. The choice of the word *section* was not accidental. It conjured up images of the sections of the Parisian sans-culottes and was also a direct imitation of the Socialist party. By 1933 there were just under 2,500 sections, which varied in size from a couple of dozen members to several hundred. In large centers (Lille, for example), sections of over 1,000 members were not unknown. The sections passed on the admissibility of members—often a hotly debated issue—as well as their exclusion for activity unworthy of the League. In time, the League had become so large and the number of sections so numerous, that the League introduced an intermediate body between the sections and the central leadership: the departmental federation. Once again, this action was in direct imitation of the Socialists, and once again *Fédération* had a distinctly revolutionary resonance.[36]

Not every section was active. The League forever complained of sections that were "asleep," but anyone reading the provincial press and the local bulletins of the League cannot help but be impressed by the energy displayed at the local level. Many sections met regularly, passing their various resolutions on to the Central Committee. Most held an annual general meeting as did all federations. In the latter case, they were almost always presided over by a member of the Central Committee. Some of the larger federations, for example, Aisne, regularly held two annual congresses.

The Central Committee was the directing organ of the League. Chosen by co-optation in the League's early years, the Central Committee, by 1907, was elected directly by the sections. Anyone could be nominated, provided he or she had the support of a certain number of sections or the existing Central Committee. In practice, the nominees of the Central Committee, usually figures in the world of academics, law, or politics with a high profile, were almost invariably chosen. This situation gave rise to annual feuds about the dictatorial tendencies of the Central Committee, although this diminished in the 1930s when a number of more or less permanent critics of the League leadership were elected. For practical reasons, virtually all of the members of the Central Committee came from Paris or its immediate environs. In 1926, the League decided to add a number of *nonresident* members representing the provinces.[37] Although these nonresidents rarely could be expected at the frequent meetings of the Central Committee, they could, and did, submit their votes and their opinions by mail. Never did all members of the Central Committee meet at once. Some members, chosen largely for their political or academic profile, rarely attended; Léon Blum, for example, only once attended a meeting.

The high point in the League's year was its annual congress. Attracting between 400 and 1,000 delegates, it was the occasion for the finest academic discourse, the display of rapierlike wit, and inevitably a personal "incident" or two. Members of the Central Committee and representatives of the big departmental federations spoke frequently and at considerable length, a fact that did not escape the rank and file.[38] Rare was the delegate who renounced his turn at the rostrum merely because he had nothing new to add. Time invariably ran out; late night or early morning sessions were the rule. To satisfy the many delegates who had not, by the end of one day, had a chance to speak, the 1937 congress scheduled a special one-hour session to begin at 9:00 sharp the next morning. Typically it began at 9:30 and was still going strong two hours later.[39] Many a humble provincial militant, having spent a year polishing his discourse, learned to his chagrin that he had five minutes in which to summarize it. Still, at most congresses, modest members of small sections managed to command the floor long enough to detail the problems of their neck of the woods or, not infrequently, the particular injustice to which they had been subjected, usually to the ill-disguised indifference of the audience. With five minutes remaining in an afternoon session at the League's 1925 congress, Salzes, a delegate from the federation of the Hérault rose to inform his colleagues that he would require at least an hour to explain the complexities of his own personal grievance. He believed himself unfit for military service, despite a medical examiner's report that concluded the opposite. Salzes had a long history of belaboring congresses with his case, and both the Central Committee and its legal experts had repeatedly examined it and found it to be without merit. To the intense exasperation of Secretary General Henri Guernut, the congress agreed to a special evening session. Of course most delegates had no intention of actually attending the session because it conflicted with a reception being held by the Masons. Others, one suspects, agreed to a night session as it would afford them a chance to ride their personal hobbyhorses. Before Salzes could take the floor, a delegate from Algeria took the opportunity to enlighten his fellow leaguers about "the native mentality." "Make the slightest concession to the Arabs," he assured everyone, "and they will immediately feel themselves entitled to strike you down."[40]

Women were present at all League congresses, although they rarely constituted much more than about 10 percent of the delegates and often rather less.
Many appear to have been there primarily in their capacity as wives of delegates.[41] They spoke infrequently; of the sixty or seventy delegates who took the
floor at an average congress, rarely were more than four or five of them women.
When they did speak, women delegates were always greeted with enthusiastic
applause. This might have reflected the fact that women were invariably more
succinct than men and that their interventions were usually rather more to the
point. The effusive reception of their remarks, especially when they involved
women's political rights, might also have been designed to mask the general
agreement on the part of most leaguers to ignore their political ramifications.

The most exciting part of a League congress was the presentation of the
Rapport Moral, roughly the equivalent of a State of the Union address. Here,
the president or secretary general, detailed the activities of the League in the
previous year, the issues that faced it in the future, and the current political situation in France (and increasingly, Europe). It was at this moment that the
great battles of principles took place between the League leadership and its
rank and file or, more accurately, the left-wing elements who claimed to speak
for the rank and file. By the interwar years, there was a more or less permanent
minority of dissident voices within the League, dating from disputes over the
origins of World War I. Although members of the minority did not always
speak with one voice (nor did their opponents in the majority), more often
than not the internal battles within the League pitted the two factions against
one another.[42] Spokespersons for the minority could be found in many
provincial federations, notably those of the Rhône, the Allier, and the Ardèche,
but the core of the opposition almost always came from the federation of the
Seine and from certain sections, Monnaie-Odéon in particular.[43]

In time these struggles became formalized. For the opposition, the Central Committee had never been energetic enough on any issue; its activity was
invariably too parliamentary, too academic, and never worthy of the League
that began with the Dreyfus affair. The Central Committee predictably replied
that the opposition had paid no attention to the organization's activities in
the previous year, was apparently ignorant of League statutes, and was not
worthy of the League founded to defend Dreyfus. The pattern of these debates
and because delegates on both sides seemed able to refer instantly to arcane
texts and documents suggest that the debates were not entirely spontaneous
and were the reflection of arguments carefully rehearsed in Paris. Provincial
delegates sensed this and repeatedly lamented that they were subjected to what

amounted to Parisian quarrels. The larger provincial Federations, those of the Charente-Maritime and the Aisne in particular, frequently engaged in polemics with the federation of the Seine about its allegedly domineering tendencies.[44] In principle, the vote on accepting the Rapport Moral was a vote of confidence; a negative vote automatically brought the resignation of the Central Committee. In practice this never happened. On those rare occasions, as at the 1935 congress, when a close vote was anticipated, the two sides worked out a compromise formulation.

Nonetheless, League congresses—much like meetings at the federation and section levels—could be very lively. This was so, at least in part, because leaguers could be extraordinarily litigious. The Duplantier affair was a classic example. In 1907 in the garrison at Poitiers, an army doctor attempted to shove a pill down the throat of a reserve soldier he suspected of faking illness in order to avoid an arduous march. The soldier, on the advice of a fellow reservist, Caillon—secretary of the neighboring League section of St. Vivien and also secretary general of the federation of the Gironde—formally lodged a complaint. The colonel of the regiment concluded that the doctor's actions had been inappropriate and confined him to base for two weeks. The Central Committee, apprised of the matter, called on Duplantier, the president of both the section of Poitiers and of the federation of the Vienne, to make a formal investigation. Duplantier turned the matter over to a friend, the editor of a local left-wing newspaper. Based on his friend's findings, Duplantier submitted a formal report to the Central Committee in which he concluded that the reservist had in fact been faking illness, that the doctor in question was well respected by his troops, and that Caillon was an outspoken antimilitarist. This report outraged both the section of St. Vivien and the departmental federation of the Gironde, which sent out circulars denouncing Duplantier who was, at that very moment, a candidate for membership in the Central Committee. In truth, their version of events was not, in substance, all that different from Duplantier's, but they took strong exception to the depiction of Caillon as an "antimilitarist" and openly suggested that the tenor of Duplantier's report owed something to his personal connections with the doctor in question, a connection Duplantier flatly denied.

Fully two hours of the League's national congress of 1908 were taken up with this question, to the obvious exasperation of some delegates who believed, quite correctly, that they were being subjected to petty personal quarrels. In the end, an arbitration committee was struck, which after two more hours of deliberation concluded, without passing on the question of complicity, that Duplantier was guilty of submitting a somewhat partial report.[45] This particular issue, trivial in itself, would have larger consequences for the League, however. Behind personal spats of this kind, there almost always lurked more consequential political tensions. Although Duplantier claimed that what was at stake was his personal honor, it was no secret that he was one of the more outspoken critics of then president, Francis de Pressensé and his efforts to take the League in a more overtly socialist direction.[46] Duplantier resigned from the League and promptly began suing everyone. In particular, he won a defamation suit against League secretary general, Mathius Morhardt who, in his capacity as editor of the League's *Bulletin Officiel,* had published the stenographic transcript of the Duplantier debate (and indeed of the entire congress). At issue here (or so claimed Morhardt's many enemies within the League) was that Morhardt had all along been in possession of documents that cleared Duplantier of any suspicion of complicity with the doctor, documents that he had either misplaced or ignored, and the resulting suit had cost the League some 20,000 francs. The League and Morhardt were silent on this last point. But shortly thereafter Morhardt resigned as secretary general, citing reasons of health. There is no evidence linking these two developments but Morhardt, who lived another quarter century, was ever after a very bitter man.[47]

For all of its disputatious tendencies, the energy of the League was undeniable. In 1930, a fairly typical year, the Central Committee sponsored no fewer than 644 meetings; the sections and federations organized a further 2,500. The government obviously took these meetings seriously, dispatching (at least until the 1930s when the archival record runs out) hundreds of agents to report on the League's deliberations. Rarely did a meeting of the League take place without some agent of the Ministry of the Interior dutifully reporting on what had been said, thus saving the government the trouble of reading the invariably extensive accounts in the press. Across the desk of various agents in the Ministry of the Interior came reports labeled "very confidential," informing the government of the latest deliberations of the Central Committee, otherwise inaccessible to all but the 20,000 subscribers to the *Cahiers.*[48]

The assiduousness of government agents was all the more inane because the League prided itself, with good reason, on being "*une maison de verre*," literally, a glass house. Its internal organization faithfully reflected its call for an open and transparent French democracy. Its house organs, the *Bulletin Officiel* and, after World War I, the *Cahiers* went to exceptional lengths to apprise League members of all aspects of its internal life, including issues about which almost any other organization might have preferred to remain silent. No letter of resignation, no matter how abusive, was refused space in the League's press. The *Bulletin* regularly published a stenographic record of League congresses, replete with all of the quarrels, spats, and insults that invariably occurred. After 1916 they were published as separate volumes. Debates of the Central Committee were also regularly published, not quite in stenographic form but with sufficient detail as to reveal to any reader the intensely personal nature of the debates that took place. Only once did the editor note that a debate had become so savagely personal that reproducing it would be inappropriate, although a record would be kept in the League's archives. Given how frank the published debates are, this debate must have been one angry exchange.[49] Dissenting opinions, including those sharply critical of the League's leaders, were routinely published, as were a wide variety of articles calculated to offend not only the League's leaders but also most of its members. The various resolutions of local sections, no matter how anodyne, would find a place in the League's bulletins. Any reader of the *Cahiers* could learn just about all there was to know about the way the League was run and what it looked like. One could discover how many members there were, who the presidents of every section were, how many members there were in any given department, as well as the percentage of the population in any department who belonged to the League. Anyone who cared could also learn what percentage of the leaguers in any particular department subscribed to the *Cahiers* (ranging from 33 percent in the Aisne to 4 percent in the Vendée). It is hard to imagine that any organization as large as the League was ever as openly and as transparently democratic.[50]

None of this candidness prevented vociferous elements in the League from asserting that its apparent openness served only to mask the occult dictatorship of the majority within the Central Committee. Routine were the charges that a self-appointed group of Parisian upper-class intellectuals ignored the views of the rank and file with which it was out of touch, cynically manipulated the congresses, and restricted dissenting views from appearing in the *Cahiers*. These were predictable enough charges, emanating as they usually did from members of that same Parisian intellectual elite. But there was some basis for them. Until 1907 the Central Committee was chosen by co-option. In that year, the statutes were revised to the effect that candidates for the Central Committee could be nominated by the Central Committee itself, by local sections, or by departmental federations and would be elected at annual congresses. The Central Committee invariably nominated some dissidents for its slate but also reserved the right to indicate which candidates it had nominated, and such candidates almost invariably prevailed. Of the 204 members of the pre-World War II Central Committee, only twelve were elected without the support of the Central Committee.[51] It was also true that at any given congress, members of the Central Committee did most of the talking. Still, the Central Committee was always subjected to a vote of confidence at congresses and invariably won them. For the minority, this proved only that their colleagues were adept at bullying provincial delegates. The majority countered that votes of confidence meant that they reflected the general sentiment of the average leaguer. A reading of the many local publications of the League suggests that this was by and large true. The ritualistic claim that dissenting views were excluded from the *Cahiers* cannot, with one notable exception in 1937,[52] be sustained by any careful reading of that house organ.

Although, in practice, internal democracy within the League never reached the lofty standards it set for itself, this can in large measure be explained by the relative indifference of the rank and file. The agenda of any given League congress was to be established by the votes of local sections. To some degree, this was a concession to sections in the West who were forever complaining that the one issue they really cared about, the clerical peril, was increasingly ignored by the League. But fewer than 5 percent of sections ever expressed an opinion on an agenda. To give local sections some direct input into League policy, the League organized a "question of the month" involving some issue of public policy and invited every section to submit its opinions. Typically, an elaborate questionnaire was sent out, laying out the issues at stake and requesting specific answers to specific questions. Some sections obviously subjected the questions to careful scrutiny and submitted detailed and thoughtful responses. But they were rare. Never did as many as 5 percent of the sections respond; 2 percent was more typical. Granted, some of the questions (for example, the Kellogg-Briand Pact or the merits of interfederal organization within the League) were unlikely to prompt much interest. But in 1930 the League posed a question— explicitly directed at its numerous North African sections—concerning the extension of political rights to the native populations. This sensitive issue ought to have stirred up interest but, again, only a small fraction of the sections bothered to reply.[53]

Similarly, sections were always anxious to see their various resolutions published in the League's house organs and were indignant if they were not. But it did not escape the notice of headquarters that these resolutions were often formulaic and utterly identical to the simultaneous resolutions of a dozen other sections of the same department, all of which suggested that there was often not much original thinking at work in the deliberations of those sections.[54] Moreover, given the hard work in making the *Cahiers* an indispensable reference tool for any serious leaguer, it was a standing affront that only about one in ten bothered to subscribe. Granted, at twenty francs annually and thus twice as much as League dues (already a sensitive issue), cost might have been a factor. Many a junior civil servant might have earned less than 2,000 francs a year. But this fact alone probably does not explain the low subscription rate. Nor does the apparent indifference to the internal life of the League necessarily indicate general indifference. As a later chapter will show, the sections could be very active indeed on issues they cared about.

Ici on ne fait pas de la politique

Ici on ne fait pas de la politique. For most of its first forty years this could have been the motto of the League. Justice, not politics, was the League's mandate. It was neither Right nor Left. Rather, its spokesmen were fond of saying, the League was on the ceiling—above the partisan fray, political only in the sense that its role was to be, according to another favorite phrase, the "conscience of democracy." Lines like this were repeated whenever two or more leaguers gathered together. Scarcely was there a public meeting of the League without someone reminding his colleagues that the League did not engage in politics precisely because it was above politics. Orator after orator, at section meetings, federation meetings, and above all, national congresses insisted that the League was above politics, outside politics, and unconcerned with politics. Its ideal was justice, a noble ideal that could only be tarnished by contamination with partisan issues. Indeed, the League owed its moral authority precisely to its detachment from politics. What accounted for the intensity and frequency of such assertions, however, was the fact that in most senses they were utterly untrue.

The Dreyfus affair that brought the League into existence was, at least in its earliest stages, relatively nonpolitical. As late as the 1898 legislative elections, most politicians chose to ignore it. If Dreyfusards were more likely to be on the Left than on the Right, the Captain's defenders as well as his antagonists could be found in all political camps. Yet from the beginning, most leaguers recognized that the League could not limit itself to the plight of Captain Dreyfus. As one of the first members of the Central Committee, Senator Alexandre Isaac, noted at an early meeting, "absorbing though the Dreyfus affair" was, there were many other examples of injustice crying out for redress, notably the plight of Algerian Jews. Any initial consensus about the new organization's appropriate sphere of activity lasted exactly six days. On June 10, 1898, at the second meeting of its newly formed Central Committee, the League debated a draft of its first manifesto. Paul Viollet, a distinguished chemist but also a devout Roman Catholic, insisted that, as part of its defense of public liberties, the League should protest against the current laws restricting the right of priests and monks to teach in public schools. Since priests and monks were, after all, French citizens, Viollet's concerns were not, a priori, inappropriate for the new League. But most of its founding members, like most late-nineteenth-century republicans, were genuinely uneasy about the prospect of clergy having any role in public education. Moreover, given the hostility of many elements in the church to Jews, to Dreyfus, and to the Republic, this did not seem to be the ideal moment to focus on the grievances of Roman Catholics. The Central Committee therefore proposed to restrict its first manifesto to the issues directly raised by the Dreyfus affair. Viollet promptly resigned from the League and shortly thereafter founded a *Comité catholique pour la défense de droit.*"

His was not the only resignation. The decision to focus exclusively on the Dreyfus case disturbed a prominent left-wing university professor. He was not at all troubled by the Central Committee's lack of concern for the problems of the church; to the contrary. But he had joined the League because he believed in its broader goals of civil liberties and justice and was appalled to learn that it was becoming a "single issue" pressure group. Worse, he thought the committee was defending a lost cause; Dreyfus, he insisted, was surely guilty! Like many "Radical" republicans of his generation, he revered the army and could not believe that the sworn word of no fewer than seven senior army officers could be challenged. He too promptly resigned. Ten weeks later, of course, it became public knowledge that the documents upon which Dreyfus's conviction had been based were forgeries. The disgruntled founding member soon reappeared in the ranks of the League's leadership. His name was Ferdinand Buisson, and he was soon to have a distinguished career as a Radical deputy and, from 1914 until 1926, as president of the League. But the experiences of Viollet and Buisson clearly demonstrate that, from the outset, members of the League had trouble agreeing on exactly what its objectives ought to be and what the appropriate limits on its actions were.[1]

Although it was founded to deal with a specific case of a victim of injustice, from nearly the beginning many members of the League believed that its mandate could not be limited to defending individual freedoms. There were broader ramifications to the defense of the rights of man. Surely human rights could be secure only in a democratic society, free from the obscurantist fanaticism of the church, free from the threat of war, and free, or at least relatively so, from the social inequality produced by rapacious capitalism.

Virtually everyone in the league was an advocate of "laicité." By this they meant that although anyone was entitled to the religion of his choice, religion should never intrude on the public sphere. Not only should church and state be separated but also the educational system ought to be free from any religious interference. Similarly, most members of the League, haunted by the fear, or later, the experience, of modern warfare, also agreed that a basic right of man was the right not to be subject to the horrors of war. Finally, it seemed obvious for many of the League's adherents that the principles of legal equality and due process lost much of their meaning when applied to a society where extremes of wealth and power prevailed. Moreover, was not the right to a living wage, full employment, decent retirement benefits, and reasonable conditions of work a human right as basic as others? And if, as seemed to many to be the case, such conditions did not seem to be realizable under the prevailing economic system was not capitalism as big an obstacle to civil rights as had been, say, undemocratic government or an established church? For the next forty years, most of the debates at League meetings and most of the articles in the League's various bulletins focused on questions concerning the church, war, and the social order.

By any standards these were *political* concerns. They were, the League insisted, political issues that followed directly from the letter and spirit of its guiding charter, the 1789 Declaration of the Rights of Man. This assertion was more than a little problematic. The connection between the Declaration and the League's political concerns was, in fact, often tenuous. On religious issues, Article 10 of the Declaration said only that "no one should be troubled for his opinions, even religious ones." The document was utterly silent about war and peace. Even more awkward was Article 17, which flatly declared private property to be sacrosanct. Still, even if the literal text of the Declaration was at times unhelpful or worse, the League insisted that the *spirit* of the document was fully congruent with its contemporary political preoccupations.[2] Blessed as the League's leadership was with some of the leading academic historians of the time,[3] it was not hard to demonstrate that the 1789 Declaration had been drafted before the Revolution had been forced to deal with the thorny issue of the church, before anyone had experienced the destructive effects of modern war, and before modern capitalism had demonstrated the abusive effects of private property. The Declaration was a living document, which could be reinterpreted or even modified with the passage of time. After all, had not the Jacobins modified the document as early as 1793 to give it a marginally more social flavor? Granted, there were some logical difficulties and inherent dangers in treating the Declaration as a document that could be modified at will, but surely it was susceptible to nuanced interpretations in the light of the gradual evolution of modern society.

Emphasising the *spirit* of the Declaration both permitted an elastic interpretation of its principles and facilitated the League's political engagement. But the specific application of this more elastic reading of the Declaration was much more problematic. For example, did the principle of laïcité mean that citizens who were Roman Catholic ought not to have the right, at their own expense, to send their children to schools run by the church? If so, what was the standing of the Declaration's insistence that no one should be troubled for his religious beliefs? Did the state, by way of minimizing clerical influence on society, have the right to treat members of religious congregations differently from other citizens, and if so, did this not violate the principle that all citizens were equal? Did opposition to war mean merely a call for disarmament, international arbitration, and open covenants, all openly arrived at? Or did it mean integral pacifism and the belief that no war, under any circumstances, was legitimate? Did the social interpretation of the Declaration mean a call for progressive social reforms or did it mean the abolition of capitalism and the collectivization of the means of production? There was simply no way that any of these issues could be resolved by reference to the League's "principles." These were quintessentially *political* issues, and the League's debates about them accurately mirrored the debates going on simultaneously among and within the various political parties of the Left.

Any attempt at a more elastic reading of the Declaration of the Rights of Man was bound to alienate those members of the League for whom its mandate began and ended with the defense of individual rights and manifestly did not extend to attacks on religion, the army, or the capitalist system. Indeed, it did not escape them that the broader definition of the rights of man was both consequence and cause of the growing influx into the League of Socialists, many of whom had not, in 1898, thought the defense of a bourgeois army officer to be exactly their issue.[4] The League's leaders invariably insisted that the broader agenda was an extension of, not a substitute for, its concerns with individual cases of human rights violations. In time though, this formula failed to satisfy the more militant elements in the League who were increasingly frustrated by what they perceived to be an excessive preoccupation with individual rights. Significantly, by the 1930s, the substantial number and cost of the League's permanent employees, nearly fifty, became an issue with the more radical elements in the League who complained that far too much of their dues went to pay for people who mostly dealt with individual cases of injustice and far too little went to political propaganda.[5] In 1935, Jacques Rosner, a former employee of the League and self-proclaimed angry young man, complained that the League had become merely an organization "which deals with a few citizens who have been the victims of injustice." But times had changed, and the 1789 Declaration was past its expiry date. A League that "only brings worn-out formulae of so-called democratic defence" and which limited itself to "minor individual grievances," would become comparably irrelevant. League rhetoric about defending "current freedoms" was naive given that under the capitalist system such freedoms were largely mythical and "we are but slaves." "In a fully revolutionary period, two ideologies confront one another," the tired ideas of 1789 and the revolutionary ones of 1935.[6] In his capacity as a delegate from the ninth arrondissement of Paris, Rosner informed the 1935 congress, "we are witnessing a radical ideological rupture within the League."[7] Even far more moderate members, like the delegate to the 1933 national congress from the Saône-et-Loire, conceded that the League would "henceforth be oriented as much towards social struggles as to the defence of individual liberties."[8] Reflecting this mood, and in preparation for the 1935 congress, Léon Emery, leader of the left-wing opposition, proposed that the League adopt a new orientation, minimizing its defense of individuals and concentrating almost exclusively on the more fundamental issues of the struggle for peace and against capitalism. It received the support of 40 percent of the delegates.

For leaguers of this persuasion, the Declaration was not so much a sacred charter as a serious impediment to social change. Many questioned the relevance of a late-eighteenth-century document to the early twentieth century. By the 1930s, a number of members demanded a new Declaration, one fully consistent with their revolutionary socialism and devoid of anachronistic references to the sanctity of private property or the primacy of individual rights.[9] This challenge from the Left posed a dilemma for the League's leadership. All agreed that the Declaration of 1789 did not adequately address the social problems of the twentieth century. All saw the need for, as Albert Bayet, a left-wing Radical and member of the Central Committee, put it, for an "economic" version of 1789. Whereas the French Revolution had abolished a *political* feudalism, the League now had to mount an assault on the "new feudalism" of the trusts, the banks, the 200 families and, in general, the *puissances d'argent,* or moneyed interests. But they also recognized the dangers implicit in scrapping outright a Declaration that was 150 years old. Its principles were eternally valid and, by virtue of its historical significance, it had political and emotional weight that no new Declaration, transparently drafted to deal with contemporary concerns, could ever have. Adroitly, therefore, they proposed for the 1936 congress, a "complement" to the old Declaration, a gloss on the historic original that would tease out of the 1789 text the appropriate applications for the present. Article 17, for example, would remain but be reinterpreted to mean that private property was sacred only when it was not used to oppress the people. The private property of the peasant and the small merchant was still sacred, but that of François de Wendel and the *Comité des Forges* would not be.[10]

At the League's July 1936 congress, however, many, for whom the Declaration had become simply irrelevant, found the compromise outrageous. Retaining the Declaration amounted to clinging to "outdated values," based on "dead ideas," insisted the Parisian university professor, Gustave Rodrigues. The world was changing; as a result "all of the values of yesterday are today bankrupt." The president of the large section of Marseilles could not hide his discouragement at the retention of the bourgeois individualism implicit in the 1789 document. "One cannot," he protested, "use the pretext of individualism to subordinate the collective interest to the tyrannical interest of a handful of individuals. . . . The old revolutionary declarations have run their course," adding that "faced with the decaying cadaver . . . of capitalism and bourgeois society and with a new society that is beginning to emerge, it is time to make forceful decisions." In July of 1936, France was, or so many delegates believed, experiencing the dawn of a new social revolutionary age; yet the League seemed to be bogged down in academic discussions of a document produced for a revolution that was but a distant memory. The Popular Front had just taken power, and the wave of sit-in strikes in the previous month presaged for many a forthcoming social revolution. As Rosner insisted, the events of June 1936 eclipsed those of August 1789. August 1789 had made tabula rasa of the old regime; June 1936 should do the same for both capitalist society and the Declaration of 1789.[11]

The more radical positions were, to be sure, invariably in the minority (although as the vote on Emery's 1935 proposed reorientation of the League shows, a very significant minority) Still, the fact that the League should even be debating such issues effectively narrowed its constituency. In principle, anyone who rejected the more extravagant claims of the anti-Dreyfusards and who accepted the democratic Republic was welcome to join the League. By 1905, at the latest, almost everyone in France had rallied, with greater or lesser degrees of conviction, to the Republican form of government; partisans of Royalist and Bonapartist forms of government were few in number and politically insignificant. Nor were there very many who wished to challenge the essential justice of the outcome of the Dreyfus affair. But the League's incipient anticlericalism, pacifism, and anticapitalism, even in their most moderate form, ensured that the natural constituency for the League would be limited to those who were in one of the families of the political Left.

Of course, this had not always been so. In the early days of the League, a clear majority of the League's leadership was drawn from what was quixotically known as the *centre-gauche*.[12] As so often was the case with French political nomenclature, the label *center-left* was fundamentally misleading because those of this political persuasion actually stood on the *center-right* of the political spectrum. But politicians of every stripe were refractory to the adjective *right;* even those who actually were on the extreme Right were shunning the label long before the turn of the twentieth century. *Right* conjured up images of enemies of the republican regime and whatever else the centre-gauche might have been, it was devoutly republican. Its adherents were the political descendants of the founder of the regime, men like Jules Ferry and Jules Simon. They were sometimes also known as *modérés* because they were uneasy with the more radical claims of those on their Left but, for all that, they passionately insisted that they were republican moderates and not *moderately* republican.[13] Indeed, what separated them from the political right was precisely their adamant defense of Dreyfus. The centre-gauche was moderately anticlerical, believing that the church had no business in the politics of the nation, nor, ideally at least, in education. They were, however, defenders of the socioeconomic status quo, ardent defenders of capitalism, and sceptical about all but the most cautious interventions of the state in economic matters. Members of the centre-gauche traditionally shunned affiliation with disciplined political parties; the closest they came to a political party of their own was the politically influential but organizationally vaporous *Alliance Démocratique*.

The prominence of the moderate republicans in the early League was symbolized by its first president Senator Ludovic Trarieux, and Central Committee members like Jacques Reinach, Yves Guyot, Alexandre Isaac, and above all Anthony Ratier, one of the leading figures in the Alliance Démocratique. With Trarieux's death in 1903, however, the leadership of the League fell to Francis de Pressensé, a Socialist deputy. In the years that followed, the centre-gauche gradually lost its preponderant influence to the representatives of the two major left-wing parties in France, the Radicals and the Socialists.

Until 1936 the largest party on the Left, and indeed in France, was the Radical party. Although not officially founded until 1901,[14] the Radicals had been around in one form or another since the early days of the Republic. The official title was the *Radical and Radical-Socialist Party.* This cumbersome title, misleading in some respects, nonetheless gives a clue to the party's political orientation. The party was neither radical nor socialist in the conventional sense of those words. *Radical* was used here in the literal sense of *root*, a reference to the party's early defense of root and branch republicanism. Unlike the very conservative republicans in the founding days of the republic, Radicals had been enthusiastic defenders of pure political democracy and opposed to such politically conservative institutions as the Senate and the presidency, neither elected by universal manhood suffrage. *Socialist* was a label added by some—although by no means all—local Radical committees to indicate a concern for the social question. They advocated social reforms, such as the income tax, and articulated a hostility to extremes of wealth and large-scale capitalist institutions. Socialism, many Radicals traditionally argued, was something very different from collectivism. The former was French, reformist, and evolutionary; the latter was German, violent, and revolutionary. One thing all Radicals shared in common was an extreme anticlericalism, which often took the form of insisting that most of the problems facing republican France could be solved by depriving the Roman Catholic Church of any influence whatsoever.

There was probably no such thing as a typical Radical. But if there were, it would probably have been André Teissier, a notary from Mâcon, an activist in the local Radical committee and, significantly, president of the very large local section of the League. Teissier was given to lecturing local Radicals and his section of the League (which in the early twentieth century sometimes held joint meetings) on the need for social reform. An income tax, he insisted, was necessary to close the gap between rich and poor; more attention had to be paid to the question of pensions for retired workers; and the influence of the plutocracy of wealth on the state was pernicious. He bowed to nobody in his savage denunciations of the clergy, but he also noted that whereas the government had made *some* progress in what he called its "laic duty," its "social duty" remained pretty much at the level of "unfulfilled promises." Of course he believed that "private property was an untouchable right" but he nonetheless wished that "wealth could be redistributed in such a way as to ensure that the poor might have at least the minimum necessary to survive." Yet, legislature after legislature went by with little in the way of meaningful social reform, which meant that an increasingly impatient population was falling for the seductive promises of the collectivist Left, prone to violence and illegality. Throughout most of his career, Teissier sprinkled his discourses with roughly equal measures of anticlericalism, calls for serious social reform, and increasingly savage denunciations of the Socialists and their loosely affiliated trade unions, which he freely described as hotbeds of "anarchism, violence and revolution."[15]

Teissier's ambivalence on the social question reflected that of the Radical party as a whole. A large, sprawling, and thoroughly undisciplined party, its members could be found everywhere from the right-wing fringes of the Socialists to the edges of the formations of the center-right. The Radicals always insisted, of course, that their party was on the Left, although increasingly its only claim to left-wing status was its persistent anticlericalism. It had been the principal formation of the Left in the thirty years after 1870, but the growing parliamentary representation of the Socialists after the turn of the twentieth century pushed the party inexorably toward the political center. It also made it a party of government.

France had a multiparty system. There were five or six major parties as well as a sprinkling of minor ones. Because no party ever captured a majority of seats in the Chamber of Deputies, every government was a coalition government. By virtue of its strategic position in the center-left of the political spectrum, the Radicals were essential ingredients in any governmental coalition, and parliamentary mathematics being what they were, it was virtually impossible to form a government without including at least some of the Radicals. Depending on the results of general elections, the governmental coalitions were sometimes oriented toward the Left with the Radicals governing with the more or less reliable support of the Socialist formations (as in 1902–06, 1924–26, and 1932–34) or with the active participation of the Socialists (as in 1936–38). Rather more often, however, the Radicals were in governmental coalitions that leaned to the Right and sometimes even including members of the extreme parliamentary Right, with the Socialists in the opposition. The fact that members of the League were more often than not on opposite sides of the political divide would have severe repercussions.

The principal Socialist party of France was formally called the French Section of the Workers' International (*Section Française de l'Internationale Ouvrière* or SFIO as it was universally known). The name, every bit as cumbersome as the official title of the Radicals, also reflected the party's origins. Before 1905, French Socialists were divided into several doctrinally warring parties. Under pressure from the Socialist Second International, which was exasperated by having to deal with several different parties in the same country, the French Socialists formally unified in 1905. As the title also indicates, the united Socialist party also officially accepted the prevailing doctrine in the Second International, an orthodox and fairly mechanistic Marxism. According to this doctrine, capitalism could not be reformed from within but must be overthrown by (more or less) violent revolution. Such an outcome was also inevitable owing both to the increasing internal contradictions within capitalist society and to the increasing size and class consciousness of the revolutionary proletariat. Although, in the interest of unity, most Socialists gave lip service to this doctrine, not all of them subscribed to it with equal conviction. From the beginning there were those who had more faith in evolutionary reform than in revolution. This tendency became more pronounced after 1920 when some of the more revolutionary elements within the Socialists joined the fledgling Communist party. Although more coherent and better disciplined than the Radicals (which would not be very difficult), the Socialist party remained divided among those who were secretly or overtly reformist, those who clung to the determinist Marxism of the Second International, and those who were consumed by a kind of nihilist revolutionary zeal.[16]

Unlike the Radicals, the Socialists were not usually a party of government. It followed from the doctrine of the Second International that if capitalism could not be reformed from within, then Socialists had no business participating in bourgeois governments, as at least one of them had prior to 1905. Only under very exceptional circumstances might a Socialist deputy agree to accept a ministerial portfolio.[17] Once again, as with the party's official Marxism, some Socialists took this doctrine more seriously than did others. Socialist deputies in particular were inclined toward a more nuanced interpretation of the party's doctrinal declarations. Party congresses might pass some well meaning and apparently binding resolutions, but once in Parliament deputies tended to believe that they were entitled to some freedom of maneuver and the right to make some critical tactical decisions that might be in violation of party doctrine, literally construed. One of the standing jokes of the time was that two deputies, one of whom was a revolutionary, had rather more in common than two revolutionaries, one of whom was a deputy. A significant number of Socialist deputies believed that the nonparticipation rule achieved doctrinal purity at the cost of political impotence. As a result, the lure of a ministerial portfolio exercised considerable charm on a number of deputies, especially those with relatively secure constituencies who felt able to risk the wrath of the party's rank and file. Because the Socialist party had rather more coherence than its Radical counterpart, one could not violate party principles with impunity. Consequently, from 1905 onward there was a steady migration of "socialists" out of the SFIO. Some (Alexandre Millerand, Aristide Briand, Réné

Viviani, Pierre Laval) migrated so far to the Right as to forget any links they once had with their socialist past. Others, more numerous (Joseph Paul-Boncour, Maurice Viollette, Eugène Frot, Adrien Marquet) drifted into splinter parties with names like the Republican Socialists or Socialists of France, which occupied a nebulous terrain between the Radicals and the SFIO. Many of them, significantly, belonged to the League and, after 1910, these independent Socialists represented the effective center of political gravity within the League.

The divided political loyalties of League members were the source of more or less permanent strains within the organization. Tensions between Radicals and Socialists were least pronounced in the four years after 1902. In the 1902 elections, both the Radical and Socialist parties made major gains; the post-1902 legislatures were the years of the *Bloc des Gauches,* an informal alliance between the Radicals, forming the government, and the Socialists, according them more or less consistent parliamentary support. For both parties, this unprecedented exercise of power offered an opportunity to effect significant changes, most notably with respect to the role of the church (a subject of general agreement between the two parties) but also, albeit to a lesser degree (because Radicals were less sure on this point) the army. But consensus between Radicals and Socialists during these years was often achieved at the price of alienating more conservative members of the League.

The classic example came with the *affaire des fiches.* In the early twentieth century, the French government had serious doubts about the loyalty of its officer corps, some members of whom were suspected of preferring a more authoritarian regime—royalist or, more likely, Bonapartist. Certainly the stance taken by some officers during the Dreyfus affair provided grounds for unease. To obtain information about the political reliability of its officers, in 1903 the Minister of War, General André, asked Freemasons to compile elaborate dossiers (*fiches*) on officers, commenting on their political and religious views as well as their personal lives and those of their families. The Masonic lodges, an elaborate network of free thinking, republican, and anticlerical Frenchmen (with, it is to the point, intimate links to the League) obligingly provided the War Ministry with an extensive array of information. It was clearly understood that the information so compiled would be used to determine advancement within the ranks. Whether this secret information significantly affected the careers of individual officers is a matter of some debate.[18] What is not in dispute is that the process was highly irregular if not illegal. The files created by the Masonry were secret and not subject to any administrative checks. Much of the information was overtly partisan, concerned less with the professional efficiency of the officers or even with their political reliability than with personal or confessional issues. And much of the information was inaccurate. In short, this was precisely the kind of abuse of power that ought to have invited the prompt intervention of the League.

Some members of the Central Committee, notably the distinguished academic Célestin Bouglé, thought so too.[19] They granted that the government had the legitimate right to inform itself about the political loyalty of its officers but not by using methods that the League would certainly have denounced had they been directed against republican officers. As Joseph Reinach pointedly remarked, principles invoked "when we fear we will not be the strongest" could not be ignored "as soon as we no longer fear that we will not be the strongest."[20]

Newly elected League President, Francis de Pressensé, by contrast, saw the matter in a different light. Pressensé was the son of a Protestant pastor.[21] Like many leaders of French Socialism, he came from a solidly middle-class background; his early career had been spent in the Ministry of Foreign Affairs and later as an editor of *Le Temps,* the organ of the comfortable Republican middle class, soon to become the semiofficial newspaper of the reigning Republicans. In the 1890s Pressensé underwent a spiritual crisis, the result of which was a passionate adhesion to the cause of Socialism. Like other Protestant Socialists (his fellow leaguer Jules Moch being the best example), his conversion to Socialism was an extension rather than a rejection of his devout Christianity. He was elected as a Socialist deputy from Lyon in 1902 and became president of the League the following year. Pressensé readily conceded that the conduct of the Masons was "an error and a deplorable one." But surely it would be wrong for the League to make too much of the behavior of government officials "who could have made mistakes, even serious ones, in the heat of stubborn battle" lest such a position appear to be "a blow against the position of loyal officers and against the republic itself." The practice of secret reports on officers was indisputably an unsavory one and ought to be abolished. But it ought not be forgotten that the royalists had employed it against republican officers for the past thirty years. The current protests of the nationalist Right were therefore utterly hypocritical, and the whole affair had been "deliberately instigated by the nationalist party in order to cause trouble and provoke disarray in the, alas, too sparse ranks of republican officers." He was unmoved by the indignation of colleagues like Bouglé and Reinach. "On the pretext of remaining the purest of the pure, we have seen too many republicans—consciously or otherwise—playing into the hand of the praetorians." The League ought not to "let itself be dragged into . . . giving aid to the clever plot of the party of forgers," and ought to "choose its moment, its reasons and its allies" before entering the fray.[22]

Pressensé's reasoning is worth dwelling on because it set a pattern followed, with some exceptions, by the League during its next forty years. Pressensé was probably not wrong in suggesting that General André set no precedent in spying upon members of the officer corps. But he deliberately chose not to grasp the moral high ground by asserting that illegal actions, even when carried out in a good cause by sympathetic people, are no less illegal. Instead he chose to argue, in essence, that "turnabout is fair play." A fair enough position for a politician—Left or Right—but not exactly consistent with the principles the League professed to embrace. To be sure, in substantive terms, the harm done to the careers of Roman Catholic army officers paled by comparison with the plight of Captain Alfred Dreyfus. But in principle, religious discrimination was present in both cases, and Pressensé came perilously close to suggesting that what distinguished them in his mind was his politically motivated sympathy for one form of discrimination. By way of justification he suggested that republican officers were a distinct minority in the army and thus entitled to whatever advantages Mercier's policies would afford them Even were he right about the political orientation of the army—and the point is not obvious[23]—his position entirely ignored the fact that officers, provided they performed their assigned tasks competently, were entitled to their private political views. Finally, there was a serious disconnect between the League's principled stand to the effect that it had a duty to intervene in any case of injustice, regardless of who the victim was and who was responsible and Pressensé's contention that the League had to "choose its moment, its reasons and its allies."

Yet on this issue, at least, Pressensé still had the support of some of the more moderate elements on the Central Committee. Yves Guyot would assert that "it would be a serious mistake to render the League in any way complicit with the campaign of the nationalists against the Republic." Jean Psichari noted that "in order to judge the issue fairly one must take account of the state of exasperation of republican officers who have been spied upon by reactionaries and clericals."[24] Moreover on this issue the leaders had the overwhelming support of the rank and file. Of the 175 sections that expressed opinions on the issue, only fourteen expressed reservations, and virtually none condemned outright the official stance. The fuss about informers, the section in Antibes insisted, was just "a hypocritical, impudent, and perfidious manoeuvre"; the League had more important victims to worry about than army officers who "enjoy a situation that in its very nature is a privileged one."[25] The section in Calais regretted that "under the influence of an exaggerated and misdirected sense of impartiality," certain public figures were tempted "casually to sacrifice civil servants in response to the slightest protest by the reactionaries." Governments had to rely on "all information coming from honest and reliable sources . . . without being restrained by an excess of phoney scruples."[26] It is easy enough, in retrospect, to find this kind of reasoning and rhetoric unsettling. But the concern was shared by informed and sympathetic contemporaries. It was, after all, Célestin Bouglé, one of the League's most prominent leaders, who at the time warned that too many of the newer members of the League found "liberalism" to be outmoded and were practicing a "clericalism in reverse." Cropping up among too many leaguers were "instincts, habits and traditions that are singularly reminiscent of the traditions, habits and instincts of the nationalists."[27]

The 1905 law separating church and state provoked another crisis within the League. Until 1905 church-state relations in France had been governed by Napoleon's 1801 Concordat by which ministers of all cults (Catholic, Protestant, and Jewish) were treated as paid civil servants of the state and subject to rigorous state control. Although the Concordatory regime had ultimately worked to the satisfaction of most republican politicians, separation of church and state was a long-standing demand of both Radicals and Socialists. The high-profile anti-Dreyfusard stance of some segments of the French clergy and deteriorating relations between France and the Vatican ensured that with the 1902 government of Emile Combes, an ex-seminarian, Freemason, and archly anticlerical Radical, separation would become a government priority. Moreover, the text of the resultant law on separation, finally adopted in 1905, was almost entirely the work of the Socialist deputy, Francis de Pressensé.

Pressensé's proposed legislation received, after an extensive discussion, the enthusiastic endorsement of a majority of the members of the Central Committee, thereby profoundly troubling a conservative minority and some of the more prominent leaders of the Protestant community. As to substance, not all of them were convinced that Separation was entirely desirable; others found the proposed bill to be harsher and more punitive than necessary. But the more pertinent point they raised was: why was the League even involved in the issue? Separation of church and state may or may not have been desirable as a matter of public policy. But what did the question have to do with the Rights of Man, especially given that the Declaration, the League's charter, was absolutely silent on the point? Even were one to agree that the separation of church and state was consistent with the spirit, if not the letter, of the Declaration, surely the League should limit itself to pronouncing on the *principle* of separation. Yet here was the

Central Committee giving its benediction, ratified by the 1903 general assembly, not to the principle, but to a specific and partisan piece of legislation. Gabriel Monod, a distinguished historian as well as a Protestant leader, reminded Pressensé that the original mandate of the League had expressly forbidden it to "involve itself in the daily political struggles." Separation of church and state, much like the graduated income tax, was a *political* question about which reasonable people could disagree. Neither one was an appropriate matter for the League to discuss, still less endorse. At this rate, he warned, the League risked becoming "a mere political and electoral association, destined exclusively to the battle against nationalism and clericalism."[28] A number of Protestant dignitaries echoed this argument.[29] These were not necessarily very telling arguments in an association already filled with individuals who believed that the battle against clericalism and nationalism was an entirely appropriate mission for the League. Pressensé was particularly unmoved by Monod's arguments. He did not care what the Declaration of 1789 actually said; as far as he was concerned, it contained the "implicit affirmation" of the principle of separation. The fact that the leaders of the French Revolution, by introducing the Civil Constitution of the Clergy, the precursor to the 1801 Concordat, did not see it that way merely proved that it was inconsistent with itself, an inconsistency, he noted, for which it had paid a terrible price. He had little use for the nit-picking of "a few so-called liberals" in the Protestant community who seemed, perversely, to be fueling the campaign of the enemies of the regime. "We are beginning to grow accustomed," he thundered "to finding on the lips of our adversaries and the worst enemies of freedom, words like liberty and tolerance."[30]

Pressensé's response was both understandable and predictable. But, in some important respects, it was also disquieting. Gabriel Monod had a penchant for lugubrious moralizing, which was not to everyone's taste. But on this issue he had raised an important point of principle. To dismiss it as "so-called liberalism" (a phrase that would in time attain a disquieting currency within the League) was at best glib. It was also somewhat facile to dismiss the notions of "liberty and tolerance" merely because they were currently falling from the lips of those who ordinarily cared for neither principle. As with the case of the affaire des fiches, important and transcendent values did not automatically lose their legitimacy merely because they were adopted by and for the wrong crowd.

Pressensé's response to questions of "liberalism" and "tolerance" could be selective, however. In 1908, General Picquart, war minister in the government of Georges Clemenceau, punished a number of officers in the garrison of Laôn for attending mass (in civilian dress) and for participating in a private meeting of the *Jeunesses Catholiques*. In principle, these actions differed little from those of General André during the affaire des fiches; moreover, Clemenceau, and especially Picquart, had become legendary for their courageous defense of Dreyfus. Nonetheless, Pressensé chose to challenge Clemenceau in parliament on this issue, noting, quite correctly, that there was nothing illegal about the actions of officers merely exercising their legitimate civil rights. The argument that punishing certain officers for their religious and political beliefs constituted a small reward for loyal republican ones—current during the affaire des fiches—was, Pressensé now insisted, nonsense. At best it was "a precedent that will turn against us."[31] The Laôn episode would in time serve the League very well. For the next thirty years, a new generation of League leaders regularly cited Laôn as decisive proof of the League's willingness to defend the victims of injustice regardless of their political or confessional affiliation. What they discretely avoided mentioning was how much controversy Pressensé's principled stance had provoked within the League at the time. Clemenceau, a formidable opponent, took most of the lustre off Pressensé's polemic by pointedly reminding him how frequently sections of his own League had demanded sanctions against officers on exactly the same pretexts. Worse, many sections of the League were puzzled, if not outraged, by Pressensé's position. Seventy-three of the 137 sections that published views about the question disavowed the stance of their president, accusing him of playing into the "reactionary and clerical party." Pressensé's seeming about-face on the question, a number of sections suggested, owed less to any renewed commitment to tolerance and everything to politics. Pressensé was a Socialist, and his intervention reflected the growing antagonism of the Socialist party to the relative social conservatism of a Radical like Clemenceau.

These political tensions also surfaced during the more or less simultaneous Augagneur affair. Victor Augagneur was a prominent member of the League and until 1905 the Socialist mayor of and deputy for Lyon. He subsequently drifted toward the Radicals. In 1905, he accepted the post of governorgeneral of Madagascar. Although he was a relatively enlightened colonial administrator, he was quick to implement recent anticlerical legislation in Madagascar. In particular, this involved closing a number of Protestant schools that provided much of the education for the indigenous population. Pressensé, with the support of the Central Committee, sharply attacked the policies of his former friend and colleague, arguing, plausibly enough, that the immediate consequence would be to deprive natives of educational opportunities.[32] Radicals in the League, however, suspected that once again Pressensé's Socialist politics dictated his attacks on a fellow leaguer. Worse, they suspected that Pressensé, a notoriously devout Protestant, did not share their instinctive anticlericalism and was partial to his coreligionists in Madagascar. Some Radicals were not sure which was more troubling, Pressensé's political views or his religious ones. The President of the section of Mâcon alluded to Pressensé's Socialist politics but bluntly complained that both he and some of his fellow members of the Central Committee "display an excessive benevolence for the [Protestant] religion." The president of the federation of the Vienne, in his letter of resignation, fulminated against a League that was increasingly "more concerned to prepare for the triumph of certain economic ideas than to defend individual rights and expand the principles of 1789." He complained of the "collectivist and revolutionary doctrines" emanating from the Central Committee and announced that he was leaving the League to avoid having "to bow down . . . before Marx and Calvin."[33]

The changing political climate after 1906 had profound consequences for the internal life of the League. Until 1906, Radicals and Socialists collaborating in the Bloc des Gauches, had enjoyed a working alliance owing to their agreement on the Dreyfus affair and the religious question. By 1906 these issues had been resolved, and newer issues began to dominate the French political scene, the most important of which was the social question. In the second half of the decade, labor unrest increased dramatically. In 1907, agricultural workers in the Midi launched a massive and at times violent labor protest, one the Clemenceau government put down with the aid of the French army. In 1908 the French postal workers struck; two years later it was the railway workers. In the latter case, the government, headed by Aristide Briand, an old Dreyfusard and former Socialist but by now moving to the Right, broke the strike by mobilizing the workers, effectively meaning that refusal to perform their duties now took the form of military disobedience with the concomitant sanctions. These strikes were largely the work of the most militant of French labor unions, the *Confédération Générale du Travail* (CGT, the General Confederation of Labor). The CGT, loosely affiliated with the Socialist party, espoused a particularly violent form of revolutionary syndicalism, replete with calls for general strikes and violent overthrow of the state. In truth, the union was usually a good deal more pragmatic and reformist than its rhetoric—or more accurately, the rhetoric of a few high-profile spokesmen—suggested. By 1911 even its leaders had adopted a more conventional trade union position. But this was less evident at the time and for many mainstream republicans, the CGT was the incarnation of the class struggle, revolutionary violence, and antipatriotism. Its actions were anathema to many

Radicals and virtually everyone in the centre-gauche. In short, by 1906 the Drey-fusard coalition, so well represented in the League, had fallen apart; this rupture had immediate consequences for the League.

Pressensé and a majority of his colleagues on the Central Committee sym-pathized with the working-class protests and were indignant with the re-pressive policies followed by the governments of the day. In their view, this represented no departure from the principles upon which the League had been founded. Pressensé repeatedly noted that the current social question was more complex and less easy than had been the Dreyfus affair. But justice was no less at the heart of these questions.

At issue for many was the delicate case of *fonctionnaires* (civil servants.) Early in the twentieth century, under French law, civil servants were allowed neither to unionize nor to strike. For many in the League this was as it ought to be. Civil servants benefited from job security and pensions not enjoyed by their col-leagues in the private sector. A strike by civil servants was different from a strike in the private sector; the former was a strike against the nation that *fonction-naires* were supposed to serve. Others, however, countered that civil servants were citizens like any others; the right to unionize could no more be denied them than it could be denied to any other French citizen. The right to strike was more complex. It was inappropriate for the highest ranks of the civil service, those who had supervisory positions, but surely not for the more modest ranks. The issue was a potentially burning one in an organization in which a high per-centage of members, including teachers, were modest civil servants. A series of League congresses endorsed this position.[34] But many of the early leaders of the League did not agree. Anthony Ratier resigned from the Central Committee in 1909, declaring that the League was becoming "more and more a propaganda and combat auxiliary of an extremist party." For his part, he no longer wished to be "in complicity with civil servants in revolt" nor to support "the dis-organization of the public service."[35] Adolph Carnot, of similar political per-suasion and a member of the League since its foundation, resigned complain-ing that since the death of Trarieux, the League "is entirely infeudated with collectivism and is more and more drifting towards anarchism and anti-patriotism."[36] Many others joined them in these years, including Jean Psichari and founder and vice president, Dr. Emile Gley, Yves Guyot, Charles Richet, Gabriel Trarieux (son of the first president), and Emile Bourgeois. Of the thirty-five members sitting on the Central Committee when Pressensé became presi-dent, twenty-two resigned in the next decade, most of them because of the changing orientation of the League.[37]

Although the Central Committee invariably prevailed at its congresses, there was no denying the existence of a profound malaise within the League. In 1911, a delegate from the Seine summed up the feelings of many of the dissidents. He had been a member of the League since its foundation, had always defended the Central Committee within his section, and was sensitive to the legitimate grievances of the working class. But did this mean, he asked that "we must always support the working class, right or wrong, against both the law and the interests of the other classes of the nation"? The demands of the postal and railway workers had been legitimate ones, he conceded, but they had fallen prey to "the violent actions of revolutionary minorities which threaten the Republican regime itself." The workers were one thing, but the CGT "represented the very negation of liberty and equality." The League needed to be more evenhanded in its treatment of political issues and be "a bit fairer with respect to those who have the heavy responsibility of power" rather than persistently lining up with "the worst enemies of the Republic and of democracy." In a thinly veiled reference to the Socialists, he noted that some of those "who had stood prudently silent" in 1898 were now using the League for purposes for which it had not been intended. "For some years now individuals have been slipping into our ranks not to defend justice *per se* but to defend a special justice, a special legality . . . a Socialist or Radical justice."[38] Dissidents like this did not carry the day at League congresses, but a growing number of sections voted with their feet. In 1909, for example, 82 sections published resolutions critical of the Central Committee, whereas only 40 expressed their support.[39] Moreover, for the first time in the history of the League there was a net loss of members. In 1908, for example, there were 15,631 new members for 6,555 resignations and 105 new sections for 64 dissolved ones out of a total of 88,932 members and 870 sections.[40] The next year, by contrast, saw 21,757 members resign and only 12,346 new recruits; there were 111 dissolved sections against 76 new ones.[41] Their departure seems not to have unduly troubled Pressensé. The good old days of the Dreyfus affair, when the issue was narrow and relatively simple, could not, he observed, last forever. Even then there had been those who viewed the affair as a limited issue of one particular injustice as well as those who saw it as part of a broader and more systematic question of social injustice.[42]

By 1910 there was widespread talk about a "crisis" in the League.[43] Dissidents condemned the League's involvement in political issues, although this was usually another way of saying that they did not care for the League's current political stance. Typically, Gabriel Monod complained that the League was "exceeding its mandate" by being consumed by "political passions." In more or less the same breath, however, he also denounced "revolutionary socialists who, in the name of collectivism, fulminate against the wage system."[44] Like many moderates, Monod was disturbed that the Central Committee had dwelt at length on the illegalities of Briand but had said very little about the acts of violence of the CGT; two hundred lines in the Central Committee's resolution on the first issue as opposed to nine on the second, remarked Paul-Hyacinthe Loyson, delegate at the 1910 congress from the sixteenth arrondissement of Paris.[45] But quite apart from the question of balance, Monod insisted, was what the League was doing in this matter in the first place. The League was increasingly involved in "political pre-occupations," "socio-political crises about which the best republicans and the best friends of the people are in disagreement." Better it should stick to the "exclusive pre-occupation with justice that ought to determine all of the acts of the League."[46] It was all part of a lengthy campaign for a "return to principles."[47] He had a point, but when members of the League decried the nefarious effects of creeping politics, what many of them really deplored was the *wrong* kind of politics. What bothered Loyson, an archly ambitious political figure, was not so much the politicization of the League but the growing influence of Socialist politics.

The charges that by 1910 the League had fallen into the hands of antipatriotic revolutionaries said more about the political passions of the period than about the evolution of the League. True, the influence of both the Socialist party and the CGT within the League had increased dramatically in recent years. It was equally the case that some of the Socialist members of the League were not beyond a disquieting verbal radicalism. During a 1910 debate on the railway workers strike, one Socialist delegate cited Article 35 of the Jacobin Declaration of the Rights of Man of 1793 to the effect that when the government violates the rights of the people, insurrection is both the most sacred of rights and the most indispensable of duties.[48] This was a line that would be invoked incessantly in the years to come. But, rhetoric aside, it was also true that both the Socialists and the CGT were at that very time becoming more moderate and more reformist. Moreover, verbal flourishes aside, the position on civil servants and union activity adopted by the Central Committee was usually both cautious and sensible. Fifteen years later the Central Committee was confronted with the case of a worker in the tax collection service who was fired for circulating a letter from his union raising the possibility of job action, effectively obstructing the collection of taxes. The Central Committee dutifully, if unenthusiastically, pleaded his case on compassionate grounds but made it clear that his actions were in violation of his duty and his legal obligations.

It was not, Victor Basch would argue, as if the nation were not badly in need of tax revenue; obstructing tax collection would "paralyse national life . . . and the name for that is revolution." An alert delegate reminded Basch that he was both a Socialist and a self-proclaimed revolutionary. Basch countered that he was indeed a revolutionary, but his idea of revolution was the carefully planned, long-term, and rational variety of which the Socialist party still vaguely dreamed; it manifestly had nothing to do with the salaries of certain categories of civil servants.[49]

The critics of the prewar period were, however, right on at least one count: the issue of the labor union rights of civil servants was not an obvious one for the League. There were compelling reasons for supporting the right of French civil servants to strike but they were, in the end, political reasons. The merits of the debate simply could not be resolved by recourse to the only principles universally agreed upon in the League: the Declaration of the Rights of Man.

The crisis of the years 1906–11 had significant long-term consequences for the League. As a result of it, most of the centre-gauche and some fraction of the Radicals who had formed the early League were gone, and the League had become more or less exclusively a formation of the Left. With unconscious irony, the president of the very large federation of the Aisne, Marc Lengrand, in 1930 insisted that when it came to choosing its leaders "the vast majority of leaguers are never concerned about their [political] nuances, provided they are red."[50] The League's political center of gravity henceforth stood somewhere between the more left-wing Radicals and the more moderate Socialists. Significantly, the years 1906–11 marked the last time that the Central Committee would be consistently under fire from the more conservative elements in the League. After 1914 the attacks came from the Left.

The League was clearly on the Left. But which Left? The formation of a French Communist party in December 1920 posed a further challenge for the League. The new party, the result of a secession from the Socialist party, had an obvious appeal for members of the League's militant minority, which since 1916 had condemned the League's cautious and critical support for the French war effort and the *Union Sacrée*. Not only did the Communists excoriate the other parties of the Left for their wartime stance, but they held forth a model of a genuinely revolutionary society that contrasted markedly with the increasingly tepid reformism of the Socialist majority. Some members of the League, like Max Maurange, spokesman for the radical section in the sixth arrondissement of Paris, were clearly fascinated by the Soviet experiment. "Out of the east," he exuded, "there comes a new light which blinds us." To those who complained of the lack of formal democracy in the new regime, he responded that the "sovereignty of the worker" has replaced the bourgeois notion of "sovereignty of the citizen" and that, in any event, "the grand principles of '89 are today outmoded."[51] But simultaneous membership in the League and the Communist party was ultimately impossible given that the Communists routinely denounced the League as, at best, a representative of the "*haute bourgeoisie* of the Left." Finally, in December 1922, the Third International declared Communist party membership to be incompatible with "bourgeois" organizations like the League. Forced to choose, many, including Mathias Mordhardt, Félicien Challaye, and Sévarine, opted for the League; others, most notably Marcel Cachin, opted for the Communists.

In the years that followed, few leaders of the League expressed much sympathy for the Communist party, but many initially extended to the Soviet Union a considerable measure of goodwill. Victor Basch, while decrying the violence of the Bolsheviks, reminded everyone that France too had had its share of violence, and to make too much of the shortcomings of the Soviet regime would be "to reason like the systematic detractors of the French Revolution who execrate it because of the guillotines of the Terror." Moreover, the real issue was not whether the French Communists were sympathetic but whether they deserved the systematic harassment to which the conservative French government was currently subjecting them. Conceding that, should they get into power, French Communists would probably lock up people like himself, Henri Guernut insisted that the role of the League was nonetheless to defend them from specious charges of conspiracy and other assaults on their public liberties. In short, they ought to be treated just like the by now famous officers of Laôn.[52] The League routinely documented cases of human rights violations in the Soviet Union, although no more frequently and no less evenhandedly than with abuses in Italy, Eastern Europe, or the United States. Communists were unimpressed and responded by disrupting League meetings.[53] As on so much else, the League remained divided on Communism. For a majority, Communism was, in the words of Emile Kahn, "a system of government based on the violations of the Rights of Man." But a vocal minority within the League was selectively sympathetic to the Communists, particularly with respect to their campaigns against militarism and colonialism. As for the League's campaigns against Soviet abuses, Challaye wondered if they were really "opportune." Not only were there sufficient abuses to protest without leaving France, but "it would be a serious matter to take part in the campaign against the Soviets currently unleashed by all the capitalist powers, by our own government and by our venal press." "We are not unaware," he conceded "that the rights of man are not respected in Russia; all that we can or should say is that we would be happy if they were." What was called for, therefore, was not some "violent" attack on the Soviet Union but rather a "cordial appeal."[54]

At the end of 1935, as part of its Popular Front strategy, the Third International lifted the ban on League membership. Fearing a massive Communist infiltration and acting on the resolutions of ninety-two sections, the Central Committee proposed that newly admitted members wait a year before exercising executive functions in local sections and two years before playing similar roles in departmental federations. The leadership predictably denied that this new rule was directed against Communist infiltration, insisting, utterly implausibly, that the real purpose was to keep closet right-wingers like the *Jeunesses Patriotes,* from slipping into the League. The League congress of 1936 duly ratified this proposal but not without making it clear that it was not fooled by these claims.[55] Significantly, and to the great outrage of many members, the League saw no reason to apply this rule to membership in the Central Committee, almost certainly because it had just admitted both Léon Jouhaux and Julien Racamond to the Central Committee as soon as (and by some accounts, shortly before), they joined the League. Jouhaux had until 1934 been the head of the principal labor organization, the General Confederation of Labor. Racamond had been the leader of its Communist rival, the Unified General Confederation of Labor. As part of the Popular Front campaign, the two labor movements had united at the end of 1935. Their appointment was almost entirely symbolic, and neither one played an active role on the Central Committee. Although in the late 1930s there were periodic and predictable charges from the pacifist minority that Communists had infiltrated the League, there is little evidence for this at any level.

After 1922, the League reflected almost exclusively the views of the non-Communist Left. It therefore occupied a far narrower political terrain than it had at the beginning of the century, but it was still vast. The non-Communist Left was notoriously divided by at least as much as united it. Conservative Radicals, fundamentally content with post-1905 France and reduced to conjuring up an increasingly nonexistent clerical peril, rubbed shoulders with revolutionary socialists whose spiritual home, in the early 1920s at least, was Bolshevik Moscow rather than Republican Paris. It required considerable rhetorical virtuosity to hold such disparate elements together. Fortunately, rhetorical skills were abundant in the League, and its leaders were adept at finding formulae that might reconcile fundamentally irreconcilable principles. An overt attack on the capitalist system would surely alienate some Radicals, whereas an assault on the "puissances d'argent," an ambiguous notion but one suggesting that the target was not capitalism but merely certain abuses thereof, might not. If, instead of "big business" one used phrases like "the economic congregations," one might subliminally suggest to Radicals that a vague and imprecise anticapitalism was but a logical extension of anticlericalism. Radicals were traditionally at ease with a rhetoric that went far beyond anything they ever intended to do. Socialists, by contrast, were more (albeit only somewhat more) serious about the language they used. It followed that the League could afford the kind of radical discourse so dear to its left wing, safe in the knowledge that its more moderate members would not take any of it seriously. By embracing a passionate language that disguised a far more moderate substance, leaders of the League held their disparate coalition together. But once committed to this kind of language, they were at some pains to prevent some segment of the League from taking it far more seriously than anyone ever intended.

Where exactly did the majority of League members sit in the political space extending from the right-wing of the Radicals to the left wing of the Socialists? Historians have frequently suggested that by the early 1930s the League was effectively dominated by the Socialists.[56] But these claims must be taken with caution. In the first place, the League had no way of knowing the political affiliation of most of its 180,000 members, many of whom did not formally belong to a political party. Moreover, most of the contemporary statements about the League's presumed political orientation were made in a partisan political context. Oft cited, for example, is the statement of the ex-secretary general of the Radical party, Edouard Pfeiffer, at the party's congress in May 1934, to the effect that the League had become more or less exclusively Socialist. But Pfeiffer asserted this in the midst of a severe internal crisis of his party when its leadership was under attack by dissident Radicals, all of whom belonged to the League. At more or less the same time, and for comparably polemical purposes, League President Victor Basch declared, most improbably, that the great majority of leaguers were Radicals.[57]

Quantitative analysis yields ambiguous results. Roughly 60 percent of League politicians in the early 1930s were Radicals, the rest being Socialists of various stripes. On the other hand, a recent study of the interwar Central Committee, including both members and unsuccessful candidates, shows that fully one-third belonged, at some point, to the Socialist party as opposed to fewer than 20 percent who belonged to either the Radicals or various independent Socialist formations.[58] But given the very heterogeneous nature of all left-wing parties in

France, the vague (when not incoherent) and overlapping nature of their plat-forms and the ease with which left-wing politicians moved back and forth be-tween different formations, political labels lose much of their value. The basis of Pfeiffer's aforementioned assertion was the fact that his fellow Radical, Henri Guernut was no longer secretary general, and the Socialist, Emile Kahn was. But Guernut began his career in the Socialist party before migrating to the Re-publican Socialists and finally, in 1932, to the Radicals. In this respect he was typical of many Socialist politicians in the League (Maurice Viollette and Joseph Paul-Boncour, for example) in that their preferred space was precisely that neb-ulous terrain between the official Socialists and the Radicals. Significantly, most of the League's leaders who remained in the SFIO (Basch, Kahn, Grumbach, Frossard, Frot, and Renaudel) were those who advocated closer and less doc-trinally burdened links with the Radicals. Similarly, the most prominent Radi-cals in the party (Jean Zay, Marc Rucard, Pierre Cot, Jacques Kayser, Albert Bayet, Gabriel Cudenet, and Gaston Bergery) were left-wing Radicals who urged a more intimate cooperation with the SFIO. It was not accidental that when dissident parties emerged in the mid-1930s—the *Parti Radical Camille Pelletan* to the left of the Radicals and the *neosocialistes* to the right of the SFIO—they were led by members of the League, in the former case by Gabriel Cudenet and in the latter by Marcel Déat, Adrienne Marquette, and Pierre Re-naudel. This suggests that the political center of gravity of the League lay almost exactly in the gray areas between the Radicals and the Socialists.

All of this said, it was the case that congresses of the League did at times re-semble Socialist revival-hall meetings. In 1927, the Central Committee prepared a document for the League's annual congress on the "organization of democ-racy." At the heart of the report was the proposition, now central to the League's thinking, that a meaningful democracy would have to be a "social democracy," one in which significant differences of wealth and power no longer stood be-tween one citizen and another. Among other things, the report called for the abolition of the "wage system." Although no one quite said so, this was per-ilously close to the position of the contemporary Socialist party.

As a result, the inevitable question arose as to the exact modalities of a tran-sition to the proposed new order of society. The issue (a burning one in So-cialist circles) of the temporary "suspension of legality" and the "dictatorship of the proletariat" could not help but surface. Indeed, as one member observed, the chances of abolishing the wage system without a temporary suspension of legality were remote. Disturbed by the discussion, one delegate had the temer-ity to suggest that in the League any mention of "suppression of legality" or dictatorships of any kind was singularly out of place. In response, a number of delegates, Victor Basch not least of them, treated this erring soul to an stern lecture on French history. Was he somehow unaware that a revolution was, by definition, a suspension of legality and that France had experienced no fewer than five revolutions since 1789, the last of which had given birth to the republic under which he lived? No one thought it relevant to observe that none of the revolutions had been directed against liberal democratic regimes or that the last of them, that of 1870, had not been, strictly speaking, much of a revolution.[59] Emile Kahn, future secretary general of the League, patiently took the same innocent leaguer through the theory and practice of the dictatorship of the proletariat. Citing the classic patristic literature, from Marx's *Critique of the Gotha Program* through the later works of Engels, Kahn sought to establish that it would inevitably be the case that after the majority had triumphed, it would still have to deal with the machinations of an economically powerful minority. Had not, one delegate helpfully noted, the democratic left-wing majority elected in 1924 been overturned two years later by the "wall of money," that is, the forces of entrenched capitalism? To prevent the forces of capitalism from destroying the new regime, Kahn insisted, a temporary dictatorship might be necessary, a dictatorship of the proletarian majority. He did not address the question as to whether such a regime might have been appropriate in 1924, but he did stress that such a dictatorship had little in common with dictatorship of a *party* that currently prevailed in the Soviet Union.[60]

What is significant about this discussion is that, for all the rhetorical extravagances unleashed, it was part of a broader debate about an exceedingly moderate clause in the Central Committee's motion dealing with "deviations" from democracy. In the end, all the motion said was that Italian Fascism and Soviet Communism were both regrettable. The first it condemned, not surprisingly, in the strongest of language and the second in only slightly more measured tones. There was nothing in the motions to suggest that the League was anything other than arch partisans of liberal democracy. Moreover, Victor Basch, for all his revolutionary rhetoric during the debate, had actually opened the congress with a plea for moderation on the grounds that the League, now a large and influential organization, had a responsibility to the French public to make the most measured judgments.

The rhetorical flourishes at League congresses served the purpose of keeping the more ardent militants more or less in line. But they also robbed the League's proclamations of much of their substance. The call for the abolition of the wage system, for example, cannot have been taken very seriously by many of the Radicals in the League, or by anyone else. Eight years later the ardent young Socialist, André Philip, was still demanding that the League pronounce on the question of wage labor. He was a member of the Central Committee so he cannot have been ignorant of past resolutions; for the same reason, he was fully aware of how little force they had.

But revolutionary rhetoric continually set the tone of League discourse. Leaguers, Victor Basch not least among them, were fond of reminding everyone of the 1793 dictum that when public liberties were threatened, insurrection was the most sacred of duties. Using language that would come back to haunt him, Basch repeatedly assured the League that if and when it became necessary to descend into the streets, he would be at the head of the insurrection.[61] Basch almost certainly did not mean any of this literally, but many rank and file took the language seriously and began to talk of "descending into the street" and preparing "a decisive riposte to the fascist provocations." As the keynote speaker at the 1934 federal congress of the Calvados admitted, there were some "who claim that the League has gone too far and is abandoning its principles." But, he countered, "it seems to us that the days are gone when we could afford such a formal definition of freedom, now that we are confronted by people who, in the name of that same freedom, beat up people, burn public monuments and are invariably armed." The League's choices, it appeared, were coming down to "submission or insurrection."[62] All of the talk of insurrection, to say nothing of the casual dismissal of "formal" freedoms, seems oddly misplaced, the more so because France remained a democratic nation. But the public statements of the League's leaders seemed to indicate that the democratic nature of the regime was more apparent than real. The secretary of the section of Vincennes announced that "there are some of us in the League who think that the Third Republic is in the process of dying," adding that "we will not stop to mourn" this moribund institution.[63] The League was unsparing in its attacks on the corruption of the democratic process by the "puissances d'argent" whose nefarious hold on so many deputies perverted parliament and whose domination of the mass-circulation newspapers short-circuited the democratic process. No one listening to speeches at the League's congresses in the early 1930s would have concluded that the existing regime had many redeeming qualities.

Nor would they have received much guidance from the League's leaders. In 1932 César Chabrun, the treasurer, presented the Rapport Moral before the annual congress. It consisted largely of a sustained invective against the "puissances d'argent" who were currently corrupting French democracy. He concluded, logically enough, that some would suggest "that this leads us to revolution." At this point, he reminded everyone of the famous Jacobin dictum of the legitimacy of revolution when faced with tyranny and pointedly asked his audience if it seriously believed that France was not currently living under the tyranny of the moneyed interests. So, was this a call for revolution? Ah, but this was a political question. "Leave this to the political parties," he insisted, "for this does not concern us. But as Leaguers, let us enlighten the parties, let us show them the way." What did any of this bafflegab actually mean? It is unlikely that Chabrun, who entered politics as a moderately conservative deputy and who as recently as 1930 had agreed to accept a ministerial portfolio, took his own inflammatory rhetoric very seriously. But some members of his audience certainly did.[64]

Again, inflammatory language served to mask a rather more conventional substance. In practice, most of the League's leaders wanted to preserve the republican regime, warts and all. Indeed, they clung rather tenaciously even to the warts. Two of the more scandalous features of the Third Republic were its failure to enfranchise women and its preservation of an undemocratically elected upper house, the Senate. An exclusively masculine suffrage made France an anomaly among democratic nations by the early 1930s and stood in overt violation of the League's stated principles. Yet its leadership resisted any attempts to give women the vote, even at the municipal level, lest enfranchised women vote for clerical and conservative candidates. A Senate, elected by restricted suffrage and explicitly designed to put a conservative brake on the policies of the democratically elected Chamber had always been an affront to the League's principals as well as those of democracy, the more so since the Senate exercised its powers to topple the kind of progressive governments the League championed.[65] Yet the League resisted appeals for the abolition of the Senate, arguing that although its social conservatism was regrettable, it nonetheless was a solid defender of the republican principle. In essence, then, the League's rhetoric appealed to revolutionary Socialists, but its substantive positions catered to the sensibilities of conventional Radicals.

There was, to be sure, more to the leadership's defense of the existing regime than appeasing the Radicals. By 1934, at the latest, the League's leaders began to recognize that attacks on the deficiencies and scandals of the democratic regime were no longer the exclusive province of the Left. Antiparliamentary rhetoric was ideally suited to the growing fascist leagues for whom "descending into the street" was manifestly not an empty phrase. It escaped few that the League's periodic assertions that insurrection was the most sacred of duties served primarily as a ritualistic commemoration of the association's republican heritage; when uttered by Colonel Charles des Isnards, one of the Parisian leaders of the protofascist Jeunesses Patriotes, the same phrase explicitly justified a very real assault on the democratic regime. Socialist deputy and Central Committee member Paul Ramadier sat on the parliamentary committee investigating the antiparliamentary riots of February 6, 1934. He pointedly reminded his colleagues that in this capacity he had been treated to a steady diet of lectures coming from the extreme Right justifying insurrection in the name of the sacred duty of the oppressed people.[66] Basch, therefore, began to remind the rank and file that for all its faults, the democratic republic provided a degree of public liberty that was becoming rare in Europe. Exclusive concentration on the regime's shortcomings served no purpose save providing ammunition for the enemies of democracy. One ought not, in the name of a purer democracy, adopt a language that was perilously close to that of the fascists.

But the distinction between legitimately revolutionary language and fascist discourse—absolutely clear to Basch—escaped many leaguers. Conditioned over the years to immoderate language, many began to feel entirely at home with statements that, by any standards, were foreign to the spirit of the League. By the mid-1930s, members of the League felt comfortable asserting that while the ultimate goals of fascism were clearly inimical to the League, fascist tactics might not be. In 1935, the uncontested leader of that wing of the League that wanted to adopt a radical new approach, Léon Emery, boldly asserted: "We must, albeit reluctantly, employ certain of the methods of fascism."[67] When, at the 1935 congress he declared: "that Parliament has, in the last twenty years, done nothing for democracy strikes me as utterly and literally true" and that as a consequence "the distinction between fascist states and democratic ones is merely a question of degree and not a fundamental one," he received a standing ovation. When Eugène Frot, deputy and former minister, attempted to dispute these assertions and argued that "parliament is, after all . . . the reflection of the wishes of universal suffrage," he was literally booed off the podium. Victor Basch was rightly aghast at Emery's language, noting that it was perilously close to the antiparliamentary rhetoric of the extreme Right. In time Basch's suspicions about the implications of Emery's language would prove to be only too well founded. But in 1935, Emery could counter, with some plausibility, that there was nothing in his highly pessimist view of French democracy that could not be found in the more "lugubrious" declarations of Victor Basch. Both sides were right. Emery was a protofascist in the making; Basch was a principled defender of the parliamentary republic. But, as late as 1935, they still spoke the same language.[68]

When not engaging in revolutionary rhetoric, the League was often engaged in issues of day-to-day politics. In 1924 the Central Committee seriously debated whether to attempt to persuade the Socialists to enter into a government with the Radicals in the recently elected *Cartel des Gauches.* The Committee decided not to, but the fact that such a debate took place at all indicates how much the League thought that one of its legitimate functions was to be a coordinating agency of the parties of the Left.[69] No less purely partisan was a 1929 debate concerning the ratification of the interallied accords on war debts. This was an issue that had embroiled French politics for much of the 1920s. During World War I France had borrowed heavily from Great Britain and, above all, the United States. Although no one contested that the debts had been contracted, French public opinion felt uneasy about allied demands for repayment. These, after all, were not ordinary commercial debts but sums of money expended, at least after 1917, in a common cause against a common enemy. American expenditures in dollars had been more than matched by French expenditures in human lives. Moreover, at a minimum, the French tended to argue, surely repayment of loans should be tied explicitly to German payment of reparations. Unfortunately these arguments made little impression on the American government, which was notoriously uneasy about the entire question of German reparations and denied any logical link between them and French debts. Finally, in 1926 with the Mellon-Beringer and Caillaux-Churchill accords, France agreed to a repayment schedule that made few concessions to her concerns of principle but that effectively absolved her of about half of the debt she had actually incurred.

The accords, however, were not submitted to parliament for ratification (although the Poincaré government began repayment anyway), and the issue did not come up for parliamentary scrutiny until spring 1929. By this time, important elements in the Socialists and the Radicals, since the 1928 elections comfortably in the opposition, were increasingly vocal in their opposition to the accords. Three days before the issue was to be discussed in parliament, Basch demanded a special meeting of the Central Committee to discuss the issue, despite the resistance of a number of deputies on the Central Committee, notably the socialist leader Léon Blum who argued that such a debate would be "awkward" for "the many members of the League who are at the same time members of [the Socialist] party."[70] Basch agreed that on the face of it the issue might appear to be a purely political one and thus outside the League's jurisdiction; indeed, this had been the position of the Executive in 1926.[71] But there were broader issues at stake. The question of the debts was one of "public morality" and thus far more important than the parliamentary maneuvering of the parties of the opposition. Surely the League believed that living up to freely consented contractual obligations was a principle worth defending. To be sure, given the political orientation of the League, the principle of the sanctity of commercial debts was not self-evident. Basch himself would alternate between describing the debts as "sacred" and insisting that talk about the respect for contracts amounted to a "vain and demagogic phraseology."[72] Moreover, as Emile Kahn reminded him, another of the League's principles was that although it was acceptable for the victor to demand that the vanquished pay for the damage he had done, the League had strenuously, in the past, rejected the notion that the vanquished could be obliged to pay for the general costs of the war. Yet without some safeguard clause ensuring that German reparations exceed French war-debt payments, German payments would merely be transhipped to the United States, meaning that Germany would, indirectly, be paying for the cost of the war. The militant left-wing pacifist, Félicien Challaye came, most unusually, to Basch's defense with yet another principle: the debt was sacred because French people needed to be constantly reminded of the financial consequences of the war in order that they might be rather more critical of France's role in 1914 and more dedicated to preventing a repetition of that catastrophe. Ernest Lafont, usually an ally of Challaye but also a Socialist deputy, charged that the League was "meddling in a question over which it had no competence," in a debate serving no useful purpose save that of "stabbing in the back the two parties who support democracy." No one quite wanted to acknowledge that Basch was attempting to import a debate, currently raging in (and perfectly but also uniquely appropriate for) his Socialist party, into the League. For all his passion, Basch's real concern about the war debts was pragmatic rather than principled, and fundamentally, although he chose not to admit it, those of Raymond Poincaré. The interallied accords were, *pace* some of Basch's fellow Socialists, the best France was likely to get; failure to ratify them would saddle France with more onerous terms and, worse, jeopardize the implementation of the Young Plan and the evacuation of the Ruhr thus imperiling a rapprochement with Germany. In the end the discussion was little more than a dress rehearsal for the one that would soon take place in parliament. The Central Committee voted, as would parliament, in favor of ratifying the accords.

This kind of public stance troubled some prominent members of the League. The recently elected Socialist deputy from the Drôme, Jules Moch, a leaguer as had been his father before him, pointedly wondered why the League

was involved in this issue in the first place. The League had begun as an organization dedicated to the rights of Alfred Dreyfus. It soon became an organization dedicated to defending the rights of everyone persecuted by the state. In
time it expanded its mandate to defending public liberties in France. This was
already, he insisted, a very vast terrain. Should not the League stick to this
mandate and let the politicians take care of the messy issues of commercial
debts?[73] At the League's 1927 congress, one delegate from Paris suggested that
perhaps the League should limit itself "exclusively to the pure defence of the
rights of man and citizen, excluding all the large problems of general politics
which ought not to be its concern." No one paid the slightest attention to his
plea.[74] Granted, whenever the Central Committee was discussing some purely
political matters, some kind of platonic demurral was to be expected. A debate
on the 1931 Hoover war debt moratorium prompted Jean Bon to remind
everyone that "we are not a council of ministers," an assertion that was literally
true but that would not have been scant years earlier.[75] Prior to 1927, Ministers
could and did sit on the Central Committee, and its deliberations did at times
have a ministerial quality. When Central Committee members confronted
questions of colonial policy they did so in the most direct manner—by asking pointed questions of their fellow committee members: Theodore Steeg,
minister resident in Morocco; Alexander Varenne, his counterpart in Indo-
China, and Maurice Viollette, governor general of Algeria.[76] Anyone following the Central Committee's 1927 deliberations about impending legislation
on the organization of the nation in wartime might have thought they were
witnessing a miniature version of French parliament. Defending the project
was the author of the law himself, Joseph Paul-Boncour, an independent Socialist deputy and currently minister of national defense. Leading the attack
was Ernest Lafont, a left-wing Socialists; mounting a defense was the more
moderate Socialist deputy, Pierre Renaudel. All were members of the Central
Committee, and all were repeating arguments previously made in the chamber. Not altogether surprisingly, Paul-Boncour responded to the predictable
pacifists laments by insisting that "the League need not concern itself with
the problem of national defence."[77] But this was an argument appealing only
to those, mostly deputies, who approved of the bill. A debate about a parliamentary proposal to eliminate the run-off ballot in legislative elections moved
Victor Basch to wonder if the Committee had not approached the limits of
"the problems the League is qualified to deal with." But no one else thought so
if for no better reason than the fact that the proposal, were it adopted, would
strengthen the parties of the Right. As Emile Kahn bluntly reminded Basch,

the issue self-evidently concerned the League precisely because it had "a politically reactionary purpose."[78]

However much it continued to claim that it was "above politics" the League was, from very nearly its beginning, deeply enmeshed in the day-to-day politics of France. Defining human rights in the broadest possible manner meant that there were few political questions the League did not feel called upon to address, including those that seemed at best tenuously connected to even the most expanded definition of the rights of man. Not only was it intimately involved in politics but those politics were almost invariably left-wing politics. At one level, this was a logical consequence of its very broad definition of human rights and therefore of its mandate. But adopting the broader mandate was also a clear political choice. Put another way, the League was not ineluctably driven into the political arena by its broad definition of human rights; to a substantial degree, the broader definition of human rights was a consequence of the political orientation of its leaders. As a result, the League's self-appointed role as "the conscience of democracy" was effectively reduced to being the conscience of the Left. To be sure, there was arguably a role for a "conscience of the Left" in Third Republic France. But such a role presupposed a critical detachment from both electoral and parliamentary politics. As the next chapter will show, this proved impossible.

THREE

Politics, Yes, but Not Electoral Politics

In one of his more candid moments, Victor Basch observed: "Every spokesman for the League, from Trarieux, through Pressensé, Buisson, myself, Bouglé, Guernut and the rest have consistently stated that the League does not involve itself in politics. In reality, however, and let us admit it, that is all it does, it does nothing but politics."[1] But, he hastened to add, it was *politics* in the broadest and best sense of the word: public policy. When members of the League asserted that *on ne fait pas de la politique,* they meant that the League did not engage in electoral politics or in parliamentary politics. Even as modified, his claim about the League's stance on politics was highly misleading.

In fact the League always paid special attention to elections. Prior to the 1902 elections, the Central Committee published a manifesto reminding the electorate that it had been the first to spot, lurking behind "a judicial affair," the "imminent danger of a counter-revolutionary plot" and to have "opened the path to the organization of republican defence." Neither the League nor its local sections were to be confounded with "electoral committees" of course. Nonetheless, the Committee insisted, "we have the duty to come to an agreement on what . . . we must ask of the candidates to whom our votes will go."[2] The League, in short, could support only sincere republicans. Local branches of the League often took these principles a step further. In 1902, the president of the section of Angoulême in the Charente reminded his members that "we must necessarily occupy ourselves with political and electoral questions in order to defend the sacred principles of '89 and '93 which are inscribed in our statutes."[3] Francis de Pressensé, the newly elected deputy from Lyons and shortly to become League president, proudly read a report from his section that boasted of its active role in his election.[4] And despite President Trarieux's assertions that the League must "have nothing to do with politics properly speaking, must not have plans for government and must not be confused with electoral committees," Article 16 of the League's statutes nonetheless explicitly permitted local sections to join electoral committees.[5]

That very article began to trouble members of the League who believed that it should "abstain from all involvement in electoral questions."[6] The issue was debated at great length at the 1904 congress. Marius Moutet, future Socialist deputy and leading member of the Central Committee, expressed concern about "the attitude of the younger and more recently formed sections" that seemed to think the League was primarily "an electoral organization."[7] Others, however, protested that any modification of article 16 would render the League "a purely philosophical association." One delegate remarked that, especially in the south of France, "there are a host of sections of the League which are the only existing republican organization." Denying those sections the right to participate in electoral politics was tantamount to surrendering those regions to the forces of reaction.[8] Nonetheless, the congress agreed to change Article 16 to expressly forbid any section of the League from joining, as a body, any electoral committee.

Article 17, however, still permitted sections to formally endorse and support a candidate under certain circumstances. Except in 1919 and 1924, French legislative elections involved a system of single member constituencies with two ballots. To be elected on the first ballot, a candidate required an absolute majority of the votes cast. Given that in most constituencies in France there were three or more candidates on the first ballot, it was frequently the case that no candidate obtained the requisite majority. In such cases a second "run-off" ballot would be held, at which time a simple plurality sufficed for election. Because typically the Left was more likely than the Right to present several candidates on the first ballot, victory on the second ballot often necessitated what was known as "republican discipline," whereby the least favored candidates of the Left on the first ballot would desist in deference to the most favored left-wing candidate for the second ballot. Article 17 stipulated that local sections could support a candidate on the first ballot only if he were the sole republican (by which it meant left-wing) candidate in the race. On the second ballot, they could actively support any candidate who had abided by the rules of republican discipline. In principle, this modification was designed to ensure that in forthcoming elections the internal unity of the League would not be disrupted by sectarian electoral quarrels between different parties of the Left.

In practice the issue was more complicated. League sections were often indifferent to, or ignorant of, the association's statutes. Two years later, the Central Committee was still forced to remind sections that they could not be formally attached to local branches of the Radical party. The statutory provision permitting sections to actively support a first-ballot candidate provided he was the sole republican running was often not a very useful guideline given that, by 1906, in most parts of France *all* candidates claimed to be republican. In the 1906 elections, the section in Sisteron in the Basses-Alpes supported a candidate against Yves Guyot. Guyot was a founding member of the League and was sitting on the Central Committee. Once identified with the Radical party, he was by now on the centre-gauche and would be one of those early League leaders who would soon resign from the League because of its growing political radicalism. Members of his section, dominated by Socialists, were obviously unimpressed by his "republican" credentials and, the strenuous protests of the Central Committee notwithstanding, maintained their support of his rival. Even the principle of republican discipline on the second ballot, so logical in theory, proved uncommonly difficult in practice. Where the danger of a conservative victory was slight (in itself a highly subjective judgment), it was frequently the case that no party on the Left felt bound by republican discipline. Left-wing candidates and their supporting committees were adept at finding reasons why the most favored candidate on the first ballot ought not to be the "republican" standard bearer on the second. Radicals in particular, faced with the superior first-ballot performance of a Socialist candidate, tended to argue that even with a Radical withdrawal, the Socialist, too extreme for their region, would be unable to garner sufficient additional votes to be elected. Socialists tended to counter that many of the votes gained on the first ballot by their Radical rivals had come from "reactionaries." Such a candidate, if supported and elected on the second ballot might be, in the words of Pressensé himself, "a Trojan horse." In the 1906 elections, in the fifteenth arrondissement of Paris, Pierre Aubricot, a Socialist and an employee of the Central Committee, received slightly fewer first-ballot votes than his Radical rival. He nonetheless maintained his candidacy on the second ballot. Faced with a high profile and embarrassing violation of Article 17, the Central Committee issued a formal condemnation of Aubricot, without, however, dismissing him from his functions. Aubricot's intransigent supporters replied that, Article 17 notwithstanding, "the struggle between the Socialist party, on the one hand, and the bourgeois parties, on the other, will continue." Nor was Aubricot's case in any way exceptional. There were so many cases of electoral indiscipline, including the example of the future Communist party leader, Marcel Cachin, that the League was forced to form a special commission to investigate the issue. At the 1906 League congress, many delegates demanded, in vain, that the League expel those sections, Socialist more often than not, that had been guilty of indiscipline.[9]

The partisan quarrels resulting from the 1906 elections helped fuel the growing ideological antagonisms within the League. Some believed that Article 17
was at the root of the "crisis" the League was experiencing in the latter half of
the decade. And almost everyone recognized that internal harmony, to say
nothing of League credibility, required some rethinking of its position on elections. In 1909 the League congress finally agreed on a new statute (Article 15),
which stated unequivocally that no section of the League could involve itself
in elections under any circumstances whatsoever. Individual members were free
to support any candidate they chose and run for any party they wished (with
the clear understanding that the candidates and the party be on the Left). But
the League and its sections would hereafter abstain from any electoral activity.

Despite Article 15, there were always sections and federations unable to resist
the lure of electoral intrigue. In the 1920s and early 1930s, some of the more left-
wing sections of the League felt authorized to join various progressive *cartels*,
which were, as the Central Committee constantly reminded them, essentially
Communist fronts. Prior to the 1924 elections, the federation of the Charente-
Maritime designated delegates to the Radical nominating convention, believing,
or pretending to, that owing to the importance of this election they had the quiet
blessing of the League president, Ferdinand Buisson. But Secretary General
Henri Guernut bluntly disabused them of any illusions they might have on that
score and stressed that no such confusion would be permitted in the future.[10]
In 1928, the Central Committee still felt the need to remind sections that "the
League must not, under any circumstances, on any pretext, for any reason, participate in elections and this means not merely voting but also the selection of
candidates."[11] Yet in the same year, the monthly bulletin of the League's powerful federation of the Charente-Maritime was still complaining that "there are
still too many leaguers who treat their section exclusively as a political organ designed to reinforce the political committees at election time."[12]

The only sure way to avoid the temptations of partisan politics was, as most
federations and sections did by the interwar years, to suspend all activities during the legislative elections. This was of particular importance in those departments where elections often involved rival candidates from within the local
League. In the Charente-Maritime, for example, five of six deputies elected in
1936 belonged to the League. But in La Rochelle, the immediate past president
of the department's powerful federation (a man destined for a distinguished
record in the Resistance) confronted the *current* president of the federation (a
man destined to be a Vichy collaborationist.) Both were running against the in-
cumbent deputy who, scant months earlier, had been an active member of the

League, purged only with some difficulty owing to the awkward revelations that he had been seriously compromised in the great political scandal of the era, the Stavisky affair.[13] Scruples about avoiding electoral contamination tended to vanish during moments of perceived political crisis. In 1935 the entire League joined the left-wing Rassemblement Populaire, one of whose functions was the coordination of left-wing candidates in the 1936 elections. Joining the Rassemblement Populaire was, as by then ex-Secretary General Guernut would later remind everyone, a violation certainly of the spirit and probably also of the letter of Article 15.[14] Given the troubling atmosphere of the mid 1930s, few in the League agonized about the issue.

Whatever the stance of local sections, the League continued to elect deputies in abundance. After the 1902 elections, there were fifty-four deputies who belonged to the League; after 1906 there were eighty deputies and fifty senators. By the 1932 legislature, there were at least 222 deputies (out of just shy of 600) who belonged to the League.[15] Some of those who sat in parliament were deputies who happened incidentally to belong to the League. Many were not. The League was nearly thirty years old before it had a president, Victor Basch, who was neither a senator nor a deputy. Henri Guernut, secretary general from 1913 to 1932, was a deputy between 1928 and 1936. His successor Emile Kahn was a perennially unsuccessful candidate for the deputation. A significant number of deputies who belonged to the League had been presidents of sections or federations prior to, and often after, their election. In any given year, nearly a quarter of the members of the Central Committee were deputies. Nor were League deputies minor members of parliament. The list of deputies who, at one time or another, occupied important positions in the League reads like a *Who's Who* of prominent politicians in post-1900 France: Gaston Doumergue, Léon Blum, Edouard Herriot, Paul Painlevé, Pierre Cot, Eugène Frot, Pierre Renaudel, Marc Rucart, Joseph Paul-Boncour, Vincent Auriol, Maurice Viollette, Marius Moutet, Henri Guernut, Paul Ramadier, André Philip, and Jean Zay.

All the rhetoric about being above politics could not mask the fact that professional politicians, to say nothing of aspiring ones, were abundantly represented in directing circles of the League. In fact, nearly half of the governments in the interwar years were headed by men who belonged, or who had once belonged, to the League. Some, Gaston Doumergue, Pierre Laval, and Edouard Daladier, had almost certainly parted company with the League prior to heading a government.[16] Others, Paul Painlevé, Edouard Herriot, and Léon Blum, members of the League from its beginning and having served on the Central Committee, were active leaguers. Remarking on the abundance of deputies, ministers, and premiers in the League, many observers, notably those on the Right, saw the League as an all-powerful arcane dictatorship within the republic.[17]

The League's incontestable parliamentary connections were also a constant source of tension within the organization. It did not go unnoticed, for example, that in many cases the deputies and senators had held office in the League before obtaining an electoral mandate, giving rise to the widespread suspicion that the politically ambitious joined the League primarily for the electoral opportunities it afforded them.[18] Marc Lengrand, president of the powerful (second only to the Charente-Maritime) federation of the Aisne, was constantly under attack from his colleagues who suspected that he was using his post as an electoral springboard. Lengrand airily insisted on his "disdain . . . for electoral office" until he resigned his post in order to run in the 1932 elections.[19] For an aspiring politician of the Left, a membership card in the League was an eminently useful accessory. Because the League's membership, 180,000 at its height, was significantly higher than that of either the Radicals or the Socialists, the electoral advantages of belonging were obvious.

No one denied that having a healthy representation among the deputies and ministers could greatly enhance the League's efficacy as the "conscience of democracy." Whether the League sought to ensure that the law be fairly enforced or that a bad law be improved, it was always better to be dealing with a minister who formally subscribed to the League's principles than one who did not. A solid block of League deputies could, in theory, be counted on to keep the governments of the day honest and to ensure progressive reforms. Significantly, when President Francis de Pressensé was defeated in the elections of 1910, he offered to resign because he feared that he could no longer effectively represent the League's interests.[20]

This sort of influence, of course, could run two ways. Many in the League's rank and file worried that too much time spent in parliamentary corridors, not to say ministerial antichambers, could dampen the revolutionary ardor of the League's leadership. This concern became particularly acute when Henri Guernut, secretary general of the League since 1913, was elected as Socialist deputy from the Aisne. That Guernut was an exceptionally capable secretary general was never questioned. But he was politically more moderate than many in the League and representative of that wing deemed to be both excessively legalistic and, in Guernut's case in particular, dogmatically "liberal." He was legendary for his good nature and his eloquent and ironic wit, a trait that in no way endeared him to some of the more earnest *militants*. That the League was insufficiently aggressive in its pursuit of its stated goals—an article of faith for a powerful minority in the interwar years—could be traced, it was argued, to Guernut's all too cordial relations with those in power and, some hinted, his own ministerial ambitions.[21] Faced with mounting attacks from the membership and the thinly disguised resentment of Victor Basch, Guernut resigned as secretary general in 1932, became a vice president instead, and was replaced in the secretariat by the somewhat more orthodox Socialist Emile Kahn.[22] This change ended some of the more overt insinuations of parliamentary corruption but did little to reconcile the internal opposition either to Guernut or, before very long, to Kahn.

After World War I, the Central Committee founded a parliamentary group including all League deputies and senators. Its existence would prove to be a constant irritant within the League. Some sections protested the creation of a parliamentary group lest it begin to rival the authority of the Central Committee and effectively "parliamentarize" the League.[23] In fact, the parliamentary group had no such pretensions and usually kept a low profile, so much so that the whole experience struck the Central Committee as being "doubtful."[24] Nonetheless, the group continued to exist until 1935, largely because many sections wanted to keep track of the activity of League deputies.[25]

Although no one dared to admit it, the *unavowed* purpose of the group was to ensure a greater degree of concordance between the League's stated principles and the voting patterns of its parliamentary members. Women's suffrage and abolition of the death penalty might have been voted by League congresses, but many of its parliamentary representatives felt free to vote against such measures. How, after all, was it possible for deputies who belonged to the League to vote in ways that were inconsistent with the League's principles? Surely, as the ex-premier Léon Blum would declare in 1937, League deputies were *politically* responsible to their electors and respective political parties but *morally* responsible to the League. But what did this Jesuitical formula mean in practice? The standard response was that the League was, of course, *above politics* and that in any case deputies owed their mandate to, and therefore were responsible before, their electors and not the League.[26] This was a lame position because the more radical elements in the League could retort that no one was talking about depriving errant deputies of their electoral mandate, just their membership in the League. A more refined position held that, of course, no deputy could advance positions that were antithetical to the basic values of the League, but whereas the League's remit was "absolute" values, deputies worked in a more complex realm of parliamentary tactics and needed some flexibility. This was a serviceable formula, largely because it meant next to nothing. Quite apart from the fact that it was not always self evident exactly what the League's basic values were, the distinction between parliamentary tactics and fundamental principles was by no means clear. The truth, as leaders of the League clearly recognized, was that it was an utter waste of time trying to exercise control over its deputies. The Radicals notoriously could not, nor could far more disciplined parties like the Socialists. Given that the League was not a party and that its deputies were spread among a number of often mutually antagonist parties, it simply had no chance at exercising control. But why then, as some rank and file asked, have a parliamentary group? The angry young Socialist, André Philip, his distinguished parliamentary career not yet under way, observed in 1935 that it was a bit pointless to have a parliamentary group that met only on rare occasions and then for the purpose of insisting that the most recent declarations of the Central Committee were not binding on it. He insisted on a resolution that ensured the League's right of "control and censure" of its deputies when the League's "principles and doctrine," as opposed to "parliamentary tactics," were at issue. Basch and his colleagues instantly accepted this formula, recognizing that the distinction between "tactics" and "principles," clear in the mind of Philip, was in practice a hazy one.[27]

The problems associated with the parliamentary group were not limited to the issue of voting discipline. The existence of a formal group tended to draw attention to the prominence of League members in public life. This was not necessarily a good thing. The least of the problems was the fact that the virulent Catholic Right poured over the relevant pages of the *Cahiers* in search of proof of the arcane dictatorship the League exercised over French politics.[28] More to the point, not every leaguer whose elevation to public office the League so publicly celebrated, was, or would be, an exemplar of the ideals of the Declaration of the Rights of Man. When Gaston Doumergue became president of the Republic in 1924, the *Cahiers* proudly remembered his long services to the League, including a prewar stint on the Central Committee.[29] Ten years later, *Premier* Doumergue had become, in the eyes of the League at least, the tool of the fascist Right. Similarly, by the 1930s, no one cared to remember that the *Cahiers* had congratulated then leaguer Pierre Laval on his appointment to the cabinet.[30] When the parliamentary group was established in 1922, Secretary General Guernut confessed to being "stupefied" by the number of deputies now professing an allegiance to the League's principles, which had heretofore been nowhere apparent in their public conduct.[31] In 1932, many members of the League were again disagreeably surprised by the names they found on the published list of the parliamentary group. Emile

Kahn noted ironically that, after the 1932 electoral victory of the Left, the League's parliamentary group had suddenly become very popular. All kinds of unlikely individuals suddenly announced that they were leaguers, including a number of long-serving parliamentarians who had not heretofore revealed themselves as such.[32]

A case in point was René Besnard, senator from the Indre-et-Loire. In the 1920s Besnard had formally denied being a member of the League, a wholly appropriate stance for a man who, from 1924 until 1928, was French ambassador to Rome. In the late 1920s, he had been involved in the Oustric affair, a scandal involving the corruption of deputies by certain shady banks, which made him the subject of an investigation before the High Court. Acquitted on technical grounds, he was nonetheless the kind of more or less corrupt politician that the League routinely execrated. The departmental federation had not been pleased by his re-election in January 1933 and was frankly astounded when his name appeared on the list of the League. How, it rather belligerently asked Kahn, had Besnard got into the League and why had the *Cahiers* not exposed him and other corrupt members of parliament? As for the first, Kahn patiently explained, if Besnard was a member of the League it was because he had managed, some time between his legal difficulties and his re-election, to persuade some section of the Federation of the Indre-et-Loire to accept him. Because only a local section could admit, or expel, a member, Kahn thought this was something the federation might well investigate. As for the silence about the questionable practices of Besnard and others, Kahn admitted with some embarrassment that he had been under pressure from certain sections not to publish the details in an election year lest some members of the Right leap on such revelations to prove the corruption of certain parliamentarians of the Left. "Bowing before such electoral reasoning," he admitted, was probably wrong but also understandable.[33]

It says something about the culture of Third Republic deputies that many who did not in fact belong to the League nonetheless applied to join its parliamentary group. By May 1933 when the League was still reconstructing its group, no fewer than seventy-one senators and 262 deputies (just under half of the deputies in the Chamber) sought entry into the group. The League, however, had no record of many of them ever having been leaguers. There followed a lengthy series of inquiries directed at individual deputies, local federations, and sections. When it was apparent that candidates did not belong to the League, they were informed that League membership was essential but also that they could sign up on the spot. Many apparently did not do so because the final lists established in February 1934 contained only 222 deputies and sixty-seven senators. Until 1934—after which time the parliamentary group became a serious embarrassment—it is obvious why the League should have wanted it to be as large as possible. Why so many deputies wanted to belong is less clear. It certainly was not because of a desire to play an active role in the group's activities. The group met about once a month, and rarely were more than a dozen members present. It seems likely that for deputies of the Left and center-left, formally belonging to a group with a progressive title was just another electoral asset.[34]

All of this was revealed in sharp relief in 1934 when France was transfixed by the Stavisky scandal. Serge Alexander Stavisky was a charming but also utterly ruthless financial swindler. His name had been on the police blotter since at least 1926 but, owing to administrative inefficiency and assorted rivalries within the judicial system, his appointment with the courts was repeatedly postponed, leaving Stavisky free to engage in a growing variety of criminal enterprises. This delay, to say nothing of Stavisky's remarkable ability to persuade otherwise serious businessmen that he was something other than a low-class crook, owed something to his charm but more to the contacts he assiduously cultivated with prominent Radical deputies and ministers. Some acted as his attorneys, and all facilitated his entry into milieus to which he would not otherwise have had access. By the end of 1933, however, time finally ran out for Stavisky, and French justice began to close in on him. With his altogether too-convenient suicide early in January 1934, the details of his political connections began to leak out.[35] It could not have come at a worse time for the Radical government then in power. Although the Left had won the 1932 elections, the perennial quarrels between Radicals and Socialists had rendered a stable parliamentary majority impossible. There followed a string of short-lived Radical governments, all of them distinguished by their inability to address the economic crisis France was facing. The revelations about political corruption intensified a growing public anger and led to massive street demonstrations on the night of February 6, 1934. These demonstrations, led by various movements of the extreme antiparliamentary Right turned violent and seemed to threaten the Republican regime itself. The recently formed Radical government of Edouard Daladier fell and was replaced by a center-right government headed by the former president of the Republic, Gaston Doumergue.

Under ordinary circumstances such an egregious example of political corruption would have been tailor-made for the League. It had long called for a "purer" republic and specialized in denouncing the corrosive role of business,

legal or otherwise, in the conduct of public affairs. In this particular case, however, the League's indignation was constrained by the awkward fact that virtually all of the deputies and ministers incriminated in the Stavisky affair were
members of the League![36] True, later, often much later, the (frankly, indulgent)
courts would clear all but two of them of any criminal offense.[37] For the most
part they were guilty only of injudicious conduct and an appalling lack of discrimination in the company they kept; their deportment was only a degree or
two removed from that of most politicians in the *république des camarades*. But
given that the League had always publicly excoriated that very "republic of
pals," none of this could be of much comfort. It wanted to mobilize French
society against the threat to the Republic represented by the activity of right-
wing leaguers on February 6, much as it had done in the wake of the Dreyfus
affair. But unlike in the days of the Dreyfus affair, this time the Right had a case:
the regime *was* corrupt, and the corruption extended into the League itself. It
did not help matters very much that Félicien Challaye, the member of the Central Committee most ill at ease with the presence of politicians in the League,
was demanding that the League publish a complete list of its deputies and senators, something Secretary General Emile Kahn had finally completed.[38] The
demand was vintage Challaye, both mischievous and principled, and Kahn, for
obvious reasons, did not comply. But the League affiliation of the incriminated
deputies was no secret because the far Right, given as it was to rigorously scru-
tinizing every issue of the *Cahiers,* knew full well from previously published lists
exactly how many leaguers were involved in the Stavisky scandal and were currently enjoying themselves immensely at the expense of the League.

The Radical party, every bit as embarrassed as the League (and for better
reasons) solved the problem at its emergency congress of May 1934. There, at
the urging of the left-wing Radical (and member of the League's Central Committee) Albert Bayet, all but one of the erring Radical deputies were expelled
from the party. That the Radical party, undistinguished for its probity, could
expel offending members posed yet another problem for the League. Its statutes
dictated that only local sections could pass on the worthiness of individual
members. Kahn sent out a series of discreet letters to the sections of the
deputies involved, suggesting that they might want to give some thought to
the issue. But this would only pose further problems.

A fairly typical case involved Louis Proust, deputy from the Indre-et-Loire
and a very conservative Radical. Like every other deputy from the department,
he was a member of the League but he was, for a variety of reasons, an excellent
candidate for expulsion. He had served for a number of years as the president

of the *Comité Mascuraud,* an organization of small and medium-size businesses whose function was to channel its considerable financial resources for the election of worthy candidates. The business interests involved here were a notch or two removed from the puissances d'argent the League routinely excoriated, but it was no secret that the *Comité* sought to orient the Radicals away from the Socialists and toward formations of the center-right like the *Alliance Démocratique.*[39] Proust had also earned a recent notoriety owing to a very public spat with his fellow Radical deputy and fellow leaguer, Jacques Kayser—Alfred Dreyfus's nephew. Proust took strong exception to Kayser, currently sitting on the Central Committee, for his pacifist and internationalist approach to foreign policy and for his habit of criticizing Radical leader, Edouard Herriot, on this point. This kind of internationalism, Proust unsubtly suggested, might be explained by Kayser's Jewish ancestry. Perhaps, therefore, Kayser might feel more at home in the political company of another Jew, Léon Blum, and a party called the French Section of the Workers' *International.*[40] Finally, Proust's name, alongside a very substantial sum of money, could be found in the checkbook stubs of the late M. Stavisky. To be sure, in due course it would be established that the check in question never reached Proust and was cashed by a third party. But there was never any doubt that between 1928 and 1933 Proust had rendered a wide range of services to Stavisky. Prompted by Kahn, the federation of the Indre-et-Loire wrote Proust's section, Neuillé-Pont-Pierre, requesting that it take the appropriate action. But the president of the section was none other than Proust himself. He had been mayor of the town since 1908, was a local judge, and was solidly entrenched. After a protracted public and embarrassing fight, the federation finally persuaded Proust to step down as president of his section, a position he promptly resumed when in 1936 he chose not to run for re-election. In this, one of the League's most quarrelsome federations, the Proust issue was still being fought out in the summer of 1938.[41]

Nor was Proust's case exceptional. André Hesse was deputy for La Rochelle. For the previous quarter century he had been a major Radical power broker in the department. Stavisky's personal friend and lawyer, Hesse was charged, but ultimately acquitted of getting his client no fewer than ten trial postponements on the basis of falsified medical documents. He was expelled from the Radical party in the spring of 1934, but many members of his League section in La Rochelle were reluctant to expel him. It was only the following year, and over the protest of many, that he resigned from the League.[42] Albert Dalimier, former minister of labor and another one of Stavisky's associates, also enjoyed the tacit support of his section. Responding to one of Kahn's letters in the fall of

1934 wondering just what various sections were doing about those implicated in the Stavisky scandal, the president of Dalimier's section angrily replied that although League headquarters apparently assumed Dalimier was guilty, when asked by the section for hard evidence it had responded only by saying it was up to the section to make a judgment. In fact, this was quite consistent with League statutes, but it left the section unimpressed. Its president icily noted: "The section took note of your response, all the while regretting the ease with which you feel free to accuse a Leaguer without even hearing his side."[43]

The League's statutory provisions rendered any uniform or principled control over deputies virtually impossible. Scoundrels like Proust, by virtue of controlling their sections, were more or less immune from censure. At the same time, other deputies could be subject to the caprice of renegade sections, some of which gave evidence of sheer frivolity. League sections were notorious for their elastic definition of what was, or was not, proper conduct by a member. In 1932, for example, the section of Fleury was torn between a majority that circulated a petition to the municipal council in favor of renters and a minority that circulated a counterpetition defending the rights of landlords. The majority promptly expelled the minority. League congresses, recognizing for once that the respective rights of landlords and tenants were not among those fundamental issues that defined a leaguer, attempted to defuse the issue, but it was still going strong four years later.[44] Even more capricious was the section of Neuilly, which in 1936 attempted to expel Jacques Kayser. In his 1936 bid for re-election to the Central Committee, Kayser had appeared to claim that he was a member of the Parisian appellate bar. In fact, he had not belonged to that bar since 1933, and this apparent disingenuousness was, in the view of his local section, an act so unworthy of a leaguer as to warrant his immediate expulsion. Because the misleading designation was entirely the result of a clerical error at League headquarters, Kayser immediately appealed his expulsion at the national congress. There, the president of Kayser's section, who admitted that he had never laid eyes on the man, was pointedly reminded that he and his section had been fully apprised of the clerical error prior to Kayser's expulsion. At this point the flustered president lamely explained to an increasingly irritated congress that the real reason for the attack on Kayser was the fact that he, preoccupied by his own re-election campaign in the provinces, had been, in the eyes of some members of the section, insufficiently active in the electoral battles against right-wing candidates in the Parisian suburbs. The expulsion was duly overturned.[45]

In the end, the parliamentary group of the League became something of an embarrassment. Its obvious lack of concern for League doctrine amused the

Right and irritated the militants. As more and more sections demanded information on how members of the group voted on issues like the proposed extension of military service, Victor Basch began to wonder whether the group served any useful purpose. Henri Guernut, president of the group, took this as a public disavowal and promptly resigned.[46] What really motivated his resignation, of course, was not Basch but the two women members of the Central Committee who had had the temerity to ask why the majority in the parliamentary group had recently, yet again, voted against women's suffrage. Without further ado, and with visible relief, the executive promptly dissolved the group.[47] Curiously though, the League still wanted to know who its deputies were. In 1936 it wrote its federations asking for the names of all deputies and ministers who belonged to the League. Most federations did not bother to reply.[48] But knowing who one's deputies were was one thing; having anyone else know increasingly involved the kind of transparency the League could not stomach. In 1937 the Socialist deputy, Maurice Thiolas, attempted to reconstruct the League's parliamentary group but desisted at the strenuous insistence of Kahn.[49]

More serious than the question of deputies was that of ministers. Ministers were, of course, in positions of executive authority and, unlike the votes of mere deputies, their actions could not as easily be dismissed as "parliamentary tactics." Rarely was there a government without League members in it, not infrequently including the prime minister. In Edouard Herriot's first government after the left-wing electoral victory of 1932, twelve of eighteen cabinet ministers belonged to the League. When Léon Blum formed his Popular Front government in 1936, the one thing most of his otherwise ideologically divided cabinet ministers had in common was the fact that virtually everyone possessed a League membership card. Blum himself had been a member of the League since its creation and, for a while, a member, albeit a not very assiduous one, of the Central Committee.

But left-wing cabinets were the exception rather than the rule. In the 35 years after 1906, the Left, by any meaningful definition, was in power for only six years (1924–26, 1932–34, and 1936–38). The rest of the time the governments of the day were coalitions of the center-right, which invariably included some Radicals, and so by extension some leaguers, in the cabinet. Worse, it was notoriously the case that left-wing legislatures elected in 1924, 1932, and 1936, yielded right-leaning governments within two years and that this was possible only because the Radical party consented to this rightward shift. This was a matter of extreme sensitivity within the League. As André Philip caustically observed in 1935, one might as well rewrite the textbooks on constitutional law to the effect that parliament sits for four years if elected by the Right and for two if elected by the Left.[50] What this meant was that the League was often confronted by members sitting in right-wing governments, which in some cases those members had helped bring into existence.

No more than with deputies could the League exercise any effective control over its ministers. But the actions of ministers loomed larger than the votes of deputies, and inevitably there were cases that even the most adroit League dialecticians could not avoid confronting. One such case was the legendary *cas Painlevé*, which embroiled the League in the late 1920s. Paul Painlevé was one of the more distinguished politicians of the Third Republic as well as a very prominent member of the League. He was an internationally renowned mathematician and an early pioneer in astronautics (he was the first French civilian to fly in an airplane). At Dreyfus's 1899 trial, Painlevé was an able witness for the defense, and he was a founding member of the League. From 1904 until 1927 he served on the Central Committee, and his prestige within the League was such that in 1926 Victor Basch nominated him as Honorary Member of the Central Committee, a distinction traditionally awarded to League members whose contributions to the defense of the rights of man were particularly outstanding. He entered politics in 1910 when he was elected as an independent Socialist. His obvious talents and his relative independence from the more orthodox Socialists made him obvious cabinet material, and he served in a dozen ministries from 1914 until his death in 1933, three times as premier. In 1924, he and his fellow leaguer, Edouard Herriot, were the architects of the victorious left-wing electoral coalition, the Cartel des gauches. In that same year he was a candidate for the presidency of the Republic, losing to his fellow leaguer, Gaston Doumergue. Throughout the 1920s, he was unambiguous in his support for the League of Nations, disarmament, and the cause of world peace. By any standards his career, both in politics and in the League, was distinguished.

By the interwar years, however, significant elements in the League had become rather more demanding of their high-profile leaders. As the former president of the federation of the Drôme noted at the time, the mystique of the Dreyfus affair, and therefore of old Dreyfusards, was fading. "An impatient young generation has flocked to the League," and they were altogether less patient with the tactical compromises of their elders.[51] Painlevé's difficulties began when, after the collapse of the Cartel des Gauches government in 1926, he opted to stay on in a succession of center-right governments as minister of war (a post he had frequently occupied in the past.) It is an open question whether any minister of war could have satisfied the more ardently pacifist elements in the interwar League. But Painlevé, the leaguer, was subject to special scrutiny and on a number of counts was found to be wanting. The dossier was long, but in particular he was reproached for his failure to adequately reform, or preferably to abolish, the exceptional military jurisdiction of the Courts Martial. This was a sensitive issue in a League that had been created to protest the procedural abuses of military justice during the Dreyfus affair and which still had vivid memories of comparable abuses during World War I. Moreover, during his tenure at the war ministry, he had directed the military repression of the anticolonial insurgency in the French protectorate in Morocco, another sore point for a League, many of whose members had serious reservations about the legitimacy of French colonialism. Worse, when the French Communist party, in opposition to his "pacification" campaign in Morocco, appealed for French soldiers to revolt, he resorted to the infamous "scoundrel" laws (*lois scélérates*) of the early 1890s. Originally drafted to deal with an anarchist campaign of terror and bombing, the scoundrel laws were a classic example of the kind of "exceptional" jurisdiction that the League quite rightly saw as an affront to the principles of justice. (As a result of the selective amnesia that periodically afflicted the League, no one chose to remember that the legislation in question had originally been drafted by Senator Ludovic Trarieux, first president of the League!)

In short, Painlevé's actions as minister of war were calculated to outrage any leaguer who took at all seriously the association's principles. As it happened, Painlevé belonged to the Monnaie-Odéon section of Paris which was also the most militant, the most pacifist, and the most left-wing section of the entire League, legendary—not to say notorious—for its intransigent insistence on League principles, as it defined them, and its willingness to denounce the League's leadership for its failure to live up to those standards. In 1926, therefore, the section voted to expel Painlevé from the League. Painlevé, as was his right under League statutes, appealed his expulsion to the national congress. Owing to assorted debates about principles and procedures, the cas Painlevé dragged on through three annual League congresses and spilled over into a fourth.

Painlevé and his defenders within the League hierarchy insisted that whereas absolute principles were easy enough to draft at League congresses, the actual conduct of the day-to-day affairs of the nation were rather more complex. The Monnaie-Odéon section had its own reading of what League principles dictated, but because not all leaguers agreed with that section it was not obvious why Painlevé should feel bound by its decrees. Yes, Painlevé agreed, French military justice still left something to be desired, although he had improved it significantly (and here his supporters in the Central Committee agreed). But, he reminded everyone, as a politician, especially one in a conservative coalition, he simply could not get his way on every issue. As for the war in Morocco, it had been conducted as humanely as possible and with an eye to the most peaceful resolution possible—an argument unlikely to convince the League's left wing for whom a humane war, to say nothing of a humane colonial war, was a contradiction in terms. With respect to the scoundrel laws, Painlevé conceded that they were an imperfect instrument, but what was he to do? Communists were urging military disobedience within the army and, as far as he could see, the scoundrel laws were the only laws on the books that would permit him to quickly suppress what he took to be unqualifiedly antipatriotic conduct.

The most articulate opponent Painlevé faced was the militant and dogmatic pacifist Félicien Challaye. Every bit as doctrinaire as his colleagues in the Monnaie-Odéon section, Challaye was an old leaguer with an acute ear for the liberal sensibilities of his colleagues on the Central Committee. Without conceding anything of substance, he agreed that perhaps reasonable men could disagree about what was politically possible for a minister of war. But what about Painlevé's ministerial decrees denying Communist party members access to noncommissioned and junior officer ranks? This, surely, was an overt violation of the most elementary principles of the Declaration, which insisted that Frenchmen were entitled to open access to positions in public service regardless of their private opinions. To make matters worse, he noted, Painlevé had not taken comparable measures against French royalists or fascists—something he, Challaye, would also have opposed—again on the basis of the Declaration. Innocently, but also maladroitly, Painlevé replied that he had not taken comparable action against royalists because, as far as he could tell, they, unlike the Communists, were not calling for disobedience within the ranks of the army.

Strictly speaking, Painlevé was right. Whatever else they may have been doing, the royalist and fascist Right were not advocating mutiny. But this was a very feeble argument for many segments of the League who believed that the army was a hotbed of reactionary sentiment just waiting to overthrow the democratic regime. Clearly at issue here was a generational conflict. Painlevé, thirty-five years old at the beginning of the Dreyfus affair and by now well into his sixties, was simply dumbfounded at the suggestion that he, a civilian into the bargain, was in any way comparable to General Mercier or that Communist dissidents could somehow be likened to Captain Dreyfus. Mercier had dishonestly and illegally convicted an innocent man; he had not. Dreyfus was a thoroughly patriotic soldier innocent of any wrongdoing; the same could hardly be said for French Communists. Was he, having been chased from office in 1917 by the Right for his allegedly insufficient firmness against the defeatists within the military, supposed to sit on his hands while Communists carried out their antipatriotic campaign against the army? Were he to be expelled from the League for his actions, he concluded, one might as well retroactively exclude Trarieux and the bulk of the founders of the League because their concept of patriotism and his were the same. Although they were astute enough to avoid saying so at the time, Challaye and his followers basically agreed.

Faced with these arguments of principle, and the frankly unsatisfactory response of Painlevé, Basch and the majority of the Central Committee had to fall back on less exalted, more pragmatic and, in the League context, less attractive arguments. If, they argued, one were to expel Painlevé, then it would follow that any deputy, senator or, if it came to that, municipal councilor, whose actions or votes were not entirely in accordance with League principles, should be expelled as well. Unfazed by this reductionist logic, some dissident members of the League fully agreed that this was precisely what they had in mind. Basch and his allies did not do much better when they asserted that one did not expel an old comrade with an admirable record of past services merely because at the moment his actions seemed to deviate from League principles. Their opponents were quick to point out that the political landscape of France was littered with ex-members of the League and ex-Dreyfusard allies. Georges Clemenceau and Colonel Picquart had once been held in high esteem but had subsequently evolved in ways that were inconsistent with League principles. But no one now regretted the parting of the ways even though both men had during the Dreyfus affair, of which younger members of the League were growing tired of hearing, rendered rather greater services than Painlevé ever had. Moreover, if past services guaranteed immunity from present accountability, then surely Benito Mussolini would have the right to protest his expulsion from the Italian Socialist party.

The only recourse was rhetoric, something Basch and his allies possessed in abundance. Basch and the Socialist deputy Maurice Viollette made dark allusions to the Reign of Terror. Already this represented something of a departure in League discourse because the period 1793–94 was usually seen as the epoch of the first great French Republic rather than the rule of the guillotine. But now it was a question of "the execution carts." As the revolutionaries gradually devoured themselves, asked Viollette, will I be next? As a former governor of Algeria and future minister of colonies, he was a plausible enough candidate. At the end of the congress of Rennes in 1928, Basch pulled out all the stops, made all the necessary references to execution carts, and blocked the motion to expel Painlevé by a two to one majority. The congress limited itself to a motion of censure, platonically regretting some of Painlevé's actions, recalling his sacrifices for the League, and declaring that he was still a worthy member. Because nothing in the League was ever settled permanently, at the next year's congress there were no fewer than eight motions directed against Painlevé, but most delegates were tired of the issue, and it died by the end of 1929 when Painlevé more or less simultaneously ceased to be a minister and stopped paying his League dues.[52] But Basch and Viollette were right that there would be more cas Painlevés.

Within five years the League was again convulsed; this time it was the *cas Herriot*, a far more disruptive quarrel than the Painlevé affair had been. Strictly speaking, there were two Herriot affairs: one involving his ministerial conduct and the other related to his conduct as mayor of Lyon. The ministerial question was a direct consequence of the upheaval in French political life beginning in 1934. One immediate result of the Stavisky scandal was the mobilization of a number of antiparliamentary, sometimes paramilitary, and invariably virulently antidemocratic movements, most notably the Croix de Feu, the Jeunesses Patriotes, and the Action Française. On the night of February 6, 1934, they descended into the streets of Paris, converged around the French Chamber of Deputies and appeared, at least to contemporaries, to be mounting an assault on the democratic regime. By the end of the evening they had been dispersed, with some fatalities, by the forces of order. Nonetheless, the recently formed Daladier government, the last of a string of center-left governments dating from the left-wing electoral victory of 1932, resigned despite retaining the confidence of the Chamber. It was replaced by a center-right government headed by the former president of the Republic, Gaston Doumergue. The League, along with most of the French Left, believed that France had narrowly avoided a fascist coup. The Republic was in greater danger than it had been since the days of the Dreyfus affair. Daladier's resignation and his replacement by Doumergue augured badly for the fate of French democracy. The democratic verdict of 1932 had been overturned by the violent action of right-wingers in the streets. It may have pleased Doumergue to call his government one of "National Salvation" but, from the League's perspective, it was a government that owed its legitimacy only to the intimidating tactics of fascists and was nothing short of "an embryonic fascist" administration.

There was an element of overstatement here. There had in fact been no plans for a coup on the part of the various leagues in the street on February 6. Even had there been, the various right-wing leaders, badly divided among themselves and in general quite irresolute, would have been incapable of putting such plans into effect. Moreover, however disquieting the actions of the right-wing leagues, it was hard to deny that they tapped a legitimate anger on the part of much of the French population. One could not conjure away the undeniable evidence of serious parliamentary corruption, the League least of all, given that most of the offenders came from within its ranks. Nor could one deny the demonstrated incompetence of a string of Radical governments in dealing with the Great Depression. Of course their task had not been made easier by the doctrinaire refusal of the Socialists, their notional partner, to accept governmental responsibility. The point could hardly have escaped Basch or Kahn, Socialists both, because they had written enough articles deploring this fact throughout the previous year.

Doumergue had always been a fairly conservative Radical and had moved further to the Right in his old age. Yet he was not, for all that, such a ferocious reactionary. He had, after all, a long history in the League and had been a member in good standing as recently as a decade earlier (a fact that no one in the League now chose to recall). All that really happened in the aftermath of February 6 was that a series of center-left governments was replaced by a succession of center-right ones. There was nothing unprecedented about this— it was precisely what happened in 1926 and what would happen again in 1938. What made these shifts to the Right possible was not the latent menace of the extreme Right but rather the general willingness of so many notionally left-wing politicians to abandon governments of the center-left for ones of the center-right. Common to both sets of governments was the presence of a number of prominent Radicals and independent Socialists (albeit rather fewer in center-right governments), most of whom happened to belong to the League.

Still, the League did not enjoy the kind of perspective afforded by hindsight. The events of February 6, 1934, came barely a year after Hitler's accession to power and on the very day of the destruction of the Austrian Republic. The *Croix de Feu,* its singularly cautious attitude on the night of February 6 notwithstanding, was growing exponentially. Whatever its legitimacy, the Doumergue government was incontestably a more conservative one than France had seen for a number of years. To deal with the growing economic difficulties, Doumergue made ample use of "decree laws," technically constitutional expedients but, by virtue of (temporarily) short-cutting parliamentary control, ones that the League had always denounced as contrary to the spirit of democracy.[53] Moreover, many of the decree laws took the form of budgetary measures to reduce the salaries of public employees, a group heavily represented in the League. Worse, Doumergue, in an effort to deal with what he thought was parliamentary sterility, proposed constitutional changes permitting the president to dissolve parliament and call new elections. This measure, invoking the unhappy experience of the monarchist president MacMahon in 1877, was treated by the league as a foreshadowing of the destruction of the parliamentary regime. In the realm of foreign policy, Doumergue's government was no more appealing. His foreign minister, the center-right senator, Louis Barthou, was a convinced advocate of diplomatic firmness with respect to Hitler's Germany and a man who worked assiduously to strengthen France's international alliances. Because this was precisely the kind of politics that so many in the League believed had been responsible for the outbreak of World War I, it seemed to presage the end of the policy of peace that it had worked so hard for since 1918.

Given what they took to be the entirely deplorable policies of the Doumergue government, it was a source of consternation rather than comfort for League militants to learn that sitting in the cabinet were no fewer than five current members of the League, two of them former members of the Central Committee. And one of them was Edouard Herriot, founding member of the League, past member of the Central Committee, many times premier, and the president of the Radical party. Of course it was true that unlike Painlevé, who had a serious and delicate portfolio, Herriot was a minister of state, a purely symbolic position, and his inclusion was designed to give the government some credibility with the Radicals. But the more militant members of the League would be well aware that Herriot's fellow minister of state, Louis Marin, president of the ultranationalist and clerical Republican Federation was there to assure the extreme Right. Moreover, they believed, Marin seemed to be doing a rather more credible job.

Even if Herriot's ministerial conduct could be justified by political necessity (a point the left-wing members of the League would not concede) his actions as mayor of Lyon struck many as being an even more egregious violation of League principles. On November 23, 1933, the prefect of the department of the Rhône ordered the workers in the municipal slaughterhouse in Lyon to participate in an air-raid drill designed to parry the threat of a gas attack from the air. Twenty three workers, under the influence of the Communist trade union, refused to participate. Herriot responded by firing ten of them, all temporary employees, outright. He sent the remaining thirteen permanent employees before the establishment's disciplinary council, which sentenced eight of them to a one-month suspension and deprived the other five of their vacation rights. Upon reviewing the case on February 16, 1934, Herriot chose, as was his right as mayor, to aggravate the sentences by reducing the seniority of all of them.[54]

Herriot, like Painlevé, had the misfortune of belonging to a particularly militant and pacifist section, that of Lyon, presided over by Léon Emery, the young, dynamic, and very articulate representative of the Central Committee's minority. Emery and most radical pacifists in the League were outraged by Herriot's actions. How could a leaguer throw proletarians out into the street in the midst of a depression merely for having the courage of their pacifist convictions? By an overwhelming vote, the section of Lyon expelled Herriot. He promptly appealed his expulsion to the Central Committee. The committee did subject Herriot to a fairly rigorous grilling.[55] But a majority found the grounds for expelling Herriot to be specious. What civil rights had he violated? Public employees did not have the right to refuse to obey legal orders. What pacifist convictions were being trampled? No one was asking the Lyon municipal workers to kill anyone, merely to participate in an exercise that might save lives in the event of war. As Herriot incessantly reminded everyone, drills of this kind were common in the Soviet Union where, he pointedly noted, workers who refused to participate would face rather more grave sanctions than he had levied. And yes, France was in the midst of a depression, but the ten workers he had fired had been replaced by ten others. With his trademark caustic wit, he would later observe that he had also insisted on the vaccination of children in local hospitals. Did this make him a proponent of typhoid epidemics?[56]

A minority on the Central Committee were unconvinced. Relying on no less an authority than Paul Langevin, distinguished man of science, determined pacifist, and a member of the Central Committee, Herriot's antagonists replied that the scientific evidence clearly demonstrated that there was no defense against gas warfare. If the government was insisting on these civil defense drills, it could only be for the purpose of instilling a "war psychosis" in the population. Some measure of the intensity of the debate and the passions unleashed can be derived from the decision of the majority in the Central Committee to engage the services of another distinguished professor of chemistry who proceeded to rebut Langevin's findings.[57]

At the 1934 League congress, held shortly thereafter, the cas Herriot became the center of a debate considerably more rancorous than the one surrounding the Painlevé affair. Whether it be his handling of the municipal workers of Lyon or his participation in the Doumergue government (distinct issues in the minds of League jurists but inseparable for most rank and file), Herriot's actions struck many of the delegates as simply treasonous. If League principles, as they understood them, were to mean anything at all, there was no longer a place in the League for a politician like Herriot. As in the Painlevé case, Basch and his allies broke out all the emotional rhetoric they could muster. But this time it did not work. Many delegates were even less interested now in hearing about Herriot's service to the Dreyfusard cause (for many now a very distant memory) or about his past services to the League. A motion to "denounce" Herriot (the French *flétrir* is considerably stronger than the English *denounce*) passed by a comfortable measure. Stunned by the outcome, Victor Basch promptly resigned from the presidency of the League. No amount of gracious appeals, coming from all sides of the debate, could change his mind, and he stomped out of the congress.[58]

Basch's resignation, to no one's great surprise (he had a history of flamboyant resignations), was short lived. He and his allies in the Central Committee were quickly at work annulling both the vote of the congress and the exclusion of Herriot by the Lyon section. The members of the Central Committee were unanimously of the opinion that, in its haste to expel Herriot, the Lyon section had not followed the most rigorous requirements of due process. Even Emery conceded that they had a point, albeit a tendentious one. But lest the Lyon comrades simply repeat the exercise with more care to due form, which they had every visible intention of doing, the Central Committee, by a much closer vote (twelve to eleven) declared Herriot's exclusion invalid on a second ground: it was motivated by partisan political concerns, which were inappropriate to the noble mission of the League.[59] Of course, they were not wrong on this point. The political motivation behind the expulsion of Herriot was patent. But, Emery and his allies within the League asked, with mounting exasperation, what were Basch's motives if not political? The best argument Basch could muster was that the expulsion of Herriot would bring with it the departure of all the Radicals, which he now, quite implausibly, estimated to represent 160,000 of the League's 180,000 members. This wasn't political?

In fact, each side consistently accused the other of turning the League into a *ligue politicienne*. Emery would insist that "the League must cease counting on a discredited political elite and on unpopular and ineffective parliamentary institutions." Emile Kahn would counter that Emery and his associates really wanted to turn the League into a "new party." The choice as he saw it was between "the old League with its principles" and a ligue politicienne.[60] There was nothing very new in all of this. Eight years earlier, during the Painlevé affair, Jean-Marie Caillaud, the pugnacious president of the federation of the Seine, had charged that the League had become little more than a "parliamentary stepping stone," its Central Committee (to which he aspired without success) a glorified "ministerial ante-chamber." Kahn predictably countered that it was people like Caillaud who, by virtue of being stalking horses for the French Communist party, were bringing politics into the League.[61] Both sides, of course, were right.

Victor Basch's 1934 stance was indisputably political, but it was also consistent with political reality. Like it or not, virtually any government in the Third Republic would contain members of the League. Herriot, after all, was but one of five leaguers in the Doumergue government. The governments of Flandin and Laval that succeeded Doumerge, every bit as unpalatable from the League's perspective, were also filled with League ministers: five (out of twenty) in Flandin's government and eight (out of twenty) in Laval's. Some, to be sure, were fairly marginal members of the League. Others, like Aimé Berthod, a distinguished French academician, had been a former Central Committee member. As minister of national education in a series of Radical governments, he chose to stay on in that post under Doumergue. Berthod was in the thankless position of having to defend the government's deflationary economic policy, which meant a 10 percent salary reduction for schoolteachers. Worse, he was under attack from a resurgent Right for tolerating the "revolutionary" attitudes of public schoolteachers. In a widely published exchange with Gustave Gautherot, the archly reactionary senator from the Loire-Atlantique, a man who had made a career out of denouncing subversives in the school system, Berthod insisted that the public deportment of the great majority of teachers was exemplary and that they were entitled to their "freedom of opinion." He conceded, nonetheless, that "respect for legality and for the defence of the nation are not opinions that teachers have, under any circumstances and for any pretext, the right to dispute." Consequently, he levied some modest sanctions against a teacher who, during a union meeting, publicly advocated a general strike in the army. Talk about general strikes, Berthod remembered from his past, could be dismissed as youthful exuberance; reference to the army represented a boundary that no public servant should be allowed to cross. This was but a nuance or two removed from the position the Central Committee had traditionally taken on the rights of public servants, but in the climate of 1934 it was a provocative stance. Berthod's section promptly voted his expulsion. Berthod, convinced that the League had by now been engulfed by "anarchistic discontent" chose, to the evident relief of the Central Committee, not to appeal this decision.[62]

Nor were all such ministers Radicals. Ernest Lafont, deputy from the Hautes-Alpes, and minister of public health in Pierre Laval's 1935 government, had been a Socialist deputy since before World War I; from 1920 to 1923 he had been a Communist, expelled only because of his attachment to the League. In the late 1920s he had been one of the more radical members of the Central Committee, distinguished by his adamant pacifism and his defense of labor-union rights. His decision to enter government was of a piece with that of many Socialists in the 1930s who believed that the traditional policy of nonparticipation amounted to sterility. His entry into the Laval government was every bit as "treasonous" as had been Herriot's actions, but no faction of the League wanted to address the problem.

In its broad outlines, Basch's position was a solid one. A League that ceased to represent anyone but the pacifist wing of the Socialists (and not always them, witness Lafont) would no longer be able to play the role it had assigned itself for the previous quarter century: holding together the diverse fractions of the Left. With the threat of domestic fascism looming, this was hardly the ideal moment for sectarian quarreling on the Left, a critical precondition, he was acutely aware, for the triumph of fascism in Italy and Germany. Because the Radicals were still the largest formation on the Left, alienating them—something the expulsion of their president was sure to do—was suicidal. But this kind of reasoning would have little impact on Emery and the League minority. The prospect of the imminent departure from the League of most of the Radicals did not trouble them very much. The best way to fight fascism was, in their view, a concerted attack on capitalism and on war, issues on which the Radicals were most uncertain allies.[63]

By 1934, however, some members of the League would have an idiosyncratic definition of fascism. A classic example was Maurice Weber, president of the section of Viroflay. Weber distinguished himself at League congresses in the early 1930s by his vitriolic attacks on the League's leadership and his persistent demands that League resources be concentrated on political propaganda rather than on cases of individual injustices. He also declared: "Herriot equals fascism." The Central Committee could not resist reminding Weber that he was calling a Dreyfusard and founding member of the League a fascist in the pages of *Nouvel Age,* one of whose prominent editors was a certain Georges Valois. Valois, also a former Dreyfusard, had gravitated to the *Action Française* before World War I and had, in the late 1920s, founded the ephemeral but avowedly fascist movement, the *Faisceau*. Weber and his associates countered that whatever Valois might once have been, he was now an avowed antifascist. Indeed, noted Elie Reynier, president of the federation of the Ardèche, Valois's political evolution was "a hundred times" more admirable than the Central Committee's "stubborn immobility and contemptible conviction about its own infallibility." There were more than a few ironies here. Valois had evolved and would continue to do so in ways that would ultimately dismay Reynier because, by the late 1930s, he was firmly in the camp of those who would reject further appeasement of Hitler. He fought in the Resistance and died in Bergen-Belsen. Maurice Weber, by contrast, would rally to Vichy and to Marcel Déat's avowedly fascist *Rassemblement National Populaire* for which he would be deprived of all political rights by postwar courts. [64]

Although each side accused the other of bringing politics into the League, the issue was more complex. The League was thoroughly immersed in politics, as it had been since its inception. The problem was that there were different politics and different political strategies. For Basch, his occasional inflammatory rhetoric notwithstanding, the central issue was and remained that of saving the Republic from its enemies, and this required as broad a coalition as possible. In important respects, this was a strategy as old as the Dreyfus affair. The younger Emery had not experienced the Dreyfus affair, and the rhetoric of "republican defense" had no magic for his ears. The merits of saving the republican regime were not obvious to him; he and many of his fellow leaguers believed the existing regime to be old, corrupt, and bankrupt. Certainly there had been little in the language widely adopted by the League in the past decade to cause them to reflect seriously on this verdict. It followed that what France needed was a revolution, the only certain way to save it from both fascism and war. There were simply no good reasons to believe that catering to old style Radicalism would further this end.

Ultimately the Herriot case dragged on for two more years. The Central Committee's 1934 decision was upheld on technical grounds at the 1935 Congress. The Lyon section dutifully went through the motions of again expelling Herriot who promptly, and yet again, appealed to the Central Committee, noting, as always, that to condemn his actions was to condemn the entire Radical party. The ideologues of the Lyon section, he asserted, had transformed a "noble institution created for protecting individual rights" into "an agency for passionate politics." Emery replied that what was at issue was not the Radical party but the League's principles, most of which Herriot had violated, much like Berthod who, he reminded everyone, had been expelled from the League.

Hoping to avoid public discord in the year of the Popular Front, the Central Committee postponed dealing with the matter. But controversy was inevitable once Emery began to campaign actively against Herriot in the first round of the 1936 elections. Herriot, outraged by this "irrational fanaticism" promptly and very publicly resigned from the League. The Central Committee of course refused to accept the resignation and waited until the elections were safely over before deciding in May 1936, by a vote of thirty to nine to annul, yet again, his expulsion. For the minority, Herriot was responsible for most of the political problems in France since 1932; for the majority, he was a central architect of the Popular Front. Each side insisted that its position was in no way influenced by party politics.[65]

The divisiveness occasioned by the cas Herriot prompted 159 sections of the League to call for a modification of the organization's statutes to provide for the incompatibility of League membership and ministerial rank. The question seriously divided the Central Committee because it posed some logical and moral problems. What did it mean to say that a minister of the French Republic was, by definition, not worthy of belonging to the League? And where would it stop? The same logic that might exclude a minister could extend to a deputy, a municipal counselor, or even a forest warden. These were telling arguments, but as Emile Kahn noted: "Many [militants] do not understand the essential difference between the League's activities and parliamentary or governmental activity and they treat as fraud or treason what, usually, is no more than difference between a Leaguer's duty and governmental activity." He might have added that there was precisely nothing in the League's doctrine that would permit its members to make those distinctions. For Victor Basch and about half of his colleagues on the Central Committee, the principal advantage of an incompatibility statute was that it would bring to an end the debilitating feuds that occurred over Painlevé and Herriot. They rallied "without enthusiasm" to this expedient, because they were simply tired of watching local sections, headed by latter-day Fouquier-Tinville's, playacting at being revolutionary tribunals. A divided Central Committee uncharacteristically left the question up to the 1935 congress.[66] A majority of the delegates, unwilling to relinquish an inquisitorial role, rejected the idea of ministerial incompatibility.[67]

But the Herriot affair had lasting consequences for the League. Kahn, remarking on the increasingly bitter and unproductive sessions of the Central Committee, the deluge of protests from the rank and file, and the "wave of resignations," expressed "serious concerns for [our] future."[68] Charles Richet, a founding member of the League, Central Committee member before World

War I, and honorary member of the Central Committee since 1921, resigned in 1934, informing Basch: "I joined the [League] in the nineteenth century during its heroic phase" but "I cannot accept the current intrusion of the [League] into politics."[69] Jacques Raynal, a League member since its foundation, resigned declaring that the League had "totally deviated from its original goal" and had become "a mere political agency, both anti-French and anti-colonial."[70] Two Radical deputies from the Rhône resigned from the League charging that it was "departing singularly from the goals stated in its statutes" and was "losing its raison d'être [and] appears to have no other concerns but politics."[71] Exactly how many resigned over this issue cannot be established, but by the end of 1936 membership had declined by a quarter and stood at 136,000, only 119,000 of whom had paid their dues.[72] Although there were other possible reasons for the sharp decline in membership, the infighting over Herriot, most contemporaries seemed to believe, was a major factor.

The issues raised by the Herriot affair temporarily lost most of their immediacy when Léon Blum formed his Popular Front government in May 1936. No one in the League seemed troubled by the fact that virtually every one of his cabinet members belonged to the League, nor by the fact that no fewer than five of the new ministers were current members of the Central Committee. Indeed, the principal concern of the League's 1936 congress, held shortly after the Blum government came to power, was the fact that in 1927 the League had, in a well-meaning attempt to separate itself from parliamentary politics, decreed that ministers could not continue to sit on the Central Committee. Perhaps, suggested Emile Kahn, this had been a hasty decision. He and other members of the executive therefore rammed through, over the objections of more principled members, a resolution giving the five ministers honorary status which, according to league statutes, assured them of deliberative powers in the Central Committee.[73]

The triumph of the Popular Front seemed, for a brief and fleeting moment, to simplify, if not solve, the League's political problems. It was, after all, a government composed almost exclusively of League members, the closest the League had ever got to power. The sense of euphoria was evident at the League's 1936 congress. Even Léon Emery, the most tenacious of Herriot's antagonists, conceded that the affair was now a "secondary issue."[74] This era of good feelings lasted only a few months.

FOUR

Liberty with All Its Risks

The leaders of the League were, by 1911 at the latest, men with impeccable left-wing credentials. They were also individuals with equally impeccable civil libertarian reflexes who took some pride in their hard-nosed willingness to push the cause of liberty wherever it might lead. In principle there was no conflict. To the League, one of the defining traits of the Left—as opposed to the Center and the Right—was precisely its commitment to civil liberties. Nothing seemed to illustrate this as clearly as the Dreyfus affair, the classic defining movement of the League's conscience. In practice, of course, principled stands on civil liberties could indeed conflict with the League's more general political goals. Were this to happen, the League's doctrine dictated that principles trumped politics. Henri Guernut, who took some pride in being the most unrepentant "liberal" in the League spelled it out clearly when in 1934 he declared: "To tell the truth is the first mark of a Leaguer; to tell the truth even when it might be disagreeable to one's friends is the second mark; to tell the truth when it might be to the advantage of one's enemies is the ultimate mark of a Leaguer."[1] President Victor Basch could match this language when he declared in 1928: "We are the people who bet on liberty, with all its grandeur but also with all its risks."[2] But this kind of rhetoric, impressive though it was, could not conjure away the very real difficulties the League had when faced with the political consequences of principles it theoretically embraced. Sometimes, as with the affaire des fiches, such difficulties could be written off as a momentary casualty of the heated political debates of the day. But over the course of its life, the League also wrestled for years with more fundamental conflicts between the policies that liberal and civil libertarian theory ought to have dictated and the more immediate political consequences of such policies. The debates over women's suffrage, freedom of association for religious congregations, and freedom of the press illustrate the dilemma of an association attempting to reconcile its simultaneous dedication to civil liberties and to left-wing politics.

Women's suffrage was, for a number of reasons, an obvious cause for the League to embrace. In the first place, the League had always recognized that the *homme* in *droits de l'homme* referred to members of the human race and not to the male species. In 1924 Victor Basch, soon to become the president of the League, said: "If our League is called the League of the Rights of *Man,* it is solely because there is no word in the French language that corresponds to the Latin *homo* or the German *Mensch.*"[3] The League was sufficiently sensitive on this point that in its early years it excised the language in its statutes indicating that "women can be members" in favor of a simple statement that this was an association of men and women.[4] Consequently, before World War I, when female suffrage was becoming an important issue in the Western world but before more than a handful of women anywhere had the right to vote at any level of government, the League actively engaged the issue. Future League president, Ferdinand Buisson, was a dedicated feminist and active proponent of women's suffrage. He quite literally wrote the "book" on the subject, the 1909 report of the parliamentary commission on universal suffrage.[5] In 1909, the League designated the distinguished French feminist, Marie Vérone as *rapporteur* for its commission on women's rights for that year's annual congress. On her initiative the League accepted the principle of women's suffrage and recommended immediate implementation of it for all three levels of *local* government.[6] It reiterated its demand at its 1914 congress.[7]

After 1918 the issue became more pressing. After the war, women were granted political rights almost everywhere: Germany, Great Britain, the United States, the Soviet Union, the Irish Republic, Palestine, and six provinces of Republican China. France's Latin neighbors, Fascist Italy and Republican Spain, eventually accorded women the right to vote in local elections. France stood out as the sole major nation in the interwar years which denied political rights to half of the adult population.

The League, although usually highly critical of the operation of French democracy, had nonetheless always been proud, and justifiably so, of France's status as one of the leading democracies in the world. It was therefore a source of considerable chagrin when, in the years immediately following World War I, it became obvious that on the question of women's political rights, France lagged behind all but a handful of the nations in the world. Moreover the arguments advanced by opponents of women's suffrage were transparently specious. Women, it was traditionally alleged, neither desired the vote nor were prepared for it. Insofar as any of this was true at all, members of the League could not help but reply, it had been even more true of men before 1848. One could hardly, on these grounds, oppose extending the franchise to women without simultaneously admitting that one's republican ancestors had made a serious error in 1848. Finally, of course, there was the whole question of the forces that stood in the way of women's suffrage. On a number of occasions the Chamber of Deputies had passed bills giving women the vote only to have them die at the hands of the Senate. This outraged the League on two counts. The Senate was an undemocratic body, elected by a highly restricted suffrage and a holdover from the days of the reluctant republicans who had founded the regime. Its democratization—or better yet its elimination—had always been a traditional League demand. Moreover, it was an open secret that many of the deputies who so readily voted for women's suffrage in the Chamber did so only because they were confident that their political counterparts in the Senate would reject the measure. This was precisely the kind of political hypocrisy and opportunism that the League specialized in denouncing.

At the 1924 congress of the League in Marseille, Victor Basch gave a classically passionate speech on the suffrage issue. Denying women the vote, he insisted, had always been a grave flaw in French democracy. Women were, in all respects, the equal of men and were therefore entitled to equal political rights. The stock argument against women's suffrage, he noted, was the clerical issue—the belief that women were more likely than men to follow the teachings of the Church and vote for parties of the political Right. But, even were it true that women were excessively under the influence of the clergy, whose fault was that if not that of men who refused to treat them as political equals? Making no allowances for the fact that he was in the south, traditionally refractory to women's suffrage, Basch was particularly harsh on the men of the Midi whose "ancestral, Arab . . . and roman" traditions led them to treat women like virtual servants, unworthy of eating at the same table as men. Moreover, even granting clerical influence, in the League, Basch intoned, "we do not have the right to bend our principles in the face of facts. . . . For us principles are eternal and we do not permit them to be affected by the opportunity of the moment. Otherwise there would be no point in having a *Ligue des Droits de l'Homme* . . . If we become opportunistic, we might as well close the doors of the League and dissolve it."[8] All of this was classic League rhetoric, repeated endlessly at every congress and, one suspects, calculated to put the better part of the audience to sleep.

Actually, Basch seems to have hoped so since shortly thereafter he found himself saying that while the League was, of course, above politics, its individual members belonged to political parties (by which he meant the Radicals and the Socialists) and had therefore "the duty to consider the destiny of" their party. "I confess," he added, "that to give women all electoral votes right away, without any transition, without steps and without stages constitutes a serious risk." Consequently, although the League remained as committed as ever to the principle of women's suffrage, he thought it appropriate to limit women's voting for the moment to municipal elections. The aging historian, Alphonse Aulard, if for no better reason than to prove he at least had stayed awake, could not resist wondering just what Basch might have proposed had he in fact fallen into the trap of opportunism! Nonetheless the congress voted overwhelmingly both for the broader principal of women's suffrage and its very gradual implementation. A half-hearted attempt to get the congress to commit itself to demanding women's suffrage for the *next* municipal consultation (that is, 1925) failed to find enough support. Neither Basch nor anyone else seemed to notice that this resolution, municipal voting only, represented a significant retreat from the 1909 and 1914 positions, which had envisaged voting at all levels of local government.[9] Four years later, a delegate from Marseilles, Bernice Lop, reminded a national congress that no progress had been made on women's suffrage and that the various parties of the left "support the reform, if at all, without enthusiasm . . . and seem indifferent to it." Basch agreed that this was an issue that ought to be addressed by the Central Committee. The discussion on the suffrage issue was only slightly longer than a discussion on the merits of adopting Esperanto.[10]

Some indication of the impact of these platonic resolutions was revealed in a talk on feminism given by *citoyen* Jean Zay, later to become minister of education in Léon Blum's government, before his fellow leaguers in the section of Orléans. Feminism had made gigantic strides in recent years and, insofar as feminism sought to ensure women's equality with men within society, he thought this to be truly admirable. Unfortunately, he noted, the feminist movement had in recent years, concentrated excessively on the conquest of political rights. This bothered him. Women, he insisted, were not inferior to men—in some respects they were superior. But, alas, the one way in which they were deficient was the ability to reason, and reasoning, he opined, was critical for political decision making. Moreover, women had no interest whatsoever in social questions. They did not want the vote and would not exercise it if they received it. Giving them the vote, at any level, was a "leap in the dark" and very dangerous. The vice president of the section, citoyenne Cormier, promptly rebutted his arguments as did several of her male colleagues, without however, convincing Zay.[11]

As the Zay incident shows, Basch's position on the suffrage issue, however conditional it may have been, was a good deal in advance of that of most of his fellow leaguers. This was clearly illustrated in 1929 at a meeting of Marie Vérone's *Ligue française pour les droits des femmes*. Basch's support for suffrage reform, cautious when speaking to the League, could be effusive before a feminist audience. Here Basch noted that some republicans feared that in a Latin and Roman Catholic country like France giving women the vote might imperil the democratic regime. But he was having none of that and openly questioned the republican commitment of anyone who challenged the democratic necessity of equal political rights for women. "Better the republic should perish," he ended by saying "rather than have her principles perish because without those principles there can be no republic." It was a good night for Basch until near the end of the meeting when a letter was read from one of those who had been invited to speak but had been unable to attend. The letter was from Maurice Viollette, former governor of Algeria, currently deputy from Eure-et-Loire, and also a member of the Central Committee of the League. Viollette allowed that he was of course in favor of the principle of women's suffrage but also a believer in "prudence." It was his impression that most women were indifferent to the vote and, were they given it, between 70 and 80 percent would not exercise the right. Even the municipal vote was fraught with peril because municipal counselors elected senators and "to give women the right to determine the political orientation of the country and even of its constitution is, at this time, a very dangerous thing to do, the more so because I think that the only women who will participate in elections are from among the extremist elements." By unhappy accident, he ended his letter with the words: "I am not one of those who says: Better the colonies should perish than their principle."[12]

It is entirely possible that Viollette's concern about the sanctity of the Senate was related to the fact that shortly thereafter he became a member of that august body. In his capacity as Senator, Viollette drafted a bill permitting women to vote in municipal elections. The bill provided for a separate college of women electors and candidates. Women would be entitled to one quarter of the positions on the municipal council, on the condition that those elected would not have a say in choosing the mayor and would not vote in senatorial elections. No less authoritative a figure than Henri Guernut drew the Viollette proposal to the attention of all leaguers, noting in passing that some members would find it to be inadequate, including, presumably, those members of the League who could remember the resolutions so solemnly passed eight years before, to say nothing of those passed eighteen and twenty-three years previously. Still, Guernut gamely insisted, the Viollette bill would be a useful trial run which, if it did not work out (and he thought it would) could cause no real harm, would certainly give women a chance to acquire their "political education," and would ensure that France would no longer be in last place among nations when it came to women's suffrage.[13]

Zay, Viollette, and Guernut were not, the 1924 resolutions notwithstanding, all that far out of line with the thinking of many members of the League. The League's *Cahiers* certainly opened its columns to proponents of women's suffrage but they were also open, although not perhaps in equal measure, to opponents like M. Flotte who belligerently met the aforementioned precedent of 1848 by wondering if anyone remembered Louis Napoleon.[14] He was in good company. A leaguer in the Meurthe-et-Moselle noted that "there have been, as history reminds us, too many disastrous examples of the vote being prematurely granted for us to make the same mistake."[15] Two years later when leaguers in the same department were debating a draft version of a new declaration of the rights of man, only one clause was rejected. It was the one calling for equal political rights for women.[16] To judge from a reading of thousands of compte rendu of local sections, women's suffrage was not a favorite topic and, when it was discussed, more often than not the emphasis was on the inherent dangers. The director of a local women's teaching college in the Charente-Maritime and vice president of the League's section in La Rochelle, recalled bitterly how the mere news that a local suffragist group was holding classes on civic education for women prompted members of her section into wholesale denunciations of women's suffrage.[17] One of her colleagues recalled being told by a fellow leaguer that even municipal suffrage for women was out of the question because "in our villages it would mean the end of republican municipalities and waiting for parliament itself to become anti-republican."[18] In 1935 the section of Nancy debated a proposed new Declaration of the Rights of Man. Significantly, all of the proposed clauses were accepted with the notable exception of the one providing for equal rights for women.[19] The president of the federation of the Creuse found himself in hot water because he had the temerity to *read* out loud the League's official position on suffrage reform at a local meeting. His colleagues somehow felt that this was an oblique and disloyal attack on Alfred Grand, senator from the department and also a leaguer who had consistently voted against women's suffrage. It was nothing of the kind, the flustered president protested. Surely everyone realized that League principles were one thing and that the timing and modalities of their application were something else again. All he had really wanted to say, he pleaded, was that women's suffrage was going to come sooner or later and that the League should prepare for it.[20] In this respect he was like many, if not most, of that minority in the League who spoke in favor of women's suffrage. Rather than present suffrage reform as a good idea in its own right, they typically chose to treat it as something that, whether the League liked it or not, was inevitable. That being the case, they suggested, the League should stop opposing the measure because, as one speaker in Chartres observed, "when the day comes that they get [suffrage reform] in spite of you" women might be lost to the republican cause.[21]

For every trenchant argument in favor of women's suffrage,[22] there was at least another insisting that it would be "dangerous to grant all women the right to vote even in municipal elections."[23] But such articles, pro or con, were the exception. Women's suffrage never generated the passion within the League that issues like pacifism, clericalism, or labor union rights did. Women were underrepresented in the columns of the League's press but they were not absent. Yet they were more likely to write about peace or the struggle against fascism than about the vote; calls for suffrage reform were whispered, reflecting either lack of interest or, more likely, a recognition that this was a "controversial" topic. What pressure there was to do something about women's political rights tended to come from the top, rather than the grass roots.

Not only were the rank and file, at best, unenthusiastic, about women's suffrage but the leaders did not seem unduly troubled by this fact. Secretary General Guernut had always publicly advocated at least some form of women's suffrage, but he knew the mentality of the militants better than anyone else in the League. In 1926 he wrote his fellow member of the Central Committee, Célestin Bouglé, concerning the wisdom of sending a woman out as a propaganda delegate to the provincial federations. "I know that my colleagues, precisely because they like women, are not very feminist; in any event they see all kinds of problems with the League sending a woman out into the provinces."[24] He might have had in mind the delegate from Paris who unblushingly told the 1923 congress: "I am an old feminist and I believe that our role is to defend women and their role is to charm us."[25] Although Guernut was clearly correct about the absence of "feminism" in the League, it was also the case that objections to women's suffrage were often couched in superficially feminist terms. When Guernut wrote an article in the *Ere Nouvelle* cautiously urging at least some steps toward woman's suffrage, the president of the section of Baux-de-Breteuil who described himself as a "determined partisan of women's emancipation" wrote to say that the immediate consequence of such a proposal would be that the department of the Eure, which currently had four republican deputies, would be reduced to one.[26] Members of the League's "Feminist Commission" cannot have been pleased to receive a letter from Madame Rouvier, with the full support of her section, asserting that she was "a convinced feminist, but above all laic, and more attached to the current regime than to my [right to vote.]"[27]

By 1935 it was therefore apparent that women's suffrage was at best the lowest possible priority within the League; at worst it was a reform that leaguers were fighting all the way. In April of that year the two (out of fifty-eight!) women on the League's Central Committee finally raised the question of suffrage reform. What, Odette Renée Bloch and Suzanne Collette wanted to know, was the Central Committee's position on suffrage reform; what had been done about it since 1924, and how was it that so many of the League's deputies and senators somehow managed to continue to vote against suffrage reform? For their pains, they were treated to a series of tortuous disquisitions on the problems of suffrage reform. Emile Guerry, for example, readily admitted that denying women the vote had been a "monstrosity," but at the same time he was under "the impression that most women did not want the vote." Of course he acknowledged that the same could have been said of men in 1848 but also insisted the vote for women now "risked bringing about the same political regression in France that has happened elsewhere." Albert Bayet, a left-wing Radical, reminded the two women that the very fact that the Central Committee was discussing the issue (for the first time in eleven years) was solid proof that the League believed in "the principle of the equality of men and women." But the League believed in other things too, such as freedom of conscience. "Now," he insisted, "we are more or less certain of losing that freedom of conscience in France if the right to vote is granted to women." He had nothing against feminism but was tired of the extremists; what he wanted was the "true and good feminism," the "feminism without danger." Jacques Hadamard, of the Collège de France, pointedly reminded his female colleagues that voting was not just a right but also a duty and what, he wanted to know, had women been doing about the "political education" of the fairer sex. Emile Kahn, the secretary general, reminded the two women—one of whom he would soon marry—that the League had other things on its mind besides suffrage reform and was frustrated by the fact that any proposal short of full and complete equality was greeted by French feminists with hostility and suspicion.

The debate was taken in hand by now ex-Secretary General Henri Guernut. As a deputy he had consistently voted for suffrage reform which, he felt, gave him a certain moral authority in these matters. He first chastised the two women for being so tactless as to bring up the voting records of League deputies. This was a sensitive issue, especially for Guernut who had often lectured militants on the reasons why the voting patterns of their deputies were none of their business. Calling League deputies to account for their votes was not, he bluntly declared, league policy—unlike women's suffrage, which apparently was.[28] He did concede that something had to be done about the suffrage issue and that one had to start somewhere. He proposed what amounted to a modified version of the Viollette bill, expanding their representation to one-third of the municipal councilors, dropping the prohibition on women voting for the mayor but continuing to exclude them from senatorial elections.

In short, and with a straight face, Guernut was putting forth a proposal that represented a dramatic regression from even the very limited reforms recommended in the previous decade. It nonetheless received the support of everyone present, with the entirely understandable exception of Bloch and Collette, who discretely abstained. Now unanimous votes were, to say the very least, not the norm in the Central Committee, which was legendary for its disputatious sessions. But that his two female colleagues could go so far as to *abstain* on this issue was more than Emile Kahn could bear. "All of the work of the Committee" he declared "risks being destroyed by the abstention of our two female colleagues." In the end, Bloch and Collette were persuaded—not to say bullied—into accepting a compromise formulation.[29] The suffrage question never again surfaced as an important issue in the Central Committee. About the only concrete result of this discussion was a decision to dissolve the League's parliamentary group thus making it harder for people like Collette and Bloch to expose the hypocrisy of so many League politicians.[30] Worse, Suzanne Collette, having endured the pious lectures of her male colleagues in the Central Committee, was subjected to roughly the same kinds of arguments a few days later from a female delegate at the League's annual congress at Hyères. Collette was visibly displeased when Jeanne Déghilage, a retired schoolteacher from the Nord, and recently elected to the Central Committee, trotted out the traditional prudential arguments against full women's suffrage, but there was no denying that her anticlerical fulminations struck a resonant chord with most of the other delegates.[31]

The clerical peril, evoked explicitly or implicitly, by most of those who opposed extending the franchise to women, was clearly central to the debate and an important part of League orthodoxy. Even in the last years of the Republic, members of the League, notably those in the north and west, insisted on the undiminished threat from the church and bristled at the suggestion that nineteenth-century anticlericalism might be outmoded. The fact that the parties of the extreme Right, Louis Marin's *Fédération Républicaine* in particular, supported women's suffrage only seemed to prove the point. The editor of the bulletin of the federation of the Pas-de-Calais asserted that the forces of the right "have high expectation of this huge and inexperienced army of female voters who, they believe, especially in our region, receive their marching orders in the confessional." He did not say whether *he* believed any of this; indeed, he asserted that by virtue of running households women were more attuned to social questions than were men and might be induced to vote for candidates of the left. But for this to happen required years of careful political education for putative female voters.[32] Even Suzanne Collette, whose bona fides are not in doubt, could write, as late as 1944, on the eve of the first electoral consultation involving women, that, "if by chance the first result of women's suffrage should be the compromising of the republican regime," women around the world would never forgive their French sisters.[33] This article was leapt upon eagerly by male leaguers for whom it legitimized their prewar reservations about the wisdom of women's suffrage.[34] But the League's arguments about the presumed voting patterns of women were, as the spokesman from the Pas-de-Calais demonstrated, often quite muddled. In 1928 Henri Guernut, while attempting to sell a local section of the League on the merits of the municipal franchise for women, noted that the chief difficulty with women voters was they were likely to go "to the two extremes, that is to say to the Communists and the nationalists."[35] Guernut never explained how a feminine electorate apparently under the yoke of a priestly caste would also be inclined to vote Communist.

The pleas by French feminists—and a handful of leaguers—that French women were, on the evidence, unlikely to vote much differently than did men usually went unheard. Even when heard, the message could have unpredictable results. Fernand Corcos, another member of the Central Committee, certainly believed that women were unlikely to vote very differently than men, but for him this was a terrible reason for giving women the vote. Corcos, of course, was a principled pacifist, given to writing books documenting in excruciating detail the degree to which French women had been at least as ardent in their support of World War I as had been men—if not more so. That French women had attempted to parlay their contributions to the war effort into postwar political rights struck him as being frankly "criminal."[36] He saw little evidence that women were any more pacifist than men, and unless and until French feminists gave evidence of being true pacifists—by which he meant subscribing to his own brand of pacifism—he really could not see the point of giving women the vote. "If," he noted, "Hitler triumphed in Germany . . . it is in large measure with the active, premeditated and militant support of women who voted for him."[37] As he told Guernut in 1927, there was not much evidence that "the average woman in real life" was naturally pacifist and opposed to pervasive militarism; to the contrary, everything suggested that they were likely "consciously or otherwise to support it."[38]

There were, of course, elements in the League who did not quite grasp Corcos`s message and took his plea that women ought to be pacifists to mean that they in fact were. One section in the Charente-Maritime, apparently inspired by a misreading of Corcos, voted overwhelmingly in favor of women's suffrage in 1937 on the grounds that it was the best way to salvage the peace. But a neighboring section, apparently less partial to pacifism, replied with a resolution that read, in part: "Considering that the political and civic education of women is in general far too incomplete and the acquisition by women of political rights would put the republican regime in danger [the section] concludes that in the current state of things, it is simply impossible to grant women civil and political rights even though they may be the apostles of peace." Yet a third section, evidently by way of compromise, suggested that women should have the municipal vote but only on the understanding that women municipal politicians should have only a "consultative" voice and then only on matters involving women and children.[39]

What is so striking about the League's position on women's suffrage is that the entire debate was conditional upon the presumed voting patterns of women. Women's participation in the electoral process was a good thing if they did not vote for conservatives, if they did not vote for Communists, if they voted for pacifists. But not otherwise. That women had the right to vote and to vote for whomever they chose seems to have been a proposition alien to virtually all members of the League. In their great majority, leaguers believed that having proclaimed, in the abstract, women's political rights, they had done their duty and could comfortably await the moment when such rights would be to their political advantage before making much effort to insist that they be applied. Overlooked was the fact that this kind of political calculation flagrantly contradicted the oft-proclaimed League policy that it was above politics, interested only in justice and prepared, should the two conflict, to sacrifice politics to justice. Rare indeed was the influential leaguer like Elie Reynier, president of the federation of the Ardèche, who had the courage to state the obvious: that all the rhetoric about female suffrage having to await women's political and moral education amounted to "a healthy dose of unconscious duplicity and [intellectual] laziness."[40]

In the 1920s the League became involved in a protracted debate that went to the very heart of the organization's vaunted liberalism: the question of freedom of association for religious congregations. In 1901 the Waldeck-Rousseau government had introduced a far-ranging law on associations. By and large the law was a liberal measure, effectively eliminating many of the restrictions on freedom of association dating from the early years of the Republic. Henceforth, most associations of French citizens need do no more than register their statutes with the appropriate civil authorities.[41] Title III of the 1901 law, however, specified that religious congregations would have to obtain official authorization from the legislature. At one level this was merely to reassert what had always been the position of French governments; in principle, religious congregations had always required explicit governmental authorization. But in the previous half century many had failed to do so and, under more conservative governments, unauthorized congregations had been unofficially tolerated. But the requirement of formal legislative approval took on new meaning three years later, with a more left-wing legislature and the very anticlerical government of Emile Combes. In 1904, the Chamber of Deputies had been called to pass on a large number of requests for authorization submitted by religious congregations. Mindful of the inflammatory role played by certain congregations in the anti-Dreyfusard cause, a majority in the Chamber had summarily rejected all but a handful.

From the beginning this posed problems for the League and its principles. Article 10 of the 1789 Declaration of the Rights of Man had stated that no one ought to be troubled for his religious beliefs. Article 6 stated that the law must be the same for all French citizens and, although the Declaration did not say so explicitly, among the freedoms taken for granted by the League was the freedom of association. Taken together these principles seemed to be in contradiction to Title III, insofar as it seemed to be *une loi d'exception,* explicitly depriving one category of citizens from the full freedom of association largely by reason of their religious beliefs. Two related but analytically separable issues faced the League: First, was it in any way appropriate to distinguish between all other associations and religious congregations? Second, did the high-handed tactics of the 1904 legislature amount to a breach of the basic principle of freedom of association?

At the time, few in the League, caught up in the partisan political strife of the Dreyfus affair, appeared to have been troubled by this law. A quarter century later things had changed. The wartime atmosphere created by the *Union Sacrée* brought something of a reconciliation between the church and the Republic. Because, for all but two years in the 1920s, the government of the day was a relatively conservative one, enthusiasm for anticlerical measures diminished accordingly. Some prewar congregations, forced after 1904 to relocate to Belgium, had returned to France in 1914, and some of their members had served courageously at the front as medics. After the war, the newly formed *Ligue des droits des religieux anciens combattants,* openly challenged the legitimacy of Title III. This was part of a general counteroffensive of French Catholics in the mid-1920s, and it had the support of even the most liberal Catholic spokesmen like Marc Sangnier who managed to persuade the League to open the pages of the *Cahiers* to his plea for a rethinking of the 1901 law.

After much deliberation, the Central Committee of the League nonetheless concluded that Title III conformed to the principles of the Declaration. Congregationists, by virtue of accepting a life in isolation from civil society, by wearing distinctive dress, and above all by swearing special vows, had effectively rejected their "civil status" and could not therefore lay claim to the same guarantees of freedom of association as could ordinary citizens.

Not every member of the League found this position to be satisfactory. Three of the most prominent, Henri Guernut, the secretary general; Marc Rucard, deputy from the Vosges and future justice minister during the Popular Front; and Théodore Ruyssen, a distinguished philosophy professor, spoke out against this interpretation. All three recognized that the 1901 law had failed to make a case for treating congregationists differently from other French citizens. It was obvious to them that the drafters of the law had failed to identify those features that characterized all congregationists and only congregationists. Not all congregationists adopted distinctive modes of dress and not all of them lived in separate communities. Even if most did, how was that different from anarchists who chose to live in a phalanstery? The single most debated issue involved the vows sworn by congregationists. But the question of vows posed two problems. In the first place, congregationists were hardly unique in swearing vows: so too did married men and women. As Henri Guernut sarcastically asked, would anyone suggest that a bachelor who swore to his concierge that he would remain in that state had somehow foresworn his civil status? Moreover, because vows of whatever kind had no standing at all in French law, how could the taking of vows be used to create a juridical distinction between different categories of citizen? No one was very troubled by the vows of poverty or chastity, but the vow of obedience seemed tantamount to surrendering one's right to freedom. But was this also not permitted? In a line destined to become celebrated, Guernut asked: "Is there not a right to renounce a right?" In short, Title III was, as Catholics like Sangnier had argued, a violation of both the letter and the spirit of the Declaration.

These arguments prompted a spirited rebuttal by Albert Bayet, a left-wing Radical, a Professor of History, and one of the more outspokenly anticlerical members of the Central Committee. Those who claimed that Title III was inconsistent with the Declaration, he intoned, simply did not know their history. It was after all the same members of the Constituent Assembly who had drafted the Declaration who also voted to suppress the congregations. They had done so, Bayet insisted, on the entirely compelling ground that such congregations were a standing affront to the very principles of the Declaration of the Rights of Man. This was, in fact, a weak rejoinder because, as his opponents within the League would not fail to remind him, that same Constituent Assembly had also passed the Chapelier law of 1791, which outlawed associations of workers. One would surely not, in the twentieth century, want to invoke the reasoning of the League's forebears to call for the suppression of the CGT!

Turning to the question of vows, Bayet was even more scornful of the suggestion that individuals had the right to renounce certain rights and freedoms. They most certainly did not! Otherwise what stood in the way of legitimizing slavery? "Let us adopt the doctrine of Ruyssen and Rucard," he snidely observed, "and twentieth century society must, by virtue of an elegant liberalism, permit slavery to be re-established." In his polemical zeal, Bayet rather overlooked the point that slaves do not ordinarily voluntarily opt, by virtue of taking vows, to enter into a state of slavery. By the same token, a monk having decided to renounce his monastic state was free to do so without fear of the repressive hand of the state. No slave in a slave-owning society could say the same.

In the end, though, Bayet opposed both the liberalization of Title III and the very existence of congregations on the ground that they were an enemy of the secular and liberal French state. Ruyssen had suggested, more or less correctly, that anticlerical passions were becoming increasingly irrelevant to French political life. Bayet, by contrast, saw "a renaissance of political clericalism and an intellectual retreat provoked by the war." He expressed "the profound conviction that the Church is in the process of attempting a supreme effort to strike down *laïcité* and to suppress freedom of conscience. Worse, I dare not believe that this effort will necessarily be in vain: the coming struggle is, in my opinion, one of the toughest that the friends of liberty will have to face and if I hope for victory I dare not predict it with any assurance." In a message clearly directed toward his wayward colleagues, he concluded: "There is too much violent revolution in the Church and too much wavering in our own ranks."[42]

Bayet was, of course, notorious for his anticlericalism. But his general perspective was shared by many authoritative leaders of the League. Alphonse Aulard, the distinguished historian and vice president of the League, justified what he frankly conceded to be "exceptional laws" because "the religious associations are in large measure the combat organizations of the Church, which, led by its authorized head, the Pope, has incessantly fought the principles of 1789." As he informed the liberal Catholic, Marc Sangnier: "On the day when Rome stops fighting the Rights of Man and when it no longer makes war on the principles of civil society, these exceptional laws will disappear. But at the current time, things are not like that and civil society cannot safely abandon these laws of self defence. The time has not come to disarm because the enemy is more aggressive than ever." Marc Sangnier pointedly observed that Aulard's (much like Bayet's) problem was not just with the congregations but with the Roman Catholic Church in its entirety. If the church were nonetheless permitted to operate freely, why not the congregations? No one bothered to reply, largely because the answer was both obvious and uncomfortable: with the separation of church and state there was little the anticlerical Left could do to tame the nefarious powers of the church at large, but Title III gave it a weapon against one branch of the church, and no one wanted to surrender it.[43]

Bayet and Aulard spoke a language with which most members of the League were entirely comfortable. When in 1926 the Central Committee canvassed its sections on this question, 94 of the 103 who replied called for the retention of Title III. Few expressed much interest in the philosophical issues involved; most, as League spokesmen wistfully acknowledged, "invoked only . . . reasons of opportunity."[44] Congregations were dangerous and should not be authorized. The question of vows struck most leaguers as a pedantic point of theory. The congregations were secret organizations with secret rituals and owed allegiance to a foreign and hostile government; their existence was incompatible with a democratic society. The odd League members noted in passing that something similar could have been said about the Communist party, although rarely did anyone draw the appropriate conclusions from this fact. No one seems to have noticed that Masonry, to which so many League members belonged, was also a secret society.

At most, members of the League were prepared to concede that the actual application of Title III, in the hands of the Combes government, had been arbitrary. In the words of L. Lebel, vice president of the Amiens section, the deputies in the post-1902 legislature had taken "unfortunate liberties with the spirit and perhaps even the letter of the law." Yet he was adamant in insisting that "when we pass judgement on a law, it is not up to us to ask if the government applied it or even how it applied it but only if [the law] was both necessary and just." This was an odd argument in an association that traditionally denounced laws precisely because they were subject to abusive applications by the government of the day.[45]

In the climate of the interwar years, it is unlikely that the arguments of the "liberals," elegant and convincing though they were, would have won over the bulk of the League. But the liberals like Guernut and Ruyssen unnecessarily weakened their case. They were unduly sensitive to the fact that their own principles were being turned against them by people who, by and large, did not share them. Although he made an effective case for what he called "the liberal or individualist thesis," Guernut could not help noting: "It is odd that Catholics should have taken over this thesis and used it to their advantage." It was, of course, irritating to have one's principles invoked for and by people who clearly did not share them. But, for many in the League, the hypocrisy of one's enemies seemed to justify a selective application of those same principles. Had not Louis Veuillot, the nineteenth-century ultramontane catholic declared to the liberal republicans he so despised: "We demand liberty in the name of your principles; we refuse it to you in the name of our principles." For many in the League, the appropriate response was "No liberty for the enemies of liberty." Marc Rucard was virtually alone in reminding the League that the only appropriate response to Veuillot's hard-nosed logic was equally tough-minded logic: we will grant you, in the name of our principles, what you would refuse us in the name of yours.[46] The League was fond of declaring, *in the abstract*, "We opt for liberty with all of its risks." When it came to practical questions, however, such noble assertions were all too often qualified out of existence.

What vitiated the case of the "liberals" still further was the patent evidence that they were reluctant to follow their arguments to their logical conclusion. Théodore Ruyssen's case against the legitimacy of Title III was forceful and unassailable; it was hard not to conclude from his argument that religious congregations should be treated no differently than any other association. But no sooner had he seemingly reached that conclusion when he abruptly confessed: "for my part I should not like to push liberalism quite that far and I . . . believe that [a new law] should explicitly deny congregations the right to exercise any political activity." The congregations were simply "too vigorous, too stable, too active" to be treated like other associations.[47] As Albert Bayet was quick to note, Ruyssen instantly destroyed his whole thesis. Here was Ruyssen, Bayet crowed, insisting that congregations were associations like any other and then, in the next breath, insisting that they should be denied rights granted to all other associations simply because they were too powerful. Because in Bayet's view all congregations engaged, in one way or another, in politics, the practical consequences of Ruyssen's position was that none of them should be permitted. It terms of outcome, he noted, nothing much separated his position from that of his colleague save that the latter had attempted, most disingenuously, to claim the moral high ground. Both agreed, although only one chose to acknowledge it, that extending freedom of association to religious congregations was simply too dangerous.[48]

Henri Guernut too made a compelling case for the complete freedom of associations for the congregations. But he also acknowledged that his position had no chance of being accepted by the League. He proposed instead what he called "the thesis of controlled liberty." Congregations could be permitted, but only under a regime of "strict surveillance." What justified this surveillance? Both logical and practical reasons. "There is no individual freedom which, if pushed to its logical conclusions, does not become to some degree a tyranny which harms and restricts the rights of society." Moreover, "history has shown the danger of giving licence to the congregations." The sisters of Saint Vincent de Paul or the Benedictine monks might be innocuous enough in their own right but they could easily become instruments of the church hierarchy, which would demand of them "attitudes and actions which civil society cannot without danger tolerate." Guernut was lucidly clear when he noted that one could not control an association that had no legal existence, and here he parted company from both Bayet and Ruyssen. The congregations should be authorized but subject to rigorous control. Did this represent discriminatory legislation? Yes, but then one could not pretend that fishing clubs or choral singing associations were in the same category as associations of congregationists or Communists, both of which "must be more tightly supervised."[49]

Guernut represented the limits of the League's liberalism. Unlike Bayet, he knew discriminatory legislation when he saw it. Unlike Ruyssen, he appreciated that if one wanted to exercise control of the congregations one first had to permit them to exist. He was seen within the League as an extreme liberal and often excoriated as such by the more militant sections. Yet not so very much separated him in the end from the League mainstream. He too worried about the practical outcome of his liberal principles. He was more nuanced, subtle, and honest in his analysis, but in the end "liberty with all its risks" was more than he was prepared to accept. He came closest among the leaguers in acknowledging that if congregations should be subjected to special restrictions, so too should the Communist party. In fact, he did not pursue this point very far and for good reason. The League's liberalism was such that any suggestion that the Communists, beloved by few in the League, should in any way have their freedom of association restricted would have been seen as outrageous. This was entirely to its credit. What was not, was its apparent belief that comparable freedom for catholic citizens was excessively liberal and a threat to the League's very principles.[50]

The clerical peril, direct in the case of the congregations and indirect with respect to women's political rights, goes far to explaining the League's blind spots on those issues. But one issue that ought to have posed few problems for the League was freedom of the press. This was a cherished principle in the League, just as it had been for over a century a cause firmly defended by the French Left. It had, after all, been the Right throughout the nineteenth century that had sought to restrict the freedom of the press. Unrestricted freedom of the press, the Right had argued, threatened the public order, to say nothing of the existing regime, and was therefore dangerous and irresponsible. The Left—whatever Left it happened to be—traditionally countered that a free and untrammelled press was an indispensable precondition for a liberal or democratic society. Certainly a free press played a major role in consolidating the democratic French Republic in the two decades after 1870—a time when its survival was altogether problematic. It was the republicans who mastered the art of the cheap newspaper, supported by advertising rather than subscriptions, with popular formats, telegraphic services, and mass distribution. As their royalist opponents ruefully admitted, the cheap, attractive, mass-circulation republican newspaper was more than a match for their own costly and fussily old-fashioned product and a major factor in the gradual consolidation of the democratic regime.

By the late 1920s, however, the League began to rethink its position. By now it was no longer concerned about threats to a free and popular press; rather, the current concern was an excessively free and popular press. What prompted this reappraisal was the appearance of the mass circulation, *L'Ami du Peuple.* This newspaper was entirely the creation of the very successful perfume manufacturer, René Coty, a man of frankly fascist persuasion, given to financing such fascist or protofascist organizations as the Croix de Feu, the *Solidarité Française,* and Georges Valois' ephemeral *Faisceau.* Coty did not much care for left-wing intellectuals, Jews, pacifists, or internationalists. Consequently he was no fan of the League and, in particular, he had little use for its president, Victor Basch, who

was, after all, a distinguished man of letters, a Jew, and, like most of his fellow Socialists in the 1920s, a partisan of Franco-German reconciliation. Typically, Coty
thought it great sport invariably to refer to the president of the League as "Herr
Viktor Basch." Coty's great innovation was to sell *L'Ami du Peuple* at a price of
ten centimes at a time when every other daily newspaper was selling for twenty-
five centimes. What made this cheap price possible was Coty's personal wealth,
all of which ensured him a wide audience—nearly a million daily sales—for his
virulent attacks on the democratic regime.

The Coty phenomenon prompted the League to seriously debate measures
to modify and restrict the existing legislation on the press. Reasoning, not altogether unlike nineteenth-century conservatives, that the untrammelled freedom of the press threatened the existing regime, the League now proposed a law
on "the effective control of the press." Among other things, the law would require all newspapers to make public their sources of funding and that a national
"press office," representing both the government and various industry stake-
holders, be created to ensure a minimum price for newspapers thus eliminating the competitive advantage of people like Coty. All of this was more than a
little problematic in light of the historic traditions of struggle for a free press.
It did not, for example, escape the attention of members of the League that,
in the past, it had been precisely the ability of the republican press to produce
cheap newspapers that gave them a decisive advantage over their royalist counterparts.[51] Eugène Frot, independent Socialist deputy from the Loiret, destined
for a prominent if checkered ministerial career in the 1930s, and currently a
member of the League Central Committee, chose to address this issue. Deftly
missing the point, Frot, observed: "Is it not paradoxical that whereas about a
hundred years ago the inexpensive press served the cause of free expression,
today the political-financial operation of M. Coty and *L'Ami du Peuple* threat-
ens the freedom of the press."[52] By this reasoning, cheap newspapers on the Left
furthered the cause of freedom whereas their counterparts on the Right had
the opposite effect. Victor Basch quickly recognized the dangers in such arguments, noting that they potentially constituted an "irreparable threat to freedom of thought."[53] The League, he suggested, would almost certainly not be
putting forth these kinds of suggestions were Coty a left-wing publisher. The
mere fact that he was on the extreme Right was insufficient reason, as he put
it, "to forget our principles." He had a point but not one that had much impact
on his colleagues in the Central Committee. His fellow Socialist, Emile Kahn,
riposted that freedom of thought was not at issue here. If anything "freedom
of expression [was] threatened by a kind of dumping by the *puissances d'argent*

" by which he meant a cheap and privately subsidized reactionary press against which republican journals could not compete. Everyone was at some pains to stress that it was not Coty's reactionary views that were at issue; rather it was the danger of his obtaining a monopoly. Jacques Hadamard, the distinguished mathematician, piously intoned that even were Coty on the Left, he would oppose any "monopoly of public opinion [achieved by] cut rate pricing." Talk of monopolies was, of course, more than a little disingenuous since, whatever temporary advantage Coty was gaining in the circulation wars, no one could seriously deny that a left-wing press continued to flourish.

The most striking contribution to the debate was that of Henri Guernut, in many contexts one of the more impenitent "liberals" in the League. On this issue he too took strong exception to the scruples of Victor Basch. The president, he charged, remained wedded to "an individualist and anarchic conception of liberty, one that dated from 1789 but was now outmoded." The time had come to "abandon once and for all that chimera of theoretical liberty" and replace it with "a real and modern liberty, a regulated liberty." In the mouth of anyone less legendary for his usual commitment to liberal principles, such language would have been frightening. The "outmoded" principles of 1789 happened, inconveniently, to include the Declaration of the Rights of Man. Guernut's observations speak to the difficulty even the most devout liberals in the League had with the practical implications of their principles. Men like Guernut were no strangers to liberal theory. But when pressed, they typically opted to transpose the debate onto socialist terrain. To the objection that no one was *forced* to buy or read right-wing newspapers, Guernut replied that no one was forced to accept work at starvation wages either, but this had not prevented progressive governments from regulating the work place. No one on the Central Committee saw fit to question the logic that somehow equated the "right" to a living wage with the "right" to a competitively priced left-wing newspaper.

Moreover, in spite of the intensity of the debate, it was never clear exactly what principles were at stake here. Was it that eccentric millionaires did not have the right to sink their money into the newspaper of their choice and thereby support one political view or another? The problem here was that Coty was hardly unique, and France had plenty of rich men prepared to subsidize the newspaper of their choice. There was Paul Lederlin, the ultrarich textile magnate and also Radical senator from the Vosges who chose to subsidize such left-wing newspapers as *L'Oeuvre* and *L'Ere Nouvelle*. Or Jean Hennessey, heir to the cognac empire of the same name and independent Socialist deputy from the Charente, who controlled both *L'Oeuvre* and the equally left-wing

Quotidien. As it happened, spokesmen for the League frequented the columns of all three of these newspapers. What then, apart from politics, distinguished those men and their newspapers from Coty and his? For his part, Coty was fond of asking precisely this question. By way of an answer, he maliciously suggested that there was at least one difference. As a political outsider, he could not be suspect of using his press empire to obtain either an ambassadorship or a ministerial portfolio, an entirely transparent reference to Hennessey, who had been appointed ambassador to Switzerland in 1924 and was three times minister of agriculture in the late 1920s.[54]

Moreover, the League had rather odd allies in its campaign against Coty. The most effective opposition to the right-wing perfume manufacturer and his cheap daily came from the so-called *cinq grands,* the five mass-circulation Parisian dailies, none of which had an editorial stance remotely sympathetic to the Left. As the publication of the first issue of the *L'Ami du Peuple* approached, Coty's printer, coincidentally also the printer for the extreme right-wing daily, *L'Echo de Paris,* suddenly backed out of his contract. The powerful *Messageries Hachette,* which enjoyed an effective monopoly on the distribution and sales of the periodical press, refused to touch Coty's newspaper. Similarly, the *Agence Havas,* the news service that doubled as an advertising agency, denied the intruding newspaper access to advertising revenue. The quasi-monopoly enjoyed by *Hachette* and *Havas* had long been denounced by the League, but in this particular case it chose to observe a discreet silence. Coty, however, fought back. He found an independent printer, set up his own distribution service, and launched a massive and ultimately very successful lawsuit against the monopolistic forces facing him, in the process effectively breaking the power of *Hachette.* Had he been a left-wing philanthropist, his struggle might have seemed like a heroic battle for the freedom of the press.

All of this was very expensive. Coty was properly indignant when the same forces that had tried to block both his access to advertising revenue and to distribution outlets protested that he was sinking his fortune into his newspaper. It was all very well and good for Georges Boris, member of the League's Central Committee and editor of the *La Lumière,* a left-wing weekly that passed for a house organ of the League, to insist that a truly independent newspaper should live on its subscription and advertising revenue alone. But was it not the case that *La Lumière* balanced its books only because Boris too sunk his personal fortune into the enterprise? Boris ruefully conceded the point but insisted that such personal subventions were intended only to be a temporary expedient. The same was true of *L'Ami du Peuple,* Coty countered. What then distinguished the two cases? For Boris it was the fact that one newspaper was trying to enlighten the public whereas the other sought to mislead it. Again, Coty could not disagree, merely noting, somewhat mischievously, that only the people would decide which newspaper was in which camp: *La Lumière* with 8,500 readers or *L'Ami du Peuple* with a million?[55] In the end, neither newspaper ever succeeded in living on its own resources. But Coty went bankrupt in 1933, whereas *La Lumière* survived until the last days of the Republic.

The question of press regulation did not disappear when *L'Ami du Peuple* did. In the early 1930s the League was obsessed by the corruption of democracy by the famous "puissances d'argent." In the light of a string of scandals, all involving the corruption of politicians by segments of the financial and business world, such concerns were hardly misplaced. One of the most consistent themes was that of *la presse corrrumpue* or *la presse pourie.* There were, the League reasoned, three forces that were systematically corrupting the French press, and a fortiori public opinion, thus perverting the very idea of French democracy. They were foreign governments, by which they meant Italy and, in due course, Germany; French politicians, by which they meant right-wing ones; and the shady businessmen of *le monde d'affaires.* Without the strictest of controls on this kind of corrosive financial influence, the free and independent press, upon which the democratic regime depended, could not survive.

At the 1933 League congress, Georges Boris, editor of *La Lumière,* presented a report on the corruption of the press, which resuscitated many of the proposals mooted in 1929 at the time of the Coty debate. No one seemed to feel that an attack on the venal right-wing press by the editor of a left-wing newspaper might involve any conflict of interest. Among the suggestions put forth by Boris were legal measures designed to sanction "false news." Of course, the logical line between the "crime of spreading false news" and "the crime of opinion" was an exceedingly fine one. Once crossed, it opened up all kinds of disturbing possibilities. Unwittingly revealing the inherent dangers in this kind of regulatory legislation, one delegate, Maurice Weber, noted that there were many ways to distort the news and that omission was as troublesome as was commission. The mass circulation *presse d'information,* for example, routinely failed to give adequate coverage to the speeches of left-wing members of parliament. Could not a law be tailored to redress this abuse? Measures of that kind, the *rapporteur* dryly noted, might be difficult to implement. Nonetheless the League was convinced that there existed a seriously corrupt press, that it was a right-wing press, and that such venality threatened not only freedom of the press but of the democratic regime itself.[56]

The League might have been somewhat less categorical on this point had it been better informed about the state of the left-wing press. A classic example was *La Volonté*, the creation of Albert Dubarry who began his career as a romantic socialist and ended up, like more than one of his ideological *confrères*, an enterprising businessman. The newspaper was vaguely socialist with a distinctly pacifist and internationalist tone. It was therefore an ideal vehicle for the militant pacifists in the League, many of whom were frequent contributors. More important still, League president, Victor Basch, wrote a regular and lengthy column for *La Volonté* from 1926 until 1934. The newspaper catered largely to a League audience; in 1929 Henri Guernut reminded Basch that placing advertisements for the League in *La Volonté* was pointless given that "all its readers are already League members."[57] What these readers and contributors did not know was that *La Volonté* was a particularly outstanding example of the venality of the press they so deplored. Better yet, it was an example of all three forms of press corruption identified by the League: corruption by foreign powers, by right-wing politicians, and by the more sordid elements in the business community. In 1926 the German government chose to subsidize *La Volonté*. In 1929–30, the French right-wing premiere, André Tardieu, funnelled money from the infamous *fonds secrets* to the newspaper. Between 1931 and 1933, a major source of income for *La Volonté* was a certain Serge Alexandre Stavisky![58] To be sure, the League could have been aware only of Stavisky's contributions, and then only at the beginning of 1934 when the details of the Stavisky affair became public. Basch contributed only one article after that and none after the editor was arrested for fraud.[59] Thereafter no one cared to talk very publicly about *La Volonté*. Privately, though, League members were clearly chagrined. Mathius Morhardt shared the general belief that whereas in the nineteenth century the press had been "the tool of the intellectual," it was now "the tool of the plutocracy." But he couldn't help reminding Basch, in a thinly veiled reference to *La Volonté*, that "many reactionary newspapers would certainly have refused to touch the 40,000 francs a month accepted by a certain left-wing newspaper incriminated in the Stavisky affair."[60]

Careful reflection on the *La Volonté* episode might have led the League to rethink its assumptions about venality and freedom of the press. Dubarry was wonderfully venal but, for all that, he really did not provide a very good example of the corruption either of editorial freedom or of public opinion. *La Volonté* was in fact a singularly "liberal" newspaper. While Dubarry was cashing secret checks from whomever was paying, his journalists had absolute freedom. There was never the slightest restraint on Basch or any of his fellow leaguers.

In 1933, it became apparent that Basch was seriously out of step with Dubarry and his associate editor, Jean Luchaire, the latter destined for a prominent career as a Vichy collaborationist. In essence Dubarry (like a powerful minority within the League) did not believe that Hitler's accession to power ought in any way to inhibit a greater Franco-German reconciliation. Basch, who would die with his wife at the hands of the Vichy milice, thought very differently about the matter. Nonetheless, Basch was permitted the editorial freedom to express his disapproval in the strongest possible terms. Dubarry, while defending his position, made it very clear that if an ideological parting of the ways were in sight, Basch's articles were, and would remain, as welcome as ever. Basch remained a regular contributor, and the content of his articles were unchanged.[61]

In the end, what real harm came from the corruption of *La Volonté*? Perhaps it explained why a militant pacifist like Armand Charpentier (also a League member) wrote in the newspaper because his essays would surely have appealed to the Germans, although they also appealed to Dubarry. Possibly it explains the periodic pieces by shady right-wing Radicals like Gaston Bonnaure and Louis Proust (both also members of the League), as this would have appealed to Stavisky (keen to corrupt them) and Tardieu (keen to co-opt them.) But the fact remains that the single most important, passionate, and lucid contributor to *La Volonté* was Victor Basch. Whatever else he may have been, Basch was utterly incorruptible, and nothing he ever had to say could have been of much comfort to the Germans, to Tardieu, or to Stavisky.

The question of restricting freedom of the press resurfaced in 1936. The Popular Front government was routinely subjected to scurrilous, slanderous, and frequently anti-Semitic attacks from the right-wing press. A particularly egregious example was the campaign launched by the virulent protofascist weekly, *Gringoire*, directed against the Socialist minister of the interior Roger Salengro. Salengro, a member of the League, had been briefly captured by the Germans in World War I. Although he soon escaped, he was routinely charged with desertion until his superiors were satisfied with his version of events, as they soon were. This had not stopped his political enemies in his constituency of Lille (Communists, in the event, although no one chose to remember that fact in 1936) from claiming that he was a deserter. Owing to his evenhanded treatment of the sit-in strikers of June 1936, he soon became the favorite target of the extreme Right and most notably *Gringoire*, which began a massive campaign of defamation involving the patently false allegations of desertion. A harried and emotionally distraught Salengro committed suicide in fall 1936. A typical

League reaction was that of the secretary of the section of Fontainbleau. "Freedom of the press is not the freedom to slander [or] to drag through the mud men who are an honour to democracy. We want, in the strongest possible way, that kind of press to be muzzled."[62]

Shortly thereafter, on November 26, 1936, the government introduced a bill designed to deal with a reckless press and intended specifically to prevent "public opinion [*l'esprit publique*] [from being] corrupted by the big financial powers." In general the bill sought to ensure a greater transparency concerning the ownership and financial backing of newspapers and to facilitate taking them to court for defamation. Of particular interest was Article 27, which dealt with the crime of deliberately and knowingly disseminating "false news." The preexisting legislation had specified that false news was a crime only if it actually troubled (*aura troublée*) the public order. The government's bill amended the article to include false news "likely to trouble" (*de nature de troubler*) the public order. Basch, Kahn, and the Socialist deputy Salomon Grumbach objected quite rightly that it was uncommonly difficult to determine what news was actually "false," harder still to prove that someone knew that the news being disseminated was false, and next to impossible to distinguish between those deliberate falsehoods that were "likely" to trouble the public order and those that were not. In the hands of a government less sympathetic than that of Léon Blum, such legislation could be extremely dangerous. Not everyone, however, was so concerned. Once again missing the point, Ferdinand Corcos, another long-serving veteran of the Central Committee, opined that since "responsible journalists" (*responsible* was a word increasingly in vogue in the League) never knowingly spread false news, the law posed no serious threat no matter who was in power.[63] In any event, René Château would note, "when the people of Paris made a revolution in 1830 to free the press from [government] domination, they did not do so for the benefit of blackmailers, enemies of the nation or professional slanderers."[64]

Having expressed their formal reservations about Article 27, spokesmen for the League nevertheless felt free to protest when the French Senate threw out the amended version of the bill. They waxed ironically about a "Senate so punctilious about freedom of the press when it is a question of protecting the worst enemies of the regime." The Senate, they noted, had not seen fit to reject similarly worded legislation concerning false news that was "likely" to weaken discipline and morale in the army. This was a legitimate comment on the conservatism of the Senate but one that overlooked the fact that the

League had not previously objected to this section of the bill, an odd over-sight among a group of veterans of the Dreyfus affair who had been accused often enough in their youth of doing just what the bill sought to suppress.

Article 14 of the same bill gave the government, upon the request of the minister of foreign affairs, authority to prevent certain newspapers from being distributed outside of France. The Senate also scrapped that provision. As-sessing the work of the Senate, a report of the League's legal specialists could not contain its outrage at this excision, especially because it was purportedly done in the name of freedom of the press. Why, the experts wanted to know, should the government not have the right to prevent certain newspapers from leaving the country when it had the right, by denying passports, to prevent certain citizens from so doing? They had a point; governments did withhold passports, usually from people they did not like, who were going to places the governments did not want them to go to; a case in point had been French So-cialists seeking to attend international congresses during World War I. The ex-perts overlooked the fact that in the past the League had quite rightly protested such exercises in governmental arbitrariness.

But there were larger issues at stake. In a language that departed somewhat from the usual tone of technical legal briefs, the consultants observed:" No Frenchman who has been abroad has not noticed that there is no foreign pol-icy possible for France as long as foreign opinion is formed by periodicals like *Candide* and *Gringoire,* which are all the more dangerous because they ap-pear to be literary newspapers rather than political ones."[65] Many problematic assumptions were being bootlegged in here. One was that the defense of a suc-cessful French foreign policy was part of the mandate of the League. Another was that the possibility that the foreign policy of the government of the day might in some way be hampered was sufficient grounds for restricting the free-dom of the press. Even if one were to invoke raison d'état (as increasingly, spokesmen for the League were doing), France was full of accredited dip-lomatic representatives and foreign correspondents, so it was unlikely that foreign opinion would be unaware of the sentiments expressed in *Gringoire* merely because copies of the newspaper had not physically left the country.

Yet precisely that possibility seems to have troubled some in the League. In 1938, just after the Munich agreement, Georges Boris, again presenting a re-port on the press before the annual congress, and making explicit reference to Article 14, noted with some outrage that an article in *Gringoire* entitled "Should we fight for Czechoslovakia" had been picked up and published in translation by the Nazi *Der Angriff.* "All these campaigns denigrating France," he intoned, "have worked for the propaganda of France's enemies."[66] Beyond the fact that Boris did not much care either for *Gringoire* or the Munich accords, the question of principle at issue here was again unclear. After all, Hitler did not have to read *Der Angriff* or *Gringoire* to know that many Frenchmen were unwilling to die for Czechoslovakia. Nor was the expression of such sentiments likely to hinder French foreign policy given that they were, to a large degree, shared by Georges Bonnet, minister of foreign affairs. When it comes to that, such views were also being published by some of his own colleagues on the Central Committee of the League.

It was not, of course, that the leaders of the League did not understand the principles of a free press. The old veterans of the Central Committee certainly showed, in their calmer moments, that they were well aware of the issues at stake. But there were not many calm moments by the 1930s. As a result, many of them were now saying things that would have horrified the League's founders. Georges Bourdon, a fifteen-year veteran of the Central Committee, was one of those most obsessed about a press that seemed to be "in the service of the powers of money and of conservatism, for the most part stubbornly defending privileges that are outdated and condemned." All of this, he noted "presents the paradox of a press that is divorced from a national public opinion which it is supposed to represent and which it is the role of the press to express."[67] Much like Frot, Bourdon had a penchant for finding "paradoxes" when it came to the freedom of the press. Did he really mean to say that the role of a free press was to reflect and to express public opinion? Almost certainly not—because a moment's reflection would have shown him that this would have excluded an opposition press that neither reflected nor expressed public opinion but was, by contrast, trying to change it—that is, precisely the role historically played by the left-wing press. In truth, he was simply expressing his exasperation with a popular and mass-circulation press that had never been very enthusiastic about the Popular Front despite the fact that the nation had, albeit narrowly, voted for it in 1936. It also reflected his frustration at the fact that a year later the Popular Front had lost much of its public—to say nothing of its parliamentary—support. Blaming the press for this development was partisan but understandable, and his language, disturbing though it might appear in retrospect, was that of a left-wing cheerleader and not an opponent of the free press. But he was an important leader of the League, and in that organization left-wing cheerleading was not supposed to trump a principled defense of freedom.

Nor was Bourdon alone. Marius Moutet had been in the League since its foundation; he had been a prominent Socialist for just about as long and had served as the very distinguished minister of colonies in Blum's first government. In 1938, no longer a minister, he was back in the Central Committee and very exercised about the abuses in the press. In theory, there were laws on the books that would permit one to haul the *Action Française* (the newspaper of the royalist and anti-Semitic movement of the same name) into court any day of the week. But rare was the judge who would convict and, when one did, the fines were invariably derisory. "You do not," he observed, "save democracy with vague press laws." What were needed were "special tribunals." Already this was language that would not have been out of place coming from a minister in the government of Napoleon III.

Warming to his subject Moutet argued: "The press has freedom but no responsibility; it is permitted to do anything—attack the regime, betray the country, ruin it even and nobody can do anything about it. When a regime refuses in this way to defend itself it is very nearly lost. This question of the press poses a serious political problem: does a regime have the right to defend itself? . . . Along with the principal of freedom there is also, for a regime and for a nation, the right to live." Was the Republic taking active steps to defend itself? Moutet did not think so; recently there had been a plot against the state involving some marginal army officers, the so-called Cagoule. "Boulangism was nothing compared to [this] plot." But where was the energetic action of the government? "A certain badly-understood liberalism leads democracy to its ruin."[68] This was certainly odd language coming from the mouth of a man like Marius Moutet. In his earlier years he had not been preoccupied with defending "the regime" for the very good reason that he was a Socialist, and the regime was, among other things, a capitalist one that he and members of his party wanted overthrown. Another reason why Moutet, in his Dreyfusard days, had not talked this way was because this was, almost word for word, the way the anti-Dreyfusards talked!

The Central Committee of the League was legendary for its protracted quarrels. But Moutet's observations prompted only the mildest of demurrals. Victor Basch, arguably the most disputatious Frenchman ever, limited himself to platonically observing that if there was a problem with the press now, the League, by virtue of a long history of defending press freedom, was partially responsible. The notoriously long-winded Emile Kahn restricted himself to a couple of sentences, noting that the special tribunals called for by Moutet did rather violate the League's principled and long-standing objections to exceptional jurisprudence. But, objected George Boris, if one wanted to repress *Gringoire* (as he apparently did), then such legislation would be necessary.[69]

The press issue was a difficult one for the League. It arose at a time when the Republic did seem to be threatened by mass movements of the extreme Right. Some of the newspapers of the extreme Right were exceptionally scurrilous. So one is tempted to dismiss the League's obtuseness on the issue of freedom of the press as a minor and understandable aberration. In fact, it was part of a much larger pattern whereby cherished League principles lost much of their appeal when it became apparent that the Right might take advantage of them.

Lurking behind most League discussion of public policy was the rhetoric of "republican defense." The slogan, *la république en danger,* was as old as the Third Republic itself. Whatever merits it had in the two formative decades of the regime, during the lifetime of the League it risked becoming a seriously shop-worn formula. Strictly speaking, after 1889 the Republic was never really in danger—if by danger one means a serious threat to its very existence. The various right-wing leagues, both at the turn of the century and after 1934, looked menacing enough but were in fact both incompetent and irresolute and no match for the vigorous action of a democratic government, be it that of Waldeck-Rousseau in 1900 or Léon Blum in 1936. To be sure, this is more obvious in hindsight than it might have been to contemporaries. In 1898 the Republic had outlived by only a few short years any regime since 1789; the riots of February 6, 1934, occurred in the context of the recent collapse of democracy in Germany and the more or less simultaneous fall of the democratic regime in Austria. The vitriolic obscenities pouring forth from some fraction of the Catholic press in the late 1890s and the more virulent right-wing press of the 1930s afforded French democrats little comfort.

It would be tempting to conclude that woman's suffrage, freedom of association, and freedom of the press, unassailable principles in the abstract, were unaffordable luxuries in a real world where the fate of the democratic regime was in the balance. Such an argument is vitiated however by the fact that the League seemed to believe that the republic was *always* in danger. The affaire des fiches took place long after the government had crushed the anti-Dreyfusard Right and when a center-left government was in power. The League's prudential equivocation about woman's suffrage coincided with the triumph of the Cartel des Gauches. Both the debate on congregations and the early discussion of the freedom of the press took place during a period of unprecedented peace and prosperity. In the late 1920s, France was as free from the threat of an anti-Republican Right as she would ever be. Yet anyone reading the debates of League congresses during those years might conclude that the triumph of fascism was just around the corner. By any standard, the "clerical peril" had been waning since the 1880s. Yet delegate after delegate at the League congresses in the late 1930s professed to believe that a return to *le régime du curé* was imminent. For far too many in the League, leaders as well as rank and file, *la république en danger* was an intellectually lazy shortcut serving no purpose but to spare them the possibly inconvenient political consequences of living up to their professed beliefs.

FIVE

The League from Below

However much the League dabbled in politics or questions of broad public policy, its raison d'être was the defense of public liberties and the cases of injustice and arbitrary justice. In 1927 the president of the federation of the Drôme noted that although the League was best known for its stance on "national or international politics, the foremost and essential function of the League is the often modest, difficult and low profile defense of minor civil servants, widows, pensioners and common citizens."[1] Most of its day-to-day activities were directed toward this end. By the 1930s the League was dealing with nearly 20,000 such cases annually, and the bulk of its substantial staff of nearly 50 employees was dedicated to handling the problems arising out of these questions.

In principle a very efficient mechanism was in place. Potential cases would first be dealt with by one of the League's nearly 2,500 local sections. Sections would examine the case in order to establish if it were an appropriate one for the League and to pass on its inherent merits. If a section thought a case worthy and believed it to be one that it could not handle at the local level, the section would compile a complete dossier and send it on to Paris. There, one of the many legal experts the League retained would examine the case, emit a judgment on its merits, suggest the most effective recourse, and if deemed appropriate, recommend formal League intervention with the relevant public authorities. The League routinely sent out circulars to its sections showing how most effectively to compile a dossier and explaining the fine points of the law and of the legal system.

In practice, very frequently nothing like this happened. Sections routinely passed on cases that were transparently not within the League's jurisdiction and more or less devoid of merit. The dossiers were often incomplete, when not totally rudimentary, thus requiring a string of letters calling for more information. By 1933, Emile Kahn, noting that the resultant postage costs were prohibitive, informed his staff that incoming cases required far more rigorous scrutiny, and requests for more details should be limited to those instances where the case seemed both appropriate and plausible.[2] Although some sections could be exceptionally tenacious with cases that caught their fancy, others apparently lost interest as soon as they had forwarded the problem to Paris. Requests for additional information went unanswered, requiring yet more follow-up letters wondering what, if anything, was happening. Even when local sections took their work seriously and screened out obviously inappropriate or implausible cases, there was no guarantee that the interested parties would not subsequently address headquarters directly, replete with caustic observations about the narrow legal views or general lack of energy of the local section.[3]

Moreover, of the thousands of cases sent annually to Paris, only about one in twenty was deemed to have merit. As the secretary of the federation of the Indre-et-Loire pointedly observed, these statistics suggested that too many sections were excessively casual in performing their duties.[4] Worse, many leaguers had an imperfect grasp of the proper role of the League and its sections. League officials, at every level, spent an inordinate amount of time reminding the rank and file what the League was *not*. It was not an employment office, a social assistance bureau, or a legal aid clinic. It did not intervene with public authorities to obtain tobacco retailing permits, reduced railroad fares, or honorific decorations. It did not involve itself in criminal cases currently before the courts, except when there was evidence of inadequate legal representation; nor did it touch matters involving civil litigation. League membership was not intended as a kind of personal insurance, and membership dues were not an insurance premium. As René Château, president of the federation of the Charente-Maritime noted, too many League members treated "the League as an insurance company, counting on it to provide guarantees against eventual misfortunes [but otherwise] do not share in its work."[5] Such injunctions were common[6] but had little impact on many League members. When not expressing their resentment at such restrictive guidelines,[7] many militants blissfully ignored them. Indeed, there were leaguers who believed that almost any personal problem or administrative inconvenience that befell them was automatically a case for the League. Whether it be litigation arising out of bicycle, motorcycle, automobile, or boating accidents or problems arising with tobacco, fishing, and hunting licenses or suspended driving licenses, there were always those who believed there was an injustice that the League must imperatively redress.

An entirely typical case in 1937 involved a war widow who wrote directly to the League complaining that the local prefect consistently refused her requests for a *bureau de tabac*.[8] Not least of the problems with this complaint was that the allocation of bureaux de tabac was the classic example of the kind of patronage that the League publicly and strenuously refused to involve itself in. Still, the legal experts carefully examined the case and patiently explained to the widow that by virtue of being a *war* widow she was the recipient of a relatively generous pension and thus not, under the existing regulations, entitled to a tobacco license. But, replied the widow, she could cite no fewer than three other widows of soldiers, all younger than was she, who *had* been granted tobacco licenses. After more investigation, the legal consultants noted that all three of these women had lost husbands who had served in the military but who had not died in combat. They were, therefore, not entitled to the generous pensions of war widows and thus were consequently eligible for tobacco licenses. Nothing daunted, the widow soon found a local leaguer who, apparently unaware of the previous involvement of headquarters, energetically took up her case. This too involved a lengthy, frustrating and unproductive round of correspondence.[9]

A significant percentage of the cases central League headquarters dealt with involved issues that had little to do with the broader principles of the League and which were explicitly excluded by League statutes. Very often local sections treated the League as a source of free legal advice. Despite various League circulars expressly excluding this kind of work, almost invariably the juridical experts of the League responded as helpfully as they could. They also often suggested, as tactfully as possible, that the interested parties might usefully consult a lawyer rather than importune league headquarters.

Many of the issues brought to the League's attention by its various sections were exclusively matters of local interest. In 1909 the section of Talmontiers-Amecourt complained about a local farm whose stables were close to the main road and spewed forth manure in an unhygienic fashion. In 1936 the president of a local section demanded that the League intervene with the Ministry of the Interior to prevent posters of the Popular Front from being torn down in his town. In both cases League headquarters patiently suggested that the sections might more usefully address themselves to the local authorities.[10] But local sections were very adept at transposing matters of transparent local interest into a broader political terrain. The section of Urepel, in the Basses-Pyrénées, was up in arms about the proposed new highway from Bayonne to Pamplona. As originally conceived, the highway was to go through the center of Urepel. But the Ministry of Public Works later decided that, because the highway was principally for tourists, the route should by-pass Urepel and go instead through the mountains which afforded some spectacular scenery. Lest League headquarters suspect—as indeed it did—that this was merely a matter of local self-interest, the section in Urepel was at some pains to remind them that lurking behind the revised highway plans was almost certainly the archly reactionary local deputy, Jean Ybarnegaray, and that only vigorous League intervention on this issue could keep up the morale of beleaguered republican forces in the region.[11]

Many cases coming to the League involved the direct interests of individual League members. The president of the federation of the Bouches-du-Rhône was forever pestering the League about some financial issues resulting from his divorce.[12] A member of the League's section in Mulhouse had twice failed a university exam owing to, or so he claimed, the political bias of his examiners. He somehow managed to persuade his section to demand League intervention to obtain him an exceptional third try.[13] Another leaguer felt that the League should be doing something about the fact that he was, unfairly, not allowed to fish without a fishing license.[14]

Frequently, cases brought to the attention of the League involved personal disputes within the civil service. The president of the section of Saint Georges-des-Coteaux was incensed at the behavior of a local schoolteacher who had taken her class, during school hours, to watch a local wedding. To make matters worse, she was very conservative and close friends with the local mayor and right-wing deputy Pierre Taittinger. Aware that the local president was also a teacher in the same school and had been subject to administrative investigation initiated by his much disliked colleague and also alert to the dangers of attacking civil servants for purely political reasons, the juridical section was inclined to ignore this case. But, protested the local leaguer, he had been one of the leading activists in the creation of the local Rassemblement Populaire but all he had to show for his pains were administrative hassles. How could it be, he wanted to know, "that under a government of the *Rassemblement Populaire . . .* a teacher who, with the support of the reactionary forces, attacks [me] has not been disturbed for a minute?"[15] Complaints about civil servants were at times less overtly political but not less self-interested. The president of the section of Recey-sur-Oure complained to the president of the federation of the Côtes d'Or about a recent appointment in the local state tobacco monopoly. In principle such posts were reserved for wounded war veterans. Yet this one had gone to a young man who had not even yet finished his military service. Although it was true that the plaintiff had not seen front line service, he was nonetheless a veteran and surely a better choice for the post. The federation's president investigated the case but discovered that the post in question had been open for two years, and the local leaguer had not applied.[16] Inevitably these kinds of disputes would pit leaguer against leaguer. In the town of Mont-de-Marsan, both the mayor and his first deputy were members of the League. But the deputy, also the vice-president of the federation of the Landes, had a string of grievances. His many interventions in the municipal council were not faithfully reflected in its minutes; worse, the mayor, during his frequent absences preferred, wherever possible, to delegate authority to his second and third deputies rather than to his first. Although it suspected that this was essentially a political quarrel, League headquarters nonetheless dutifully wrote the prefect who contacted the mayor. By way of reply, the mayor noted that the decision to limit the first deputy's activities to what was strictly required under the law had not been his but a unanimous decision of the municipal council determined to limit the contact of a notoriously quarrelsome individual with the town's constituents. Paris seems to have found this explanation compelling.[17]

At times the interventions of the League—both local and national—could be overtly political and very petty. It devoted over a year, and much paperwork, to the case of Pierre Taittinger. Taittinger was an obvious target because he was president of the right-wing and antiparliamentary formation, the Jeunessess Patriotes. He was the mayor of Saint-Georges-des-Coteaux in the Charente-Maritime but also deputy from the second arrondissement of Paris. In May 1935 he voted in the municipal elections in Paris, but in January 1936 he voted in Saint-Georges-des-Coteaux in elections for the local administrative council (*conseil d'arrondissement*). This was a violation of French electoral law. The section of Saint-Georges-des-Coteaux promptly took him to court for electoral fraud. The president of the departmental federation freely acknowledged that this was "outside the usual mandate of the League" but nevertheless insisted that unless it were pursued vigorously, "the prestige of the League in our region will be greatly reduced." Taittinger did not dispute the facts but did argue, plausibly enough, that he had not realized that it was illegal to vote in two different places (in both of which he had a residence) for two different and discrete local elections. The local tribunal accepted his arguments, found him guilty of a misdemeanor, and levied no sanctions. At the urging of the League, his case was appealed, and a higher court found him guilty of electoral fraud and imposed the token (and suspended) fine of 100 francs.[18]

One reason why so many inappropriate cases crossed the League's desk was that so many of its members had an elastic definition of "injustice." In 1936, with the support of his section, one member, an inventor, appealed to the League because he believed he had been cheated out of a patent by an elevator company. His case was not very strong, as the juridical consultants informed him in a three-page brief. Moreover, as Kahn reminded him, this was purely a "private matter." But, countered the outraged investor, surely "the Dreyfus Affair was also a private matter."[19] Moreover local leaders of the League were fully aware that even in questionable cases their persistence might pay off. The section of Cahors wanted the League to intervene in favor of one of its members who claimed that a teaching post he sought had gone to a less qualified individual. The initial reaction of headquarters was the standard: "We make it an absolute rule . . . never to intervene in the appointment . . . of civil servants." But the case hinged on the impossible question of whether or not the grade of *très bien* on one of the unsuccessful candidate's exams should be assigned a numerical value of 18 or 19 out of 20. The League's jurists, upon examining the issue, concluded that the candidate did not have a compelling case. But when the president of the section protested strenuously, Kahn relented and, in light of "the importance you personally attach to this matter" asked for a second examination from the experts. Their conclusion did not change but neither did the indignant protests of the section. In the end, Basch wrote up a three-page letter to the minister of education pleading the candidate's case.[20]

Strenuous lobbying by section presidents did not, of course, always succeed. The case of the leaguer who had lost his job as a mail carrier for being drunk and failing to deliver the mail and ten years later wanted it back was dismissed by the League despite the fact that the president of his section had given it his "strong support."[21] But League headquarters was particularly alert to the sensibility of its members. Even the most outlandish or inappropriate requests received a sympathetic and tactful response. The secretary general often moderated the frequently exasperated tone of the juridical consultants.

This extreme degree of responsiveness to people who were in the League for reasons of self-interest speaks to a desire to retain as many as possible of them. The rank and file sensed this too because they frequently threatened to resign when, or even if, their cases were not pursued more vigorously. Upon being informed that his demand for help in obtaining work in the local fire department was "a little outside our competence," one leaguer promptly resigned. Kahn nevertheless took the time to write the president of his section in the hopes of persuading him to stay.[22] The secretary treasurer of the section of St.-Emillion had been involved in an automobile accident and claimed that he had been sued (successfully) only because he was a good republican. Upon being told he had no case, he resigned in anger. Again Kahn pleaded with the president of his federation to have him change his mind.[23] The treasurer of the section of Saint-Lo had sought a position in the post office in Rennes but it went, for compassionate reasons, to someone else. When League headquarters was both slow and unenthusiastic about his case, he and other members of the section's executive promptly resigned from the League. Secretary General Henri Guernut pleaded with the section's president to have the dissidents reconsider. Indeed, to that end, President Buisson sent a long, and ultimately successful, letter to the relevant minister on behalf of the angry local treasurer.[24]

Reasons other than the disinterested pursuit of justice might motivate someone to join the League because some very real material advantages could accrue from belonging to a large organization with political clout and considerable influence in the corridors of power. For many leaguers, the association was the perfect vehicle for obtaining positions within the civil service or advancement or transfers therein. League statutes, however, explicitly forbade such requests, and the League was repeatedly on record as condemning any attempts by outside parties to influence appointments or promotions within the civil service. When it suited League headquarters, it could be utterly categorical on the point. When Hassani Said, a resident of Algeria and apparently not a League member, wrote Kahn appealing for help in obtaining a post, he was treated to an indignant reply. This was an inappropriate request for the League whose statutes "absolutely forbid giving recommendations of any kind, especially those involving appointments, transfers or promotions within the civil service." The League believed that such decisions should be made by the administration without outside interference. Given that it had always publicly objected to the whole idea of these kinds of recommendations, the League could hardly intervene in his case.[25] Individuals who did not belong to the League, members who were obscure, who lacked the support of their sections, or whose case was transparently unworthy could count on such responses. Most League members, however, were fully aware that if one went about it in just the right way the League could have a rather more elastic reading of its statutes. As a result, demands for administrative favors poured in.

There was, in fact, a fairly elaborate ritual to successful requests for League favors. It was always good form to begin with a lengthy statement of one's militant activity within the League for the last several decades or at least attaching one's League membership card to the letter. It was desirable, too, to claim, truthfully or not, that this was the very first time a personal favor had been requested. Above all, it was essential to argue that what might appear at first blush to be merely a personal favor was, upon closer examination, part of a public-spirited attempt to preserve the beleaguered Republic. The school system, the civil service, and the judiciary were literally crawling with reactionaries and if the Republic were to have any chance of surviving, it was long past time that at least a few good republicans should be admitted into the ranks of civil servants. League militants were often crassly ignorant of their organization's statutes, but they were always remarkably well informed about who was in power and where. If the relevant minister was a leaguer, they knew about it; if not, perhaps his *chef du cabinet* was, in which case the League might consider not troubling the overworked minister and go instead directly to his subordinate.[26] It never hurt for League central to be reminded that because of its heroic achievements over the years it had earned the very considerable influence it could exercise over various ministers. Standard were references to "the eminent leaders of the League . . . who have always demonstrated that they are 'the right man in the right place.' "[27] Fairly typical was the president of the section of Quimper who wrote Basch in 1937 reminding him that he had belonged to the League since its inception and had not heretofore asked a favor. "On the one hand," he noted, "I know how badly the government needs to place laic republicans in the civil service. I also know that the League is listened to with favor by the current government. This is why I permit myself to ask you to use your influence in favor of [a fellow leaguer who sought an administrative position.]" Emile Kahn replied by noting that "hoping to render a service to a minister by drawing his attention to a good republican" he had in fact personally spoken with the personnel of the ministry in question.[28] The president of the section of Chateaubriand also wrote Basch stressing his twenty years of service and the unprecedented quality of his request. One of his fellow leaguers was a local judge who sought a promotion to a higher court in Nantes. "There are few members of the French judiciary who are as sincerely republican as is he," the president noted and wondered if Basch might not use his influence with Marc Rucard, a leaguer and currently minister of justice in Léon Blum's second government. "To see one of our kind finally rewarded" would be a source of encouragement to the local section. Kahn responded by telling him that "we, like you, believe that republican judges have long been disadvantaged and that far too many judicial positions have gone to judges whose republican loyalty is more or less doubtful." Indeed this is why the League had recently called for a purge of the republican administration. Still, he noted, it was a general statement of policy only and the League could hardly ask that "a particular judge be given a particular position." To clarify matters he went on to say "that what you propose might have been possible, in an entirely unofficial capacity and as a personal favor to you, with our colleague Marc Rucard." Since the request had been made, however, the government had fallen and Rucard was no longer in the Ministry of Justice and the League had no "personal relations" with his successor Paul Reynaud.[29] Indeed, the League's response to requests of this kind was as often as not dictated by the political affiliation of the relevant minister. Kahn told one petitioner that "what might have been possible with M. Moutet [a prominent League member] would appear to be difficult with M. Mandel," the very conservative politician who had succeeded Marius Moutet in the Colonial Ministry. But he promised that "we will take up this file again when circumstances are more favorable."[30] There was often an element of nudge and wink here.

To be sure, some requests were patently absurd. One leaguer, a police officer, had just written the exams necessary for promotion. Since the exams would be graded in Paris, could Basch or Kahn prevail upon the examining board to treat this candidate benevolently?[31] Faced with an interminable string of comparable requests during the Popular Front, the League formally reminded its members that it was not a patronage machine.[32] Not all members were convinced. The president of the section of Lourdes who sought a position in the post office for his niece bluntly reminded Victor Basch that, although he did read the *Cahiers* and its strictures about patronage, he had also attended the most recent national congress and had heard Basch declare that the Popular Front should reward its own people. Another, seeking a post for his daughter, acknowledged that this was not an appropriate activity for the League but pleaded that by virtue of "being categorized as on the left in a reactionary department" he had no chance of a sympathetic hearing from his local deputy.[33] Both cases were rejected by League headquarters.

Despite periodic complaints that too many leaguers were "too quick to solicit the League for personnel services,"[34] headquarters frequently afforded such demands a sympathetic treatment. To get around absolutely explicit League statutes, secretaries general perfected formulas like *pour vous être agreeable, à titre tout à fait exceptional,* or *à titre tout à fait personel.* And it certainly helped to be persistent. The section in Cahors, working for one of its number who sought a teaching position, was initially told: "We make it an absolute rule, as you well know, to never intervene in questions involving appointing civil servants." But letters from the section continued to pour in stressing the merits of their candidate. In time Paris relented, and the president of the section was told that "in light of the importance you personally attach to this matter" the League would give it a second examination. Its legal experts still thought the matter inappropriate for the League. But in due course, after yet more letters, Basch did write the minister of national education (also a leaguer) on behalf of the candidate.[35] The archives of the League are full of letters from its presidents to ministers on behalf of various worthy candidates. When the minister belonged to the League, the salutation invariably read: *M. le Ministre et cher collègue.* Lest the ministers in question fail to grasp the significance of *cher collègue,* they were frequently reminded that this particular case had originated with *nos camarades* in such and such a federation or section. The standard formula was to request that a minister "examine [the] request with benevolence." The frequently positive responses from League ministers contained phrases like " I am very happy to have been able to . . . support the benevolent interest that you have shown for this civil servant."[36] There was more than a hint of the "republic of pals" here.

To be sure, a close examination of the files suggests that more often than not League interventions were legitimate enough. Very frequently they involved a civil servant who wanted no more than a transfer so that he—or she—could be closer to a spouse. The line between an appeal for patronage and a case of injustice could be exceedingly fine. Candidates for positions could often mount a good prima facie case that they ought to have received these posts had it not been for some administrative error or some administrative bias. The League subjected these claims to close scrutiny, and its legal experts wrote lengthy assessments—later the basis for formal letters—seeking to tease out the deeper meaning of overlapping and often contradictory administrative regulations or attempting to sort out the finer points involved in assessing someone's seniority. Writing the minister of finance to obtain a bureau de tabac for a leaguer seems scandalous at first blush. But what if she were an impoverished widow who, for reasons beyond her control, had been forced to leave her department and thus lose her place in the line for such positions?[37]

If the presidents of sections sometimes behaved like small town wardhealers, just as often they acted like the leaders of local service clubs, conducting themselves as part-time social workers. The president of the section in Casablanca took a benevolent interest in one of his members who had something of a personality disorder and was persistently in trouble at his workplace. The president repeatedly intervened to stave off dismissal or to have his colleague transferred to a less stressful position. The individual in question seems to have appreciated none of this and, when not badgering the president on a daily basis, wrote letters to Emile Kahn, indeed came to Paris to confront Kahn, about the inadequate support he was getting from his section. The local president only gave up on him upon learning that he had joined the *Croix de Feu!* [38]

So was any real harm done by any of this (apart from the flagrant violation of the League's statutes and its pious public pronouncements)? It certainly must have been galling to discover that large numbers of individuals were in the League because they thought it an effective patronage machine. One can only imagine Henri Guernut's reaction upon being informed by a disappointed petitioner: "I do not have much to show for my two years in the League."[39] Yet it could have escaped none of the League's leaders that however ignoble personal calculations of this kind were, they were also what attracted significant numbers to the League. And it was also the case that a large membership was what gave the League its influence in French society and politics. Given that individuals and sections whose requests were rejected could become quite indignant, and threats of resignation were not uncommon, bending the rules was, in important respects, the lesser of two evils. A historian of the post-World War II League has recently noted that what then distinguished the association was "the relatively limited benefits it could offer its members."[40] That this was true of the postwar League may explain why its membership was always a tiny fraction of its prewar counterpart.

Although the League's archives abound with outlandish cases submitted by its sections, the files supported by the federations were usually both more mundane and less inappropriate. In 1936, the juridical experts examined twenty cases submitted by the federation of the Nord. As one might expect in a border department, fully eleven of them involved foreigners seeking residency permits and/or attempting to avoid expulsion from France. League headquarters rejected five of them either because the cases were weak or because the file was insufficiently documented. It intervened in six cases, successfully in four. Three cases, including a messy divorce, were rejected as being purely private affairs. One case involved a religious congregation suspected of illegal teaching activities; the League intervened six times with the minister of the interior but received no satisfaction. One case involved a dispute between a civil servant and his immediate superior; the League suggested he take the matter up with his union. In another, a civil servant complained about the administration of his pension; the League did intervene—without success—with the appropriate minister. Two cases, one involving a disputed fine and another involving the disruption of a private meeting of resident Italians, were returned for more information that was not forthcoming. A final case involved an individual injured in a horse racing accident. Again headquarters requested, but did not receive, more information.[41]

However dubious many of the cases sent to the League were, there is no denying that some of them genuinely involved apparent injustice. The energy and persistence with which the League pursued these cases is striking. The

League was forever drawing attention to apparent cases of injustice to the relevant ministers, friendly or not. It rarely took no for an answer; each cabinet shuffle brought a succession of new ministerial appeals. If an appeal for a new trial were rejected, the League demanded at least a pardon. If that failed, it appealed for a reduction in sentence. All of this demanded an enormous expenditure of League resources.

Much of the activity of the League in this respect was also utterly thankless. Often the victims of injustice, real or alleged, were better at proffering lengthy dossiers than at making a coherent case for their innocence. In 1928, Camille Hannion was convicted of fraud. He quickly began to burden the League with reams of paper protesting his innocence. Twenty page single-spaced letters followed one another at regular intervals. For the next twelve years the file grew annually, amounting to literally thousands of pages and in the end about four inches thick. But from the beginning the League's juridical experts were writing Hannion and the various sections who took up his case noting very tactfully, as they invariably did, that the case was so complex, the facts so confusing, and Hannion's arguments so incoherent, that they simply could not establish what was at issue or what, exactly, were the legal points Hannion expected them to address. Hannion's response was invariably more convoluted dossiers. Increasingly he seemed to feel the best way to address the concerns of the League was to have more or less identical appeals sent from different League sections. In desperation, the League's experts suggested that because Hannion always seemed to be in contact with lawyers, might it not be advisable to have one of them present a simple and clear exposé of the issues so that the League might know exactly what to do with the case. This did not work very well either because at least one lawyer contacted by Hannion, having been utterly confused by his incoherent arguments, promptly wrote the League hoping that it might be able to make sense of his case. [42]

Even more frustrating was the need to explain to the more militant leaguers that the League had to deal with the current provisions of the French legal code, however imperfect they might be. The classic example was Articles 443 and 444 of the existing criminal code, which spelled out in a narrowly restrictive way the possible grounds for an appeal of a criminal conviction. The only acceptable grounds were entirely new evidence that pointed directly to the innocence of the convicted person and not merely to evidence of partiality by the prosecution.

The more nimble-minded of the sections had repeatedly to be reminded that "new" evidence manifestly did not mean evidence that had been wrongly ignored or imperfectly understood at trial. Similarly, these articles did allow that, should a material witness at a trial whose testimony led directly to conviction subsequently be proven to have perjured himself, this could be grounds for appeal. But the League's Parisian legal experts had repeatedly to remind provincial militants that "proof" of perjury could not take the form of a powerful suspicion or even overwhelming evidence that a witness had lied at trial. The only acceptable form was a criminal conviction for perjury.

To be sure the League strenuously objected to the narrowness of Articles 443 and 444. Henri Guernut managed to get legislation passed through the Chamber in 1934 to modify their provisions in a significantly more liberal way. Adoption of the new law, however, was blocked by the Senate. In the meantime, leaguers would have to live with the law, imperfect though it was.

League sections were rarely more patient with the League's reading of the legal code than they were with its readings of its statutes. Many were adept at finding ingenious ways around what they took to be the excessively narrow reading of the statutes that prevailed in Paris. The section of Cauderon in the Gironde was much preoccupied by another conviction for fraud where yet again the case for an appeal seemed to be stymied by the absence of new evidence. To avoid the excessive legalism of Paris, the section engaged the services of a professor in the local faculty of law. He produced a sixty-seven page brief arguing that the accused did in fact have grounds for appeal. The section and the president of the federation of the Gironde were impressed by his reasoning. The League's legal expert, who happened to be Maurice Hersant, a member of the Central Committee, was a good deal more skeptical. Law professor though he might be, the section's expert was in this instance merely another lawyer arguing his brief on behalf of his client who, Hersant noted, was the professor's primary source of information. The predictable reaction to the finding that there still did not seem to be any new evidence was that of "profound stupefaction" from the section and a gentle plea from the federal secretary that, at a minimum, League jurists could provide a more thorough rebuttal of the professor's case. In due course the rebuttal was provided. Yet in spite of all the abuse it was taking from the Cauderon section, headquarters took the case to the Minister of Justice who promptly and predictably threw it out. The section seems to have dropped the case at this point, possibly because the principle supporter of the accused resigned to avoid being expelled.[43]

Although it is easy enough to document the questionable cases, there can be no doubt about the merits of many of the cases the League chose to pursue. It was notably active, for example, in some high-profile political trials. Joseph Caillaux was one of the up-and-coming politicians of prewar France. Having already served as Premier in 1911, by 1914 he was the new president of the dominant Radical party and seemingly destined once again to take over the government. He was always bedeviled, however, by a somewhat unorthodox private life. In the spring of 1914, a prominent newspaper editor began publishing some of Caillaux's intimate correspondence. His (second) wife responded by shooting the editor to death, for which she was tried and acquitted! By the end of 1917 he was again in trouble. Caillaux had never hid the fact, either before or during the war, that Franco-German hostility was disastrous, and by 1916 he was privately calling for a compromise peace. His many enemies accused him of treasonous communication with the enemy, and he was duly charged with treason in January 1918. The truth was rather more complex. Caillaux, who had traveled widely outside of France during the war, was almost certainly in touch with individuals who may well have been in contact, via one or more intermediaries, with the Germans. But at most he was guilty of being incautious about the company he kept. None of these nuances carried much weight in the political atmosphere of 1918 when France was headed by the old Jacobin war-horse Georges Clemenceau and when many thought the death penalty was entirely appropriate. Victor Basch, then vice president and certainly no defeatist, leapt to Caillaux's defense—something that required no small measure of principle or courage.[44] The League actively mounted the Caillaux defense before the High Court and, although he was convicted on technical grounds, his sentence was reduced to the time already served. All the while actively trying to recruit Caillaux to the Central Committee, the League pushed hard for his complete rehabilitation, which it achieved in 1925. After that time Caillaux resumed his impressive career in French government, albeit in ways that increasingly distressed his former supporters.[45]

As befitted a League born of the Dreyfus affair, it was also very vigilant about the abuses of French military justice. French (like most) military justice was often procedurally unfair, arbitrary, and capricious. During World War I, many French soldiers were convicted of (and some executed for) various acts of "indiscipline." More often than not such indiscipline involved a reluctance to die in yet another pointless frontal assault. The French were actually less disposed to executing soldiers than the British or the Italians (but not the Germans.) But the League was acutely sensitive to what were in some cases little more than judicial murders and labored long in the postwar years, fighting much of the time a nearly impossible battle, to have these soldiers rehabilitated and their widows and dependants granted a pension.[46]

Although some of these cases obtained a high profile in the postwar years, the League did not wait for the end of the war to intervene in favor of those who ran afoul of the military. Three examples, chosen more or less at random from the League's copious dossiers, illustrate both the exceptional severity of French military justice during war time and the League's persistence in trying to rescue obscure individuals from at least the worst consequences of their presumed actions. In 1918, a twenty-four-year-old soldier named Louis Becherend, who had been in combat since November 1914, deserted from his company. The company had come under severe artillery bombardment and had been temporarily dispersed. Becherend, suffering momentarily from shell shock, sought out the nearest medical station. Because he was suffering from no injury more visible than a bleeding nose, he was told to rejoin his unit. But his company had moved on and Becherend, in an apparent state of shock, wandered around incoherently for a further day and a half. When he came to his senses, he presented himself to the nearest military authorities and confessed to being absent without leave. He was promptly charged with desertion. While the case against him was being prepared, he was sent back to the front for a further twenty-five days of combat. When his company was finally withdrawn from front-line action, he was brought before a court martial. His case was not helped by the fact that he had earlier served a week in prison for being absent without leave (for twenty-four hours) and he was duly condemned to death. Pleading the case of deserters in the last days of the war required some tact. President Buisson, in his letter to Poincaré, president of the Republic, readily acknowledged that "he who abandons his comrades is a coward. He must be punished and you . . . have very often had the cruel duty of ignoring heart-felt instincts for pity." But surely the confusion of battle "which at times drives crazy those who are on the verge of collapse" should be taken into consideration and the crime judged in that light. He succeeded in getting Becherend's execution delayed and ultimately commuted to twenty years at hard labor.[47]

Other cases were less dramatic but no less revealing. A soldier who deserted in November 1914 was sentenced to five years at hard labor. But he agreed to return to the front in hopes of expunging his sentence. He was twice wounded, the second time losing an eye. He was correspondingly mustered out of the services and sent to prison in 1916, although in light of his two years in combat his sentence was reduced to three years. But surely, Buisson argued, two years of hard combat leading to permanent mutilation more than compensated for a momentary defection in 1914. Two years and many letters later, he persuaded the minister of war to suspend the last five months of the soldier's sentence.[48] More banal still was the case of the soldier who while returning to the front with his unit in June 1917 got caught up in the antics of his more rambunctious colleagues and fired, as did they, his rifle out of the window of a train as it passed through a station, and one of the bullets punctured a military water tank. The soldier insisted that the bullet could not have been his because he was sitting on the other side of the train. The court martial did not believe him, in part measure because he had a long (albeit disputed) history of misbehavior, and sentenced him to five years at hard labor. The League chose not to dispute the facts of the case but was quick to engage their legal experts on matters of law. They noted that under Article 252 of the Military Code of Justice hard labor was an appropriate punishment for attacks on military property if, and only if, the property in question had been totally destroyed or effectively ruined (*devasté*). But, they contended, citing an impressive array of military case law, a bullet hole in a water tank did not rise to this standard and was therefore not punishable by hard labor. A year later the Ministry of War agreed and suspended the sentence.[49] There were hundreds of cases like these. None were, in form or substance, the equivalent of the Dreyfus affair, none made headlines, and all involved obscure and soon forgotten individuals. What they had in common was the tenacity of the League, the intellectual rigor it deployed, and the moderately satisfying outcome of its efforts.

A classic case of the difficult, if not to say exotic, cases the League dealt with in peace time was that of Madeleine Mancini. In 1915, when she was sixteen years old, a legendary bandit, Romanetti, showed up at her isolated family farm in Corsica and forced her to become his mistress. She apparently attempted to escape him on several occasions but was finally relieved of his company only in 1926 when he was murdered by a local peasant. The peasant subsequently took refuge for a while in the nearby farm of her uncle, Antoine Mancini. In 1928 three more bandits arrived at her farm seeking refuge. The next day they went next door and murdered Antoine and his two sons. Before long there were local rumors to the effect that they had done so at the behest of Madeleine who allegedly sought revenge on her uncle for having harbored her lover's killer. In any context other than the Corsican one, the case against her was inherently dubious, but it was greatly strengthened by the claim made by a different and distant uncle, Pierre Toussaint-Vallé, to the effect that he had been told by yet another bandit that Madeleine had promised him that she would become his mistress if he were to kill her uncle. At least in part on the basis of his testimony, Mancini was tried and found guilty of being an accomplice to murder and sentenced to life at hard labor.

Subsequently, however, the bandit in question, still at large, learned of Toussaint-Vallé's testimony. Somehow believing his own honor to be at stake, he promptly confronted Toussaint-Vallé and obliged him, in front of witnesses, to sign a formal retraction. Toussaint-Vallé then claimed, alternately, that as an illiterate he could not recognize his own signature, that he had signed it under duress, or that he had not had the statement read out to him before signing. The Mancini family nonetheless took him to court for perjury. The League, having long suspected that Mancini was a victim of injustice, took an immediate interest because it recognized that a perjury conviction would provide grounds for a new trial. But it was also aware that Corsica was not the ideal venue for the perjury case given that various feuding clans were making death threats against all involved. It pleaded strenuously with the minister of justice to have the case tried in Lyon (where Mancini was serving her time.) Its appeals failed, and a Corsican judge in 1932 decided, on narrow legal grounds, to acquit Toussaint-Vallé.

Although a new trial was therefore ruled out, the League nonetheless, pursued the case relentlessly. In April 1933 Kahn personally spoke to the president of the Republic, hoping to obtain at least a pardon. Five times between May and July of that year Basch and Kahn requested a personal audience with the minister of justice. They finally got an audience but no promises. A full year later Kahn managed to get yet another interview with yet another minister of justice who promised to look into the case. It took yet another year for yet another minister of justice to finally reject their plea for a pardon. Still the League persisted. It had better luck in 1936 when Marc Rucard, a League member, held the justice portfolio. He dramatically reduced her sentence. Finally in January 1938 the League persuaded Vincent Auriol, another League member heading the justice ministry, to grant Mancini a full pardon.[50]

Many of the more sensational cases pitted the case-hardened League jurists in Paris against the passionate but legally uneducated partisans in the sections. The Seznec affair provides a perfect illustration. In the late evening of May 25, 1923, in the Breton department of the Finistère, Pierre Quemeneur, a local entrepreneur and politician, disappeared. Shortly thereafter, Guillaume Seznec, a small sawmill owner, was accused of the murder. Although the prosecution's case was entirely circumstantial, although no body was ever found, and although Seznec insisted on his innocence, he was convicted of the murder after a lengthy trial and sentenced to life imprisonment on Devil's Island. From the beginning the case was a messy one. Seznec's defense was full of logical inconsistencies but so too were the arguments of the prosecution. The quality of the police investigation as well as the legal work on both sides left something to be desired. The business practices of neither Seznec nor his alleged victim were entirely above reproach, and as a result there were soon a number of lurid scenarios as to how Quemeneur had met his presumed fate. Mingled, one way or another, in the affair were assorted colorful characters of varying degrees of respectability. As a result, the Seznec affair was always good copy and every new revelation (and scarcely a year went by without one) ensured a spate of front page stories in the interwar popular press.

In 1930 the Seznec case came to the attention of Marie-Françoise Bosser, a schoolteacher, founder and secretary of the League's section in Pont-Aven in the Finistère. She promptly interviewed one hundred of the interested parties and became convinced of Seznec's innocence. In July 1931 she drew the case to the attention of the Central Committee. Overcoming her nervousness, because, as she admitted, she had never before addressed an audience more intimidating than the little children she taught, in 1932 she traveled to the League's national congress to plead Seznec's case. Before long she was speaking to packed houses, first in Brittany and then all over France. She addressed any section of the League that would hear her. In 1933 she dispatched copies of a brochure on the Seznec case to every departmental federation of the League, pleading that every section purchase at least one copy. She rounded up five members of the 1924 jury, presented them with the damning evidence concerning the trial and persuaded them to call for its reopening. In time, the entire federation of the Finistère was working on nothing but the Seznec case. In 1937 she led a delegation of Breton deputies to confront Premier Léon Blum and his Minister of Justice Marc Rucard, both leaguers. Throughout the decade she was a fixture at League congresses.

Although the Seznec case was always before the congresses and more or less permanently on the agenda of the League's executive and its Central Committee, there were constant tensions between Bosser and the League's leaders. Bosser was impatient. She fully appreciated the legal complexities involved in Seznec's case and the fact that the wheels of justice turn slowly. But while those wheels were turning, an innocent man was dying in a tropical prison! She could not help but wonder if mysterious forces in the Ministry of Justice, if not in the League itself, were conspiring to impede the rehabilitation of an obviously innocent man. Bosser's conspiracy theories were not much appreciated in the

Central Committee, aware (as was Bosser) that during many of those years, the justice ministry was headed by a leaguer. No one disputed that there were troubling aspects to Seznec's trial, but members of the Central Committee did not share Bosser's conviction as to Seznec's innocence. They patiently explained to her that unshakable conviction was one thing but what the Seznec case really required was solid evidence. But, she reposted, she had evidence. Evidence in abundance! Why just about every day brought in new evidence of Seznec's innocence. But this very fact was a source of concern for the Central Committee. Bosser, it noted, did not seem adept at discriminating between solid evidence and rumor. All too often she seemed to be citing second- or thirdhand reports that some jailer or padre on Devil's Island apparently believed in Seznec's innocence. Moreover, it reminded her, under Articles 443 and 444 of the criminal code of justice only evidence that was entirely new and pointed directly to the innocence of the accused was grounds for an appeal.

Worse, the Central Committee was uneasy about the company Bosser was keeping. Her principal associate in the case was a former judge and also a leaguer named Charles-Victor Hervé. Hervé was a man of undeniable persistence and energy, but he also had a history of mental instability, which, among other things, had ended his career on the bench. Furthermore, he sought to defend Seznec by constructing an alternate scenario of the crime. His pet theory was that Quemeneur was killed not on May 25 but on May 27 at his family estate at Plourivo, having been surprised in bed with another man's mistress. Although Hervé carefully refrained from giving the name of the other man, it was an ill-kept secret in Brittany that the person he had in mind was none other than the victim's brother Louis Quemeneur. Inevitably, although there was almost no hard evidence for this account, the story was too good for the would-be Zolas in the local press, one of whom parlayed it into a book. The result was a massive and very successful lawsuit by Quemeneur. Seznec's case was not helped unduly by Hervé's quixotic and unexpected failure to testify at the trial of the poor journalist. Hervé, in turn, was subjected to a successful defamation suit.

In due course, however, Hervé did provide Bosser with the critical new evidence. He discovered a witness who claimed to have driven someone who could only have been Quemeneur to his country house at Plourivo on the evening of May 27. Not only did the witness nicely corroborate Hervé's favorite theory as to the circumstances of Quemeneur's demise, but he exonerated Seznec who could have been nowhere near Plourivo on that date. Sufficiently impressed, the Central Committee called upon the minister of justice to open an investigation leading to a revision of the 1924 verdict. But, upon being asked the name and address of this critical witness, they were distressed to learn that Bosser did not know and Hervé, for strategic reasons that he kept to himself, would not reveal it. And they were aghast, some months later, to hear Bosser declare that the witness in question was perhaps not all that important and that the real case rested on a series of witnesses, none of whom were individually that decisive, but which taken together pointed to the innocence of the convict on Devil's Island. Nor could she hide her exasperation with the narrow formalism of the Central Committee, charging that "it seems, in effect, to grasp one pretext after another to postpone indefinitely any action." She was also given to telling the many sections she was in contact with that the Central Committee was guilty of some combination of "suppression, inertia or duplicity" on the Seznec file. These sections sometimes shared her concerns. The section of Champigny, for example, regretted the disappearing witness, suggesting that he had been bought off or otherwise intimidated. But surely the dossier on Seznec contained "ten, fifteen or perhaps twenty" other items pointing to his innocence.[51]

The internal battles within the League over the Seznec case reveal two conflicting but equally admirable sides to the League: passion for justice, on the one hand, and a hard-nosed mastery of the judicial system, on the other. There was something wonderful about the spectacle of the diminutive schoolteacher from small-town Brittany who, in 1935, announced to a congress of men who were otherwise engaged in squaring political circles, that she had ridden on the bus for exactly 1,248 kilometers to get five minutes to speak for a man whom she knew in her bones, *pace* the logic chopping of the Central Committee, to be innocent. But there was something equally impressive about Odette René Bloch, the distinguished Parisian lawyer and member of the Central Committee who rose at the 1934 congress to remind Bosser that she too passionately believed in justice but, unlike Bosser, she was also acutely alert to the significance of Articles 443 and 444 of the code of criminal justice, the very articles that governed appeals for revision. There were two kinds of leaguers here, both, for once, women: the passionate defender of rough-and-tumble justice and the professional jurist.[52]

There was no ideal ending for Seznec or his impassioned advocate, Bosser. A succession of justice ministers, many of them, Marc Rucard, Yvon Delbos, and Vincent Auriol, members of the League, examined the case without being convinced. Seznec did not, as Bosser so often feared, die in jail. She lived long enough to see Seznec pardoned, to find him a home in Brittany, and to bury him in 1954. She and Emile Kahn were still fighting for his rehabilitation in the late 1950s. The case was before the courts as late as 1996 and still, from the perspective of the Seznec family, without success. But in 1989 the famous Articles 443 and 444 were revised to permit even evidence leading to doubt to be grounds for revision. The new legislation is sometimes referred to as the "Seznec law"; it could equally well be called the "Bosser law."[53]

SIX

War and Peace: 1914–1934

In the years before 1914, the League took a firm stand on the issue of war. It was "pacifist" in the sense that most of its members felt that it was the duty of democratic governments to ensure that international conflict be resolved by peaceful means. They rejected war as an instrument of international relations and feared the nefarious consequences of militarism, nationalism, and imperialism for world—or at least European—peace. Progressive and mutual disarmament, binding international arbitration, and world government—in the form of international organizations—were the standard recipes of the pre-1914 League. The League participated fully in the spate of international and pacifist organizations that proliferated in prewar Europe, sending delegates, for example, to the meetings of the International Congress on Peace in Nîmes, Milan, London, and Stockholm. To judge by the amount of time spent discussing these issues in the years before the World War I, League members took them seriously. Nonetheless, in spite of much debate, the League was left with a series of platonic resolutions that sounded impressive but were ultimately vague as to just what active measures the League would take to prevent war and—more important—what it should do if, despite its best actions and those of other men of good will, war were nonetheless to break out.

With the outbreak of war in 1914, the League rallied to the defense of the French nation and, like virtually everyone in France, joined the Union Sacrée. Indeed, in the early months even some of the most articulate pacifists in the League were seduced by the super-heated patriotism of the time.[1] Still, although generally supporting the war effort, the League was not uncritical of the French government. It protested wartime censorship, military justice, and suspensions of civil liberties unjustified by the exigencies of war. There was, of course, always some debate about how far the League could—and should—go in its criticism of the government without undermining the war effort. Georges Clemenceau's ruthless suppression of defeatists after 1917 was a case in point. Few of the League's leaders were sympathetically disposed toward true defeatists but some, led by Victor Basch, were uneasy with the government's heavy-handed measures and its increasingly broad definition of defeatism and treason. When two prominent politicians, Louis Malvy and Joseph Caillaux, were charged with treason in 1917, Basch insisted that the League would have to intervene on their behalf. Ferdinand Buisson, the president, disagreed, and Basch promptly resigned as vice president, a resignation he retracted a short while later.[2]

Basch was nonetheless convinced that France was fighting a just war, a case he made in his *La Guerre de 1914 et le droit,* published in May 1915.[3] This little volume, soon to be the League's semiofficial position on the war, was the result of long and careful analysis of the diplomatic record. In the early months of the war, all of the belligerent powers published selective collections of their diplomatic archives in an attempt to win the propaganda war. After pouring over these volumes and subjecting each to a meticulous scrutiny, Basch undertook a masterful presentation of the facts as they were known in 1915.

He began his book by reminding his audience of prewar League doctrine, notably that the League expected all governments to do everything possible to resolve international conflicts. Only when all available means had been "exhausted" and "if a nation attacks both the territory and the honour of another nation" did the injured nation have "the most imprescriptible right and sacred duty to inflict upon the aggressor the punishment he deserves."[4] In fact this was a rather stronger position than Basch and the Socialists in the League had taken before 1914, but it obviously seemed appropriate in the context of 1915.

Basch then took his readers through a concise but admirably clear account of the diplomatic developments of the tragic summer of 1914. He demonstrated that, at every turn, the Allied powers had done everything possible to resolve the conflict peacefully; Germany and Austria, by contrast, had not. Granted, German foreign policy was at times "incoherent and contradictory," reflecting the erratic character of her Emperor, but there was no doubt as to the consistently bellicose core of German diplomacy.[5] The facts seemed to Basch to be "so clear, so obvious, so patent, that one is stupefied to see them contested" by anyone, even the German intellectuals.[6] Good pedagogue that he was, Basch nonetheless presented his readers with the best possible case the Germans could make, which he then proceeded to demolish. Great Britain had outdone herself to preserve the peace. Russian diplomacy, whatever one thought of the nation's domestic politics, was a model of "prudence, energy, initiative and the sincere and clairvoyant love of peace." Of course, the "peaceful will of France was so sincere, so frank and so consistent" that even the Germans could not dispute it.[7]

Germany alone had acted with reckless disregard for the peace. What accounted for Germany's behavior? In the end, it was the fact that Germany was united in 1866 not in 1848; united, not by democratic means but by Prussian might. The peaceful, cultured, scientific Germany he so admired was corrupted by Prussian barbarism, a venom so strong that it ultimately found its way even into the veins of German Socialists. Only by breaking the power of Prussian militarism and establishing a genuine German democracy could peaceful Europe be freed of the scourge of war.[8] All in all it was a remarkable document, a dense but highly readable argument packed into 111 pages. It went through twenty editions, sold 30,000 copies, and became the prevailing doctrine for a majority of the League for the next quarter century.

Only twice in the book did Basch's absolute confidence fail him. He conceded that the order of mobilization, later to be a point of major contention concerning the responsibilities for the war, was a "wretched" question. He dealt at length on the confusing and conflicting evidence before concluding, not very convincingly, that Austria *probably* mobilized before Russia did. But what did it matter? Mobilization did not necessarily mean war. As for Germany, who incontestably mobilized fifth among the great powers, was it not the case that even in times of peace Germany was in a state of "virtual mobilization"?[9] The second issue was the French alliance with Tsarist Russia. This was a sensitive point because Basch, like most prewar Socialists had always been uneasy with the alliance. Not only was Russia a particularly oppressive autocratic regime, but its foreign policy was calculated to drag France into war over obscure Balkan quarrels. Basch argued, however, that Germany was also an autocratic regime and in no position to lecture France about its diplomatic partners, the more so since Russia had once been an ally of Germany. Moreover, absent that alliance, what would have become of French security during the Schnaebelé affair, the Tangiers affair, or the Agadir incident? Here Basch was getting somewhat rattled. Neither Tangiers nor Agadir were clear-cut examples of German threats to French security, although they were arguably classic examples of French imperialism. As for the Schnaebelé affair, it was a minor incident, largely the fault of France, and it took place some years before the Franco-Russian alliance was in place![10]

From the internal perspective of the League, the most controversial part of the book came near the end. Basch confessed that this was war that could not now be stopped and that, in his view, no one had the right to stop it. "Whatever it costs, we are obliged to hope that it goes on to the very end" because any "hurried peace would necessarily be precarious and would simply mean future wars." This was a call for *guerre à l'outrance*, war to the bitter end. This war, in a line that anticipated Woodrow Wilson, "could put an end to war" and therefore "this frightful war could become a holy war."[11] Although he did not explicitly say so, these remarks were directed to those just beginning to find their voice who wondered if the origins of the war were quite as clear-cut as Basch was suggesting and, correspondingly, if the carnage ought not be stopped short of victory.

As early as 1915, Louis Guétant, vice president of the section in Lyon, and Mathius Morhardt, former secretary general, protested what they saw as the League's uncritical support of the Union Sacrée. In January 1915, a number of League members, many of them on the dissident Socialist left, founded an informal study group, ultimately called the *Société d'études documentaires et critiques sur la guerre*.[12] As its title suggests, the purpose of the Société was to challenge the official French, and by extension Basch's, version of the war's origins. Initially the meetings of the Société were held in the League's Parisian headquarters and were open to a wide range of leaguers. Basch himself initially attended the meetings. But, under the leadership of the pacifist historian Georges Demartial and Morhardt, any pretense that the Société was a shared League enterprise quickly evaporated. It wanted to focus exclusively on precisely those questions on which Basch had faltered: mobilization and the Russian alliance. Increasingly, it concluded that the version of the war's origins presented both by the French government and by the League was dubious. This being the case, its members argued, there was no moral justification for fighting the war to the bitter end and every reason for calling for an immediate peace. Many of those who had initially attended meetings of the Société, Basch, Charles Gide, and Charles Seignobos, appeared to be hopelessly chauvinistic; most of them stopped attending meetings dominated by what they perceived to be defeatists. In truth the Société, which met infrequently, invariably subjected to the watchful eye and the periodic harassment of agents of the Ministry of the Interior, had a limited impact on French public opinion. Its impact on the League by contrast, was considerable. The Société was at the origins of an articulate minority in the League that would consistently challenge the leadership for the next quarter century.

By the time the League gathered for its first wartime congress in November 1916, the opposition of the minority had crystallized and was articulately demanding a compromise peace or, more accurately, a call for international arbitration and mediation. After all, its members noted, the League had always been in favor of arbitration. Surely it was a bit odd to call for arbitration before conflicts broke out or after they had ended but to reject the idea at precisely the time it could be most useful—that is, in the midst of a frightful bloodbath that showed no signs of ending. The majority thought the plan to be hopelessly naive, highly impractical, and utterly inappropriate for a situation in which France was trying to defend herself from an aggressive power that was occupying large parts of her territory. When a criminal assaults an innocent person, the majority argued, the appropriate response was to call on the police, not an arbitrator. "One does not arbitrate a crime," was the stock phrase of President Ferdinand Buisson. The minority riposted that Germany was a "criminal" only if one accepted the comforting assumptions of the majority about the origins of the war. A better analogy would be the case of a duel between two otherwise civilized individuals where surely arbitration was the best and only solution.[13]

The debates were emotionally charged. In a nation at war, even the eminently reasonable arguments of the minority could be offensive. Séverine, the legendary and universally respected feminist within the League,[14] gave a passionate speech in which she deplored the horrors of the war and the pointless slaughter. Could the delegates not grasp that? Jacques Hadamard stood up to icily inform Mme. Séverine that even without her facile rhetoric, he was quite capable of appreciating the horrors of the present conflict. Although he chose not to mention it, he had already lost two sons.[15]

Leaders like Basch also insisted that the minority's call for arbitration had less to do with their perception of the *origins* of the war than with their fears about its likely outcome. Fearing that a prolonged war meant French defeat and a draconian peace settlement, the minority opted for an arbitrated end to the conflict. Having more faith in the staying power of the Allies, he rejected the idea. The dissidents angrily rejected these charges, vehemently denied that calculations about the likely outcome of the war influenced their thinking, and insisted that only a desire to end the carnage lay behind their call for arbitration.[16]

The end of hostilities did little to resolve the internal dispute within the League. Indeed, by the end of 1918 the Central Committee was complaining that the minority had formed a permanent opposition faction within the organization. The internal tensions came to a head at a meeting sponsored by the League in Bellevilloise at the end of December 1918. Here Victor Basch spoke at length on the theme of "heroes who died for France and for liberty." Coming scant weeks after the armistice, in most parts of France this would have been unobjectionable, indeed anodyne, language. But Bellevilloise, a radical neighborhood in Paris's working-class twentieth arrondissement, was not typical of

France in this respect, and fully represented at the meeting were those who preferred to believe, as one of them put it, that "our dead were sacrificed not for liberty but for the cause of international capitalism."[17] Suspecting, not altogether wrongly, that Basch's interminable discourse was intended to ensure that there would be no time for more radical orators, the crowd of several thousand became increasingly restless. By threatening to punch one of his hecklers in the mouth, Basch did little to calm spirits and soon lost all control of the hall, at which point he and other members of the Central Committee walked offstage. To the Committee's immense irritation, some members of the minority took over the podium and conducted the meeting for several more hours.[18]

The meeting was the last straw for many in the Central Committee and for Victor Basch (still technically resigned therefrom). In their view, the crowd at Bellevilloise was full of anarchists and agents provocateurs; had they not provocatively cheered every reference to Germany? The fact that they claimed to be cheering *revolutionary* postwar Germany did not, in the eyes of the majority, make this behavior any less gratuitously antipatriotic. The Right, and notably the *Action Française,* took the Bellevilloise episode as conclusive proof of their contention—now twenty years old—that the League was both revolutionary and antipatriotic. For others, the latest "crisis" in the League merely confirmed their decision to leave it some years before when it became, or so they thought, "compromised" by revolutionary syndicalism. Paul Hyacinthe Loyson saw a certain irony in Basch's recent fulminations about "anarchists." Had not he and many of his colleagues been consorting with anarchist leaders for years? Was it possible that Basch was just now learning what they stood for? If there was a scandal in the League, it was not because of the revolutionary militancy of the minority but because the supine majority permitted them to remain in the League at all. What hope was there for a League whose leaders permitted themselves to be driven off the podium by a handful of unruly workers?[19] For others the "crisis" in the League was not, as people like Loyson would have it, because of its promiscuous contact with the revolutionary masses but precisely because of the absence of such contact. Spokesmen for the minority complained that the Central Committee had "lost contact with the people and no longer speaks its language. How far we have come since the days of the Dreyfus Affair." The "petit-bourgeois conceptions of most of its leaders" guaranteed an inseparable gulf between the League and the laboring masses. As the future Communist leader, Ferdinand Loriot, put it: "the Central Committee . . . has since 1914 counted itself among the most dangerous opponents of the socialist proletariat."[20]

The internal divisions within the League continued into the interwar years. As a body, the League was critical of and disappointed by the peace settlement, troubled by the lack of progress on disarmament, and concerned about the inability of the League of Nations to effect a profound change in the patterns of international relations. This broad agreement, however, masked profound differences that the League leadership was, despite its best efforts, unable to paper over. All recognized that the Treaty of Versailles was a flawed peace, marred by indefensible territorial adjustments and, in particular, by the infamous Article 231, the so-called War Guilt Clause. This clause, all agreed, was tantamount to a confession extracted from an accused who was given no chance to defend himself. Yet, while deploring the illegitimate process that led to Article 231, the majority nonetheless believed that in fact Germany *was* primarily, albeit not wholly, responsible for the war. It followed that it was entirely appropriate to demand reparations payments from Germany. For the majority, then, the peace settlement, while imperfect, was, in its broad outlines, legitimate. The minority countered that Article 231 was indefensible *either* with respect to form *or* substance. The entire treaty, the minority would insist, was informed by a serious (and deliberate) misconstrual of the events leading to war; the result was a treaty entirely lacking in legitimacy. By virtue of a perverse reading of the events of 1914, the League leadership appeared to be sanctioning a treaty that disarmed only Germany, punished only Germany, and exempted Germany and Germany alone, from the principles of national self-determination. The least of the problems with the treaty was that it represented an elementary violation of the principles of justice; more serious was the fact that it almost certainly set the stage for a future war.

As a result, the question of the war's origins was a perennial and divisive issue within the League for the next twenty years. As late as 1935, Morhardt was still appealing to League congresses to devote more energy to elucidating this question.[21] Leaders of the minority assiduously poured over every newly released diplomatic document (usually of Soviet or German provenance) in search of evidence of German innocence and Franco-Russian guilt. Inevitably, some of their "revelations" proved to be inconsequential. Morhardt, for example, thought it of some significance that the Swiss envoy to France had approached a senior official in the French Foreign Ministry, Philippe Berthelot, on August 1, 1914, informing him of the Austrian desire to initiate a peaceful outcome to the Austro-Serbian crisis. Berthelot allegedly rejected this initiative on the grounds that it was now too late. It turned out, upon examination, that the Swiss envoy had not, in fact, contacted Berthelot, who in any case was in close touch with the Austrian ambassador to France.[22]

Nonetheless, and in spite of its penchant for conspiratorial dead-ends, the minority consistently hit upon two of the more substantial issues concerning the origins of the war about which the majority was most vulnerable. The first involved the conduct of Russia in the days leading up to the outbreak of war. It was of capital importance to the minority that Russia, *pace* Bash's 1915 version, had in fact mobilized before Austria. Moreover, it had been recognized at least since 1892, that in light of the Franco-Russian alliance, "mobilization meant war." This was a far cry from Basch's 1915 contentions about Russia's "sincere and clairvoyant love of peace." In time, but only after protracted wrangling over the entire question of mobilization, the majority would concede that Russia had in fact been the first great power to mobilize but nonetheless insisted that the sequence of mobilization was of limited significance and that mobilization in no way meant war. As leaders of the minority were quick to note, the majority lost interest in the mobilization question *only* after it became apparent that Austria had not mobilized before Russia.

Moreover, Russia was not acting alone, and her behavior was intimately connected to that of her principal partner, France. From 1912 on, the direction of French foreign policy was largely in the hands of Raymond Poincaré, premier and foreign minister in 1912 and president of the Republic after 1913. Poincaré, a native of Lorraine, was the very symbol of prewar French nationalism and the minority subjected his every action to close scrutiny. At every step, they contended, he encouraged the more militaristic and imperialistic reflexes of his Russian ally. His presence in St. Petersburg on the eve of the outbreak of war was surely not unrelated to the provocative stance taken by the Russians short days afterwards. Much of the discussion was exceedingly arcane. What exactly had Poincaré said or meant to say to his allies in the years and days before August 1914? What exactly had been the French position on Russian mobilization, what had they known about it, and when did they know? There were no simple answers to those questions, then, or even now, and their intricacies would have been lost on the average leaguer. In time, Félicien Challaye, by far the most articulate polemicist in the League, cut through the minutiae of the debate.[23] He argued that the Franco-Russian alliance, whatever it might have been at its origins, was an offensive one. France sought the return of Alsace-Lorraine, and Russia wanted access to the Straits. The Balkan crisis of 1914 provided a golden opportunity for both powers to pursue these goals and, consequently, both actively welcomed the war.[24] Reference to Poincaré was a deft stroke because few in the League sympathized with his prewar domestic politics, most notably his campaign to expand compulsory military service from two years to three. Both Basch and Kahn argued, plausibly enough, that one might deplore both Poincaré's super-heated nationalism and his domestic politics without concluding that he deliberately plotted war in 1914.[25] This was a logical enough point but one that would sit uncomfortably with many leaguers in the 1920s, when Poincaré more often than not presided over governments of the political Right. A decade later, one of the leaders of the minority, Georges Pioch, felt comfortable asserting that Poincaré was "one of the most wicked and criminal men the people have ever suffered."[26]

By and large the League's leaders treated the arguments of the minority with derision. Sorbonne-trained historians like Kahn, Charles Seignobos, and Alphonse Aulard could never quite mask their contempt for the dissident amateurs, "neo-historians" (to use Kahn's unkind phrase). Somehow, Kahn sarcastically intoned, the minority had managed to construe the leaders of the Central Powers as "victims of injustice." "Franz-Joseph would appear to be another Caillaux; William II, a new Dreyfus, minus of course Devil's Island." Some of this condescension was unfair. Few arguments of the minority would stand up to historical scrutiny today, but in the 1920s they were not far removed from the scrupulous assessment of such rigorous scholarly historians as the American, Sydney B. Fay. It is true that they leapt uncritically on the various documents emanating from the Soviet Union and from Weimar Germany but equally true that comparable French documents were slow to appear.[27] Because the Germans were a good deal more accommodating about publishing their diplomatic archives than were the French, it was not unreasonable for the minority to conclude that the official French version of the origins of the war was a weak one. Equally feeble were the arguments of leaguers like Jacques Hadamard, the distinguished mathematician and long-time member of the Central Committee, who had a penchant for reminding people like Morhardt that his views about the origins of the war were being exploited by the forces of revision within Germany. He was of course right—one would have hardly expected things to have been otherwise—but it was an odd line coming from a founding member of the League. As Morhardt lost no time in reminding him, "this is not the first time [I have] been forbidden, in the name of *raison d'état,* from searching for the truth. Already during the Dreyfus Affair, [I] heard it said: You are speaking against France and the German newspapers seize upon your articles and speeches."[28] This was excessively melodramatic and self-important language, very much Morhardt's speciality, but he was not altogether wrong either.

When members of the League declared that investigating the origins of the war was an improper activity for the organization, they often meant that it would be politically and electorally inexpedient. At the 1923 congress, the secretary general of the federation of the Aisne (and future deputy, minister, and Central Committee member) Marc Rucard argued that the question of the origins of the war, over which so many delegates were feuding, was inopportune in light of the forthcoming legislative elections. The likely outcome of these debates would be to diminish, or worse, eliminate German responsibility for the war and thus her obligation to pay reparations. In departments such as his, devastated by the German occupation, this would be an unpopular stance. "To say that Germany is not responsible amounts to saying that Germany does not need to pay and you can imagine the delicate fix into which that would place the League of the Rights of Man in [the devastated regions]." Here, Rucard, admirable leaguer though he in fact was, spoke as a future deputy from one of the departments of France occupied by the Germans in the war.[29]

The majority went through the motions of catering to the demands of the revisionists. It repeatedly urged the French government to speed up the publication of French diplomatic documents and issued a formal call for a parliamentary commission of inquiry into the origins of the war. But these were not exactly calls for an open inquiry because the leaders of the League were at pains to emphasize that the whole purpose of these efforts was, in the words of Alphonse Aulard "to proclaim to the whole world the irreproachable innocence of France, victim and not an accomplice in the great crime."[30]

Over the objections of some of its members, who could not see the point, in 1922 the Central Committee finally agreed to establish a separate subcommittee to investigate the origins of the war. As Secretary General Guernut candidly admitted, it did so primarily in order that the Committee's time would no longer be wasted on this secondary issue.[31] The meetings of the subcommittee were by and large unproductive. The futility of its deliberations owed something to personality issues. Mathius Morhard was at the best of times a difficult colleague who believed himself to have been marginalized since resigning as secretary general and eternally reminded everyone that *he*, in his twelve years at the helm, had made the League what it was. He had little use for his successor, Henri Guernut, whose management skills he thought inferior to his own. He had even less use for Emile Kahn whom he considered an arrogant upstart. Nor did he appreciate being repeatedly told by both Basch and Kahn that he and his

associates in the minority lacked the formal education, the professional formation, the critical skills, and the linguistic abilities to be able to tackle intelligently
the question of the war's origins. Since this antipathy was entirely mutual, meetings of the subcommittee usually degenerated into insult sessions, and hardly
a meeting went by without someone leaving in a huff.

More fundamentally, members of the majority believed that the war origins
question was precisely the kind that ought not to be of concern to the League.
Pouring over diplomatic documents was, in Ferdinand Buisson's words, "marginal" to the work of the association.[32] Aulard announced that "historical research had nothing to do with the rights of man" and Guernut noted that the
League was not "*une ecole de chartes* nor an association for historical study or
archival investigation."[33] These were valid points, although it was somewhat
disingenuous for Guernut to simultaneously ask why the League should investigate the origins of World War I and not those of the Thirty Years War, as
the answer was perfectly obvious. Moreover, it was all very well for Basch to insist that settling debates about contemporary history was the task for professional historians, and future ones at that. But the revisionists could counter
that it had not been so very many years ago that the League had been passionately engaged in a dispute about a piece of contemporary history: the
Dreyfus affair. Why had it been relevant to the League's mission to agonize
over the texts of this affair and not those involving the outbreak of hostilities
in 1914? In a throw-away line that augured poorly for the future history of the
League, Mathias Morhardt once observed that if the question of the origins
of the war had somehow been about Jews, Basch and his friends might be
more interested in exploring it.[34] In some exasperation, he asked if this were
not the same League that twenty years earlier had been so "touchy about the
question of a comma or problems of syntax" while probing documents relative
to Dreyfus? Why was the question of the responsibility for a war that had
killed millions less important than the guilt or innocence of one man?[35]

There was, of course, one obvious answer—one hinted at by some members of the majority. The role of the League was to defend individual victims
of injustice rather than to involve itself in the larger public issues of the day
like the origins of World War I. But this was an argument that most members
of the League could make, if at all, only sotto voce. If the origins of the war were
none of the League's business, why had it published Victor Basch's *Guerre de
Droit*? To now claim that the League should limit itself to cases of individual
human rights abuses was tantamount to accepting the thesis of the prewar
centre-gauche, which leaguers of Basch's and Kahn's generation had so readily

dismissed. Few indeed were the leaders of the League in the next two decades who did not think matters of foreign policy relevant, indeed, central, concerns of the association. It was not so much that the majority thought the war origins question to be irrelevant to the work of the League; rather it was that their minds were made up, and they did not like the implications of questioning the comfortable verdict of German guilt. What was passed off as a debate about the appropriate mandate of the League was in fact a debate about public policy. For the majority in the League the postwar settlement, flawed though it might be, was fundamentally legitimate. Their concern was to ensure that it be both preserved and enforced. Debates about the war's origins served no purpose save that of putting in question precisely that postwar settlement and, as they noted at every possible opportunity, playing into the hands of the vestiges of Prussian militarism all too preponderant in the Weimar Republic. The cause of peace, to which they were as attached as were those in the minority, would best be served by persuading Germany to accept the verdict of 1919.

For the minority, the 1919 settlement was flawed—and therefore dangerous—precisely because it rested on the dubious verdict of 1914. This was, as they saw it, both bad history and bad public policy, calculated to envenom Franco-German relations and render the peace more, rather than less, fragile. If Germany were no more responsible for the war than France, it followed that German protests, even when emanating from the extreme nationalist right, had a certain merit. As Challaye noted in 1931, even in Hitler's more extreme demands "there was something legitimate."[36]

In 1925 Fernand Buisson attempted to rescue the League from the quagmire of the war origins question by arguing that the war-guilt clause had not been intended to establish Germany's responsibility for the outbreak of the conflict. All Article 231 had wanted to assert was that Germany had invaded and largely devastated French and Belgium territory and was therefore responsible for restoring the damage. Few in the Central Committee accepted this line of reasoning when it was first made in 1925.[37] When virtually the same argument was put forward in 1931 by two distinguished historians, Pierre Renouvin and Camille Bloch, the latter a member of the League, the majority embraced it. If nothing else, the notion that the issue from which German nationalists derived so much propaganda value was just a misunderstanding, gave an increasingly uneasy group of leaguers a straw at which to grasp. For the more militant members of the minority, the Renouvin–Bloch thesis was a transparently desperate "fall back position" made necessary by the growing evidence that Germany was not responsible for the war.[38]

Divergences on foreign policy also extended, albeit far less bitterly, to colonial policy. Some members of the League were uneasily aware that French colonialism, entailing as it did the deprivation of political rights for millions of French *subjects*, was hard to reconcile with the principles of the rights of man. Once again it was Félicien Challaye who most clearly saw the contradiction. His public statements on French colonial rule, mild though they read today, outraged a French officialdom who thought them improper for a schoolteacher. The League's leaders tepidly defended Challaye's right to express himself while energetically distancing the League from his position.[39] By and large the League, with senior colonial administrators playing an active role in its Central Committee, believed that it should limit itself to protesting the *abuses* of colonial rule. At most, it would concede that in theory the League believed in the right of national self-determination but, in the words of Emile Kahn, when it came to colonial subjects, "it is not as simple as one might think." Before one could even contemplate self-determination it was the duty of colonial powers to civilize the natives to the point where they might be "capable . . . of exercising their human rights," something Kahn, like most of his fellow Socialists, thought was decades if not centuries away.[40] Unfortunately, the League's disinclination to question the principles of colonial rule was vigorously seconded by the various colonial sections that, to the general embarrassment of everyone, tended to present less subtle justification for French imperialism. An otherwise fairly sedate debate on colonialism at the 1930 congress was thoroughly spoiled by a delegate from Haiphong who protested the very idea of providing higher education for the natives. Not only would this elevate them above their station, but it would deprive native Frenchmen of career opportunities in the colonial administration.[41]

In 1930 the League canvassed its sections, particularly those in North Africa, about the possibility of extending very limited political rights to certain categories of natives, notably those who had fought for France in World War I. Some sections, including some North African ones, admitted that because natives had, in very substantial numbers, fought and died for the mother country, such proposals were worthy of consideration.[42] Many others, metropolitan as well as colonial, delivered themselves of racist diatribes. The section of Batna in Algeria complained that far too many concessions had already been made to the natives "who by and large do not share the mentality, values or civic virtues of Europeans [and who often] aspire only to drive us out of Algeria." The section of Antony, in the Parisian suburbs, assured League headquarters that even the "educated Arab aspires to only one thing: to dominate because he is . . . fanatical, prideful and full of himself. . . . He is forever on the lookout for our weaknesses in order to exploit them." It concluded by comparing the Arab to a tiger cub raised in captivity. No matter how kindly one treated it, upon maturity its first instinct would be to kill.[43] The League chose not to publish these findings. In general though, dissent over colonial policy was a minor chord in the interwar League. What obsessed leaguers of all persuasions was not Algeria or Indo-China but Germany.

From 1918 until the mid-1930s, despite the inevitable twists and turns, there were two positions within the League. The majority insisted that they were pacifists, proponents of internationalism and convinced advocates of disarmament. They could at times be highly critical of their own government to the degree that its actions seemed to violate these principles. Yet, by and large, they betrayed considerable sympathy for the difficulty faced by French diplomats, generally treated the perennial French Foreign Minister Aristide Briand as the incarnation of international understanding, and remained sensitive to the legitimate security concerns of the nation. The minority, by contrast, remained convinced of French bad faith and saw every action of the government as designed to antagonize Germany and to render a lasting peace impossible. The divergent positions were anchored in different assessments of the same diplomatic reality. The divergence was intensified by conflicting conceptions of pacifism. The majority was pacifist to the degree that it rejected war as an instrument of national policy and believed that disarmament, the new diplomacy, and international government were the best means of banishing forever the scourge of war. What it did not say was that war, under any circumstance whatsoever, was unthinkable. Within the minority there were integral pacifists who said precisely that.[44]

Until the beginning of 1933 the divergences within the League with respect to international relations, although fundamental, could be papered over with rhetoric. The debate, bitter though it often was, remained somewhat abstract. Hitler changed that. Victor Basch clearly appreciated that Hitler's accession to power meant that France was no longer dealing with a "pacifist and democratic Germany" but with a very different kind of regime whose aggressive and expansionist appetites were patent. This clearly called for a change of course on the part of the League. The shift was, however, gradual. The majority continued to call for disarmament, international cooperation , a strengthened League of Nations, and Franco-German reconciliation. The League's leaders clung to this line gamely even while they watched the disarmament talks sputter from one abortive proposal to the next and the League of Nations gradually lose whatever

moral authority it might once have had. German withdrawal from both the disarmament conference in Geneva and from the League of Nations in the fall of
1933, brought an anguished protest from the majority of the Central Committee but no end to its traditional calls for disarmament, "adjustment" of the 1918
treaties, and pleas for a reinvigorated League of Nations. As late as 1935, Basch
was prepared to see some evidence of the peaceful intentions of Hitler.[45] But
conviction was obviously lacking, and the traditional pacifist discourses were increasingly interspersed with dire warnings about the dangers of pan-German
nationalism. Entirely new was the appeal for France to strengthen her alliance
system. Of course given the odium attached to the pre-1914 system of "entangling alliances," Basch preferred to talk about a "bloc," or better yet, a "club"
of the democracies. France must strengthen her ties with both Great Britain and
with the United States and make any sacrifice to do so. Among other things,
he thought that this meant a resumption of war debts payments, suspended
by France at the end of 1932. Moreover, although it did some violence to the purity of the concept, he thought, for the first time, that the Soviet Union should
be drawn into a tight alliance designed to restrain fascist aggression and to keep
the peace. All of this, he insisted, was consistent with the values the League
had always preached.

The League's minority—and ultrapacifists in general—did not agree. Domestic policy was analytically separate from foreign policy. Much as one might
deplore the domestic developments within Germany, they did not render a
Franco-German reconciliation any less necessary. Indeed, logically, they rendered it more pressing than ever. The rhetoric about a "bloc of democracies"
struck them as merely the latest euphemism for the very old idea of entangling
alliances that, just as they had before World War I, rendered war more, rather
than less, likely and that threatened once again to draw France into a horrible
conflagration because of events in some part of the world about which most
Frenchmen cared little. Finally, they noted that merely waving one's past pacifist credentials around was not enough. Everyone in the League was in favor of
peace, just as everyone was in favor of democracy. The only important question was: which came first? The minority made it abundantly clear that peace
came first, if only because, in their view, without peace there would be no
democracy. Basch, they charged, was reversing the order of priorities.

Basch thought most of this to be the product of muddled minds. Leaving
aside that the persecutions within Nazi Germany were of direct concern to the
League, the fact that Hitler was in power had self-evident implications for
foreign policy. As for the two "antagonistic blocs," Basch hastened to remind

his colleagues that he had not created them; they already existed. He was not proposing some kind of "democratic crusade," still less a preventive war. But he did feel that a solid alliance of democratic nations would deter the belligerent reflexes of the fascist states. It followed that the *peace versus democracy* choice was a fallacious one. The union of the democracies was the necessary and sufficient condition for maintaining the peace.

Basch, as usual, had the better mind, and in hindsight his analysis was clearly more perceptive. Yet his critics among the minority did have a point. As Jean Luchaire observed, there was something of a logical gap between Basch's insistence on Hitler's expansionist designs and his own rejection of the possibility of preventive war. If Hitler really were the ogre depicted by Basch, was not preventive war precisely the correct remedy? Three years later, this was a point that Basch would grudgingly concede.[46] Moreover, although Basch may well have been correct to insist that the hostile blocs already existed, if the desired end was to prevent them from becoming *more* antagonistic, his increasingly violent anti-German diatribes were not helping matters very much. Possibly, close cooperation of the democracies, assuming always that it could be achieved, would deter Germany or Italy from aggressive war. But there was no absolute guarantee that this would be the case. Certainly there could be no guarantee unless it was certain that, in the last resort, the democracies would go to war. But this was just a couple of nuances away from the position that the best way to defend the peace was to prepare for war, a position that no one in the League yet endorsed. Basch would have replied that he intended no such thing, although he was becoming less and less convincing on this point. And although Basch would maintain throughout the 1930s that the minority was invariably and consistently wrong, it was right in at least one prediction: France did ultimately go to war over a part of Europe most people in France did not care about.[47]

No one could dispute that Nazi Germany was not Wilhelmine Germany, and Hitler's persecution of political dissidents and racial minorities could hardly be ignored. The *Cahiers* published a series of articles on Nazi persecutions, just as it had in the past highlighted civil rights abuses in the Soviet Union, Fascist Italy, and the United States. Basch and his allies paid special attention to the plight of anti-Nazi refugees in France. New, however, were the growing concerns about the apparent willingness of certain elements on the French Left to reach an understanding with the new regime. A critical turning point came in April 1933 when Jean Luchaire, editor of *Notre Temps*, a left-wing weekly to which many of the younger members of the League frequently contributed, sponsored a meeting of assorted French youth groups with their counterparts among the Nazis. The German youth attempted to explain the "German revolution" of 1933 as a Teutonic equivalent of 1789. They rehearsed the standard postwar German grievances, arguments which the League, or a good part of it, would not find entirely unsympathetic. But they also insisted that Nazi anti-Semitism was but the legitimate protest of a people that had suffered far too long under the Jewish yoke. German Jews, they pleaded, were far more domineering and less assimilated than their French equivalents. In time some kind of reconciliation with a domesticated Jewry might be possible but, for the moment—and just as had been the case during the French Revolution—drastic measures were required.[48] Basch and his associates on the Central Committee could barely hide their "stupor and indignation." Yes, the peace imperative dictated continuing *diplomatic* contact with Germany, but this did not legitimate private contacts between representatives of the French Left and Nazi spokesmen. *A la rigueur* it might be possible to concede the shortcomings of allied diplomacy during the previous fifteen years. But it defied common sense, not to mention common decency, to permit Nazis to *defend* and *justify* anti-Semitism as if it were merely an opinion about which reasonable people could disagree.[49] What intensified Basch's outrage was the awkward fact that representatives of the League's notional student auxiliary, *Ligue d'Action Universitaire Républicaine et Socialiste* (*LAURS*), felt authorized to accept the invitation. Somewhat mollified to learn that LAURS spokesmen had used the occasion to protest Nazi persecutions, the Central Committee nonetheless urged LAURS to consult the League's leadership before taking comparable initiatives in the future.[50]

The meeting sponsored by Luchaire was, of course, the beginning of a long and sordid collaboration between a critical segment of French intellectuals and Nazi Germany. Less than a decade later, Luchaire and some of his collaborators in *Notre Temps* would be active in collaborationist and anti-Semitic circles in Vichy. But in 1933 things were still very much in a state of flux. Many members of the League, Pierre Cot, Jacques Kayser, and Pierre Mendès-France were still frequent contributors to *Notre Temps*, none of them—the last two for obvious reasons—the least bit suspect of pro-Nazi or anti-Semitic sentiments. Significantly, one of the representatives of LAURS at the meeting, and still a close associate of Luchaire, was André Weil-Curiel, one of the early leaders of the Resistance. Nonetheless, there were distressing signs that certain elements in the League were uncomfortable with Basch's and Kahn's preoccupation with German domestic policies and above all with their concern for Hitler's racial policies. No one, of course, attempted to justify Nazi anti-Semitism, but a number treated the question as an irritating detail that ought not to be blown out of proportion and that most certainly ought not to impede a Franco-German reconciliation.

In an article entitled "Germany, 1934," René Georges-Etienne, president of the section of the fifth arrondissement of Paris and soon to become League treasurer, shared his impressions of a recent trip to Germany with a group of students from LAURS. It was hard, he admitted, to find any political or ideological common ground with representatives of the new Germany. On economic questions, by contrast, "the national socialist movement deserves to be better understood and more carefully studied." The racism, nationalism, and authoritarianism of the new regime represented the antithesis of democracy but, he noted, Weimar democracy had offered little for the Germans because "true freedom consists of being able to work and to live." A controlled press was evil but "is the public more deceived by a press it knows to be censured by the state than by a press which it believes to be free but which is, almost entirely, under the secret control of economic forces"? One surely had to admit that the assorted "flaws" of democratic regimes were such as to "offer the supporters of authoritarian regimes arguments which are *apparently* not without value." "Ought we to descend on Berlin to impose the virtues of democracy on a fascist government at precisely the moment when the Stavisky scandal demonstrates so vividly the flaws of our own current democracy?" In retrospect, such lines might appear to reflect a willful moral blindness. The conditions of the French press were not even remotely like those of its German counterparts; to compare the destruction of German democracy to the corruption of a handful of French politicians (most, although he chose not to mention it, members of the League) was grotesque. In reality, Georges-Etienne, a man who would have a perfectly honorable Resistance record was simply like most Leaguers in his laudable preference for addressing the shortcomings of his own nation before castigating his neighbors.[51]

Others in the League, however, began to go further and to suggest not only, as did Georges-Etienne, that France was not without its shortcomings, but also that Nazi Germany was not without its redeeming features. The starting point of their analysis was invariably that Hitler's advent was but the perfectly predictable consequence of Germany's humiliating treatment by France since 1918. The protest by the Central Committee majority against Hitler's withdrawal from the disarmament talks and the League of Nations prompted a counter manifesto by the Committee's minority (itself something of an innovation.) Anger at Hitler's withdrawal from the disarmament talks was pious hypocrisy—much like the talks themselves. The *only* power that had disarmed (or been disarmed) was Germany; no one else gave any serious evidence of doing likewise. As for the League of Nations, was it not self-evidently the agent enforcing the patently unjust postwar treaties? "No matter how odious the internal German regime may appear to be" or "whatever our aversion for its domestic politics," representatives of the minority pleaded, a Franco-German rapproachement was more imperiously necessary than ever.[52]

Beneath this careful phraseology, however, there lay a startlingly benign assessment of Nazi Germany. Jacques Ganuchaud, an ally of Léon Emery, found the League's theoretical stance on Nazi Germany to be weak. "It limits itself," he wrote, "to examining the negative aspects of fascism. It seems not to realize that [fascism] has a positive aspect, capable of seducing the masses."[53] In the fall of 1933 André Berthet, a former Communist and now secretary general of the powerful federation of the Rhône, complained that for some in the League the new situation in Germany seemed to pose a choice between "the struggle against Hitler and the struggle against war." These alternatives, he insisted were false and artificial ones, as a careful assessment of the Nazi regime would show. What brought Hitler to power? The iniquitous Treaty of Versailles, to be sure. But also the demonstrated inability of the "old parties" (among whom he included both the German Socialists and Communists) to deal with the economic depression. The Hitler movement was in fact part of a "revolt of youth against the old beards." The recent invitation to French youth to meet their German counterparts, that had so recently disturbed the majority, was, for Berthet, "the excellent initiative of M. Luchaire"; the young Nazis had struck him as being "sincere," and he thought it appropriate to celebrate the "realism of the young generation." What irritated him was the dogmatism of French Socialists who seemed incapable of appreciating that Nazism was a "popular movement" including important segments of the German working class.

Was Hitler a threat to the peace? "I do not think so," he opined. True, Hitler had written *Mein Kampf,* but this was an old tract likely to be forgotten, like most campaign statements, now that he was in power. Of course there was a nationalist component to Nazi Germany, not unlike France in 1792 or any other "new regime." But it would likely disappear with the inevitable "normalization" of the regime. Indeed, the real question about Hitler was not whether he threatened the peace but whether "Hitler's moderation [would] inconvenience the arms manufacturers," anxious to exploit this new opportunity for profits just as they had the alleged menace of the Soviet Union and Fascist Italy. Throughout this analysis there was no recognition that Hitler had the more or less overt support of most of the traditional German elites. Nor was there a word about his persecution of Jews.[54] Berthet was not an exception within the minority. In the same issue of the *Cahiers* Challaye presented an only slightly more nuanced version of the same argument.[55]

Anxious to minimize the significance of the change of regime in Germany, members of the minority were uncomfortable with the League's apparent obsession with Nazi atrocities. Challaye, for example, was uneasy with the term "concentration camp," preferring the more *neutral* "labor camp."[56] When Suzanne Collette presented a carefully documented article on human rights violations inside Germany, Lucien Cancouët, one of the more outspoken leaders of the minority, protested that her tales simply did not ring true. He held no brief for a regime that had destroyed the worker's movement. But, reminding everyone, as he habitually did, that as a combat veteran, all too familiar with the horrors of the front line, he knew something about human brutality. Collette, by contrast, did not and seemed too ready to naively accept horror stories that seemed reminiscent of the *bourrage de crane* of 1914–18. Whatever else he might have been, Hitler was not "a wild beast that must be destroyed."[57] It did not escape the minority that Hitler's victims and the League's majority shared one thing in common: Jews were prominent in both groups. One contributor to the local bulletin of the federation of the Meurthe-et-Moselle wondered if fellow members shared his concern that the League seemed to be unduly preoccupied with the fate of Jews in Germany. "Do we not see here the influence of the principal leaders of the League, Basch and Kahn, both of them Jews, something they never forget."[58] The energetic intervention of Kahn quickly terminated that particular editorial initiative but others persisted. Georges Demartial also wondered if the Jewish presence on the Central Committee did not explain its diminishing commitment to peace. Demartial, a perennially unsuccessful candidate for the Central Committee, suggested that there was something wrong with a mode of recruitment that invariably ensured that nearly a quarter of its members (including the president and secretary general) were Jewish. Although the League was not a Jewish organization, it seemed incapable of learning how to "fight anti-Semitism without exposing itself to the charge of being pro-semitic."[59] Even less subtle was an opinion piece that somehow managed to appear in *Université Républicaine*, the house-organ of LAURS. Jean Florac, a regular contributor, noted that much of the current Franco-German tension was a function of the plight of German Jews. But had German Jews given any thought to the reasons behind their "eternal grievances"? Had it occurred to them that their refusal to identify with the "popular masses" was at the root of their difficulties? Could it be that "ethnic pride" and "a sense of superiority" made it impossible for them to treat the average German as anything other than "customers"? Once, to be sure, legal restrictions had prevented Jews from agricultural occupations; now, however, low profit margins were a better explanation. "Jews," he concluded, "should be smart enough to understand that certain privileged occupations are not exclusively reserved for them."[60] Erratic opinions like this were, to be sure, very much the exception in League publications. Nonetheless, in their disagreements on foreign policy, it became more and more common for members of the minority to make gratuitous reference to racial origins. In 1934, in the context of a protracted dispute with fellow Committee member Georges Gombault over disarmament, Challaye felt it appropriate to remind everyone that Gombault was born Louis Weiskopf. Although he had nothing against Jews as such, he confessed to a marked preference for those who chose not to hide their Jewish identity behind Christian names.[61]

The question of the Soviet Union also divided the League. Throughout the 1920s, the majority continued to express dismay at the human rights violations in the Soviet Union, although often in a highly qualified form. Fernand Corcos, for example, would inform a meeting of the federation of the Indre-et-Loire that while the Soviet Union was "obviously under a very harsh dictatorship . . . a revolution should be judged only in retrospect." League members, therefore, should withhold judgment and "allow Russia to undergo the experiment."[62] The minority protested that when not entirely the product of counterrevolutionary propaganda, such abuses paled by comparison to abuses in the West, most notably with respect to the colonies. It applauded the Soviet Union's intense antimilitarism and was untroubled by either the Soviet Union's growing military establishment or by the fact that the only war the Soviets denounced was an imperialistic one. The minority continued to hold that view as late as 1933 when Challaye insisted that the League should concentrate on French colonies where France "adopts . . . policies compared to which those of the U.S.S.R are very humane." Georges Michon flatly declared that "the League must not attack Russia." Jacques Kayser was less categorical but thought it a "poor time" to be asking awkward questions about the Soviets lest the League appear to be "involuntarily complicit with Japan, Hitler and England, all enemies of the USSR." In the same debate members of the majority countered that unless the League showed some concern for the problems in the Soviet Union it hardly had the right to denounce comparable abuses in Nazi Germany.[63] On this point they were clearly correct, although exclusively from the perspective of civil liberties. Matters of foreign policy, with which both sides were clearly obsessed, were an entirely different matter. Although neither side had yet fully grasped the point, the rapidly changing diplomatic landscape soon made it uncommonly difficult to be equally critical, or equally indulgent, toward Nazi Germany and the Soviet Union. René Martel, president of the section of Versailles and candidate for the Central Committee dimly grasped this reality when he noted that France needed to work for a Franco-German reconciliation, whatever her legitimate aversion for German domestic politics, "provided always that such an accord not become a threat to the Soviet Union."[64] This was a circle that could not be squared, and before long both sides would abandon their respective positions.

All elements in the League saw a critical connection between domestic politics and foreign policy. But they saw them in very different places. For the majority it seemed self-evident that Hitler rendered Germany a far more dangerous country. The minority dismissed this view as the product of ideologically (if not racially) blinkered minds. Germany's grievances, legitimate into the bargain, were not a Nazi invention. Moreover, it was surely naive to believe that fascist regimes were somehow more prone to war than were bourgeois democracies. Prewar France provided a classic counterexample. Why, in any case, focus exclusively on German fascism? Any Frenchman who worried about the threat of fascism need not, after February 6, 1934, look beyond his own doorstep. Was it not the case that in the Doumergue government—for many in the League an embryonically fascist one—Foreign Minister Louis Barthou was industriously (and irresponsibly) trying to shore up France's alliance network? If there was a threat to the peace, it was coming from France.

Worse yet, the majority, obsessed as it was by developments beyond the Rhine, failed to appreciate either the nature of domestic fascism or the only way to fight it. The current domestic fascist menace was not just a new version of Boulangism or the anti-Dreyfusard leagues. Fascism grew out of the corruption of bourgeois democracy by the malignant forces of capitalism (an analytical framework the minority rarely applied to fascism in Germany.) It was both pointless and regressive to attempt to stave off French fascism by shoring up a corrupt, discredited, and clearly dying bourgeois parliamentary democracy. Only a genuine social revolution, leading to a true social democracy, could save France from fascism. But the existing leadership of the League was all too intimately connected to the decadent old order to make that conceptual leap. In a formula that was widely used, minority spokesmen insisted that the essential precondition for an effective antifascist response was for the League to "separate itself completely from all governing milieu (high politics, administration and

official press.)"[65] As Léon Emery noted, the League would have to "cease counting on a discredited political elite and on unpopular and ineffective parliamentary institutions." A purely defensive response was a waste of time or worse;
what was needed, "to put it bluntly, is a revolution."[66] Attacks on Nazi Germany and defense of bourgeois democracy could only lead to war. Only a social
revolution at home, sweeping away the regime of corruption, could ensure international reconciliation.

Seen in retrospect, and especially in the light of the subsequent evolution
of many of the *minoritaires*, many of these statements have a decidedly sinister
ring to them, combining as they did a pronounced indifference to the horrors
of Nazi Germany and a savagely antiparliamentary rhetoric. But in the context of the times—and well into 1935—the position of the minority was calculated to win the support of a substantial segment of League activists. For many
militants the minority was merely applying consistently the formulae to which
the majority had only given lip service. There was little in the slogans of the minority that could not be found in the previous public statements of the League
leadership. That the slogans meant something quite different to Basch or Kahn
than to Challaye or Emery might not have been obvious to the rank and file.
Even when the differences were clear, for many, Challaye and Emery seemed
to be more consistent with League values—or at least League rhetoric. Had not,
after all, the 1933 congress unanimously endorsed the idea that French democracy was subservient to and corrupted by the puissances d'argent, the "economic congregations," and the "industrial feudality"? The spectacle of many
of the earlier leaders of the League serving in or even (if one cared to remember the previous affiliations of Doumergue and Laval) presiding over right-wing
governments was not calculated to weaken the case of the minority. The Herriot affair, which to the dismay of Victor Basch, monopolized League energies
in 1934, was a boon to the leaders of the minority.

By 1934, war seemed closer than ever before and the intransigent pacifism
of the minority, correspondingly, more appropriate. With the Right once again
in power and Louis Barthou, not Paul-Boncour, in the Quai d'Orsay, the case
for focusing exclusively on the shortcomings of French diplomacy had a certain compulsion. Nor did it help the majority that at least some of its representatives did not seem altogether uneasy about Barthou. In 1934 Challaye rather
pointedly reminded the Central Committee that one of its members, and one
of the most outspoken of the leaders of the majority, Salomon Grumbach, had
accepted a position under Barthou as technical councillor to France's League
of Nations delegation. Although this particular sally prompted great indigna-

tion (in no small measure because the leadership suspected, correctly, that Grumbach's Jewish origins were at least as important for Challaye as his governmental positions), Challaye did have a point. Given that the Central Committee was, in principle at least, hostile both to Barthou and the Doumergue government in which he served, what was Grumbach still doing on the Central Committee?[67] One might have countered that having Grumbach on the Central Committee was hardly an innovation; in the past the Committee had been comfortable with the presence of Paul Painlevé and Joseph Paul-Boncour, both serving as *ministers* in the conservative government of Poincaré. But in the climate of 1934 such an argument would have been unlikely to disarm the militant minority.

In the years 1934 and 1935 the viewpoint of the minority seemed to be in the ascendancy, and many were confident that the minority would soon be a majority in the League. The advent of Hitler appeared to confirm, not infirm, the minority's excoriating critique of French diplomacy in the previous decade and a half. Political developments in France only reinforced the minority's pessimism about the state of French democracy and its responsibility for the deteriorating international situation. The majority was increasingly on the defensive. No amount of casuistry could quite mask the fact that it was the majority, not the minority, that was shifting its views on foreign policy. The prominent (and embarrassing) role of League deputies in the Stavisky affair and the presence of so many League ministers in the right-wing governments of Doumergue, Flandin, and Laval substantiated the minority's charge that the League had become a *ligue politicienne* as did the majority's tenacious defense of one of them, Herriot. The condemnation of Herriot at the 1934 congress, an unprecedented revolt against the authority of the Central Committee, seemed to presage a fundamental reorientation of the League.

As the 1935 congress approached, many expected a dramatic shift in League policy. Léon Emery would be presenting a motion demanding that the League replace its classic human rights orientation with one dedicated almost exclusively to fighting war and capitalism. Anticipating a major confrontation at the congress, Jacques Rosner of Lyon crowed: "In this revolutionary period two ideologies will come face to face . . . there is no reconciling them." This time, the radical differences would not be papered over by the rhetorical compromises for which the League had become infamous. This time the League of the politicians would be replaced by a genuinely revolutionary one.[68] Rosmer represented the radical wing of the League and was a self-appointed angry young man. But others of more moderate persuasion shared his views. P. Gateaud, an executive member of the federation of the Saône-et-Loire, had little use for the constant sniping of the minority, but he too believed that the League was about to experience a "necessary bifurcation" and would "henceforth be oriented as much towards social struggles as towards the defence of individual liberties."[69] All of them, however, reckoned without the League's ability to fudge issues. Although the two theses did confront one another at the congress and although Emery's motion received the support of 40 percent of the delegates, in the end everyone settled for a compromise resolution which papered over but did not resolve the fundamental differences. Emery's strong showing provided Rosmer with a "moral victory" but, as he ruefully acknowledged, it remained the same old League.[70]

Rosmer's disappointment reflected the larger truth that political developments in France were inexorably working against the calculations of the minority. Its inflated hopes had largely been conditioned by significant shifts within and among the parties of the Left. The events of February 6, 1934, had knocked them out of their sectarian lethargy of the early 1930s; there was increasing talk of unity of action; and, most important of all, the Communist party was poised to abandon its self-imposed isolation. A unified and reinvigorated Left, soon to be known as the Rassemblement Populaire, in which the Communist party now played a central role, seemed likely, on past performance, to be one in which the combined struggle against war and capitalism would now be the central tenet. It did not seem unreasonable to assume that this new revolutionary ardor would be reflected in the League. In fact, however, members of the minority seriously misread the Rassemblement Populaire. They were correct to see it as new development on the left and equally right in seeing Communist participation as a significant feature. What they initially failed to appreciate, however, was how radically the Communists were rethinking traditional assumptions about both foreign and domestic policy, a rethinking that brought them, paradoxically, far closer to the majority than to the minority. In essence, and making allowances for innumerable twists and turns and many second thoughts, the Nazi threat to the Soviet Union caused French Communists to abandon their traditional antimilitarism and to become passionate advocates of a rearmed and diplomatically firm France, allied with the Soviet Union. If a France that succumbed to fascism was an unlikely partner for the Soviets, so too was a France that perceived itself to be threatened by revolution. It followed that, were France to be a reliable ally of the Soviet Union, she must be saved from fascism not by revolution (itself more than a little problematic) but by the rigorous defense of a more socially progressive bourgeois democracy. Here, important elements in both the Radical and Socialist parties were more or less in agreement. So too, and more to the point, was the majority in the League. Thus, by the end of 1935, it was increasingly apparent that the Rassemblement Populaire that the minority so eagerly embraced a year earlier, was, ironically, working to reinforce the position of the majority.

As usual, Emery was one of the first to grasp the significance of the changing climate. In March 1935, and two months before Stalin made his famous statement approving French rearmament, he noted that the war fever continued to mount. If Great Britain, at least, seemed to be restraining its bellicose instincts, the same could not be said for France where a "phantom parliament is no longer anything more than a cover for every reactionary initiative." "But, without doubt, the most tragic and serious [development] since the arrival of Hitler is the total reversal of the USSR." In 1928 the future Soviet Foreign Minister Maxim Litvinov had correctly declared "regional mutual assistance pacts" to be but a polite term for the dangerous entangling alliances that had led to war in 1914. Now the Soviet Union was actively pursuing precisely such diplomatic arrangements, all of which doomed any serious effort to revise the Treaty of Versailles and would "force Germany to accept as permanent the conditions imposed on her by her defeat." He still was "in no way" either anti-Soviet or anti-Communist but he now felt the need to criticize Soviet diplomacy "as much to save the Russian Revolution as to save the peace."[71] This was a Jesuitical, and desperate, formulation to which Emery could cling only for a short while.

The men who had founded the League in 1898 could not have envisaged that within a generation, the energies of the organization would be consumed with questions of diplomacy. Few could have imagined future leaders of the League being embroiled in the arcana of the exact timing of a telegram reaching Paris in the summer of 1914, the precise wording of a foreign diplomatic dispatch, or the complexities of mobilization timetables. Nor could they have anticipated the feverish debates in future Central Committees concerning the occupation of the Ruhr, the Treaty of Locarno, the Young Plan, disarmament conferences, and so forth. At most they would have acknowledged that questions of international diplomacy would interest members of their League, questions about which they might often disagree but that were generally irrelevant to the League's mandate. They lived, however, in a world where war and fear of war were remote from the lives of most Frenchmen and questions of foreign policy a matter of general public indifference. But 1914 changed all that. Nor could they yet appreciate the consequences of a relentless logic that dictated that the League's mandate would extend to a far wider range of issues than

individual cases of injustice. This logic was, in fact, compelling. If the imprisonment of one man on Devil's Island was an injustice, then surely too was the
death of 1.4 million Frenchmen in an arguably avoidable and apparently fruitless war.

Yet in practical terms, the two cases were radically different. It was relatively
easy for men of good will, armed with a sense of justice and a solid knowledge of legal procedures, to demonstrate that Alfred Dreyfus had been wrongly
and illegally convicted. All that was needed was to convince the public and
public authorities, something that required courage, skill, and determination,
which the League possessed in abundance. The questions of who was to blame
for World War I and whether or not it could have been avoided were infinitely
more complex. A century later historians still debate them, whereas the question of the innocence or guilt of Dreyfus has been settled for a hundred years.
Basch's case for German guilt, intelligent though it might have been, was far
weaker than the League's 1898 case for the innocence of Dreyfus. The minority's case for German innocence, specious though it now appears to be, was a
far stronger case than the one presented by the anti-Dreyfusards. Even had
there been greater uncertainty about the innocence of Dreyfus, the League's
course would have been clear; reasonable doubt would have sufficed to re-
habilitate Dreyfus.

The disputed origins of World War I dictated no such clear path. Diplomacy, after all, rarely lends itself to the elegant clarity of the judicial system.
Although the point often escaped members of the League, even someone convinced of German guilt might conclude that the 1919 settlement violated the
declared principles of the victors. Even in the face of overwhelming evidence
that Germany had deliberately sought war in 1914, it was still possible to argue
that France's involvement in that war was exclusively a product of her misguided and unnecessary alliance with Russia. From either of these positions,
it might follow that France had only herself to blame for Hitler's advent and
that an alliance against Hitler was as irrational and as dangerous as had been
the prewar alliance against Wilhelmine Germany. As good an argument (and
also one not dependant on the verdict about 1914) would have been that Hitler
was not even remotely the equivalent of the Kaiser and that his ambitions went
far beyond righting whatever injustices may have been done in 1919. The latter
was almost certainly the better case but only in light of our subsequent knowledge. The critical point is that there was absolutely nothing in the League's
principles, however broadly defined, that would permit it to decide the issue.

Leaders of the League were at times dimly aware of this elementary reality, but rarely did they internalize the proposition. Seldom did anyone say that foreign policy is something about which reasonable people in the League might legitimately differ, and it is simply not our issue. Those who declared, correctly enough, that the League ought not to be debating the war's origins, manifestly did not mean to suggest that questions of diplomacy were outside the League's mandate. All they meant was that their minds were made up or that they were weary of the harping of the minority. It was the majority, however, that started the debate (with Basch's 1914 book on precisely that subject) and continued publicly to advocate what it thought were the appropriate diplomatic policies. There was, therefore, no reason for the minority to withdraw from the debate. Moreover, as war drew nearer, the debate would become more intense, indeed ferocious, with deleterious consequences for the League.

SEVEN

From the Popular Front
to the Fall of France

The Popular Front was a critical turning point in the history of the League. In the wake of the frightening events of February 6, 1934, all elements on the French Left began to recognize the need for unity, aware as they were that, as had been the case in Italy and Germany, left-wing disarray threatened to open the door to fascism in France. In addition to preserving the democratic Republic, left-wing unity would rescue both the Socialists and the Communists from the counterproductive sectarian strategies in which they had been enmeshed. Entry into a broad left-wing coalition of republicans also served the Radicals because it might lead the public to overlook the fact that the crisis of 1934 owed not a little to their governmental incompetence and corruption. Long and difficult negotiations between the Socialists and Communists began in the spring of 1934; by the summer of 1935 they were joined by the Radicals and several score of other minor groups in the Rassemblement Populaire.[1] The union was sealed with a triumphal manifestation in Paris and in most major towns of France on July 14, 1935. In Paris, a majority of the speakers at the founding rally of the Rassemblement Populaire (Basch, Ferdinand Herold, Paul Rivet, Julien Racamond, Eugène Frot, Léon Jouhaux, and Marc Rucard) were or would be members of the Central Committee. Victor Basch presided over the organizing committee of the Rassemblement Populaire whose permanent headquarters were also those of the League at the Rue Jean Dolent. A contemporary observer described Emile Kahn as the "work horse [of the committee] . . . conciliatory, discreet and adroit."[2] Both Basch and Kahn were in their element, deploying their considerable energy and diplomatic skills to minimize the often serious disagreements with the coalition's partners. Indeed, the League and most of its subsequent historians considered the Rassemblement Populaire to be very much its own creation.[3] Not since the Dreyfus affair had the League played such a prominent role in the defense of the Republic.

In fact, however, association with the Rassemblement Populaire would be the source of almost endless problems for the League. In the first place, joining the Rassemblement Populaire was not easily reconciled with the famous Article 15, which appeared to prohibit precisely this kind of adhesion—a fact that League leaders would only later and reluctantly concede. But the internal regulations of the Rassemblement Populaire stressed that it was not a party or even a super party but rather a center of liaison between entirely autonomous organizations. Whereas previous left-wing coalitions like the Cartel des Gauches had involved only political parties, the Rassemblement included several score of notionally nonpolitical organizations.[4] Sticking to this technicality, the League managed to overlook the fact that the Rassemblement Populaire was clearly a coordinating agency for the forthcoming legislative elections and actively drafting what were at least general legislative guidelines for a future government.

In its broad outlines, the platform of the Rassemblement Populaire was unproblematic for the League. Parrying the fascist menace, preserving the peace, and implementing major social and economic reforms were issues virtually everyone in the League could agree on. But the devil, as always, was in the details. Was the struggle against fascism limited to French fascism? Or did it extend to foreign fascism as well? If the latter, how exactly did this help the cause of peace? In his many torturous articles on the subject Basch had contended, rightly, that diplomatic actions to contain Nazi Germany did not necessarily mean war. But others in the League had countered that such measures were, to say the least, unlikely to ensure peace either. Even were the focus to be restricted to French fascism, the exact policy prescriptions were not obvious. If, as many in the League believed, the root cause of fascism was capitalism, or as they preferred to put it, "the trusts" and the puissances d'argent, merely outlawing the various right-wing antiparliamentary formations was unlikely to deal decisively with the problem. Nor, strictly speaking, would the proposed social reforms, valuable though they incontestably would be for the working class. Only a genuine social revolution, or at a minimum the kind of dramatic structural reforms advocated by the Socialists, could render France immune from the fascist temptation.

Not only were these issues in dispute within the League but, by virtue of entering into the Rassemblement Populaire, it also became hostage to the partisan squabbling among the parties of the Left. Despite the rhetorical flourishes and some critical differences, the Rassemblement Populaire was, in important respects, just a revamped version of earlier left-wing electoral coalitions.

Common to all of them was the role of the Radicals. The problem with the Radical party, whom everyone on the Left still expected to be the largest party after the forthcoming elections, was that its claim to be on the Left, plausible enough at the turn of the twentieth century, had weakened progressively thereafter. It still mouthed the increasingly irrelevant anticlerical slogans and the increasingly meaningless calls for peace. But for those in the League who hoped for a genuine revolution with assorted economic Bastille's falling, the Radicals were a dubious ally. When not utterly incoherent, the social and economic program of many Radicals was essentially conservative. Edouard Herriot's claim that there was little in the program of the Rassemblement Populaire that could not be found in the 1901 platform of the Radical party was designed to reassure nervous Radicals but was also calculated to disquiet those who hoped for genuinely revolutionary change. Both Léon Emery and his fellow Central Committee member Gaston Bergery, deputy from the Seine-et-Oise, who had resigned in disgust from the Radical party in 1932, began to fear that the Rassemblement Populaire might, like earlier left-wing electoral coalitions, win the forthcoming elections, only to achieve little in the way of radical change.[5]

What made the Rassemblement Populaire different from previous left-wing alliances was the presence of the previously isolated Communists. In principle, the inclusion of the Communists ought to have reassured the more radical members of the League. But the Communists, at least in their post-1935 incarnation, were at least as serious a problem as were the Radicals. Although it pleased the more radical elements in the League to find capitalism—or at least the kind prevailing in France—to be the root cause of fascism and, although on the theoretical terrain the Communists might have agreed, by 1935 the Communists had adopted a more pragmatic approach to the question. They were acutely alert to the fact that what gave fascism its dynamism was the support of the embittered and marginalized members of the middle and lower-middle class. It therefore seemed logical to cater to the Radicals, the classic representatives of just those critical strata of society. This was the same logic that, after 1935, led the Communists to a series of "outstretched hands" to peasants, small businessmen, and even to progressive Catholics (an oxymoron for many in the League). As a direct result therefore, in the six months of elaboration of a common program of the Rassemblement Populaire, Communists and Radicals allied successfully to oppose the more fundamental assault on capitalism—massive nationalization of heavy industry for example—advocated by the Socialists.

The resulting program of the Rassemblement Populaire was, at least in some respects, calculated to trouble many in the League. Certainly it contained a number of far-reaching social reforms—indeed the most progressive in the history of the Third Republic: the forty-hour work-week, two weeks paid vacation, full government support for collective bargaining, nationalization of both the Bank of France and the war industries, and creation of a wheat marketing board. It also called for the dissolution of various right-wing leagues. But its purely financial platforms were vague. Members of the Central Committee, of all political hues, complained that it was most unclear precisely how the Rassemblement Populaire, assuming it got into power, would be able to finance many of its proposed reforms. As Léon Emery noted, with his usual acute eye for detail, there were elements in this program that even Pierre Laval could live with. Nor could he find anything resembling a clear monetary or fiscal policy.[6]

Much more significantly, at least from the perspective of the League's minority, were the platforms dealing with foreign policy. As Emery observed "there is everything here, but also nothing." Yes, all the classic language was present: collective security, disarmament, even revision of the 1919 treaties— although as Emery was quick to remark "revision," a classic demand of the Left, had now been modified to "adjustment" (*assouplisement*). But he asked, what did any of this mean? Was multilateral disarmament the necessary precondition for collective security? If so, the program did not say this. Or, as he rather feared, was it the other way around? Disarmament was being relegated to the status of something one would like to do but only after the German menace had been dealt with.[7]

He was of course quite right. The document was deliberately ambiguous and reflected the increasing divisions within the French Left about foreign policy. He was also correct in suspecting that for many in the Rassemblement Populaire, and most notably the Communists, disarmament had become distinctly secondary to the creation of a block of states designed to stop Hitler. As a result of their growing anxiety about the threat represented by Nazi Germany, by the spring of 1935 both the Soviet Union and the French Communist party had abandoned their dogmatic stance on "bourgeois militarism" and were openly sympathetic to French rearmament. Emery found it bitterly ironic that when he and Bergery had been forcefully advocating left-wing unity the previous year, people like Basch treated them as "communist agents." Now Basch was claiming paternity for the Rassemblement Populaire, and they were reduced to expressing their growing reservations about the Communist role.[8] This was another way of saying that they, unlike Basch and his colleagues, had failed to notice the dramatic shift by the Communists in the previous year.

The tumultuous feuds of 1935 were temporarily forgotten during the heady days of the late spring and early summer of 1936 which brought the victory of the Popular Front. Even Emery would declare in July that the Herriot affair he had so tenaciously pursued for two years was now "secondary."[9] Although the actual shift in votes was slight, the electoral coalition of the Left, owing to second ballot cooperation, had a commanding majority in parliament. Also, for the first time, the Socialists had replaced the Radicals as the largest party in parliament, and Communist representation had gone from a handful of deputies to over seventy. As a result Léon Blum formed the next government, with the participation of the Radicals and the parliamentary support of the Communists. The electoral victory coincided with, and largely stimulated, a wave of sit-in strikes mobilizing very nearly two million workers. The combination of a Socialist government in power and the massive mobilization of an important segment of the working class ensured that during its first two months France saw more progressive social legislation than at any other period in its history. This represented a triumph for the forces of the Left and above all the League. Not only had it some claim to paternity of the Popular Front government but it could, and did, point with pride to the fact that virtually all the ministers of the new government were members, often prominent members, of the League.[10]

The League had, therefore, a great deal invested in the Popular Front government, very much *its* government. Never before had a more sympathetic government been in power. Indeed, the Popular Front has traditionally been treated as the League's finest hour since the heroic days of the Dreyfus affair. As a direct consequence, however, the League became hostage to the fortunes of that government. League principles, which had been easy to articulate under previous and less sympathetic governments, became more problematic under this one. It had, for example, always been an article of faith that a government could not dismiss civil servants merely because it did not approve of their political views. It had quite properly dismissed out of hand the argument that civil servants with dissenting political views might somehow obstruct the work of government. In 1923 President Buisson complained that the (then conservative) government acted as if all its civil servants must "share the political opinions of the government."[11] But shortly before he formed his Popular Front government, Léon Blum called for a *souffle républicain* (a breath of Republican fresh air), by which he meant that civil servants suspected of disloyalty to the government would be purged. In practice, and to the bitter disappointment of the socialist Left, only a handful of senior civil servants were dismissed.[12] But

Blum's desire to ensure that he could count on loyal supporters in the administration, understandable though it was, differed in no way from similar reflexes of previous more conservative governments, reflexes the League had correctly denounced.

This point, however, seems to have escaped both the League's leaders and, more markedly still, the rank and file. At the beginning of 1937, prominent Central Committee member, Albert Bayet, deplored the continued presence of conservatives in the civil service and openly called for the suspension of *inamovibilité* (effectively tenure) of judges. It seems not to have occurred to him that the "tenure" he found so regrettable was another name for the political independence of the judiciary. For Bayet it sufficed to fall back on the slogan: "For new times, a new spirit." The possibility that this rhetoric would come back to haunt him in future but very different "new times" appears to have escaped him.[13] That this was in any way a delicate issue certainly escaped many of the militants. No sooner had the Popular Front been elected than the federation of the Alpes-Maritimes began demanding "regional tribunals of Public Safety to seek out, judge and punish" right-wing civil servants. Its section in Nice went considerably further and requested permission to be able to intervene "diligently and with determination before the [Popular Front] ministers so as to ensure as soon as possible, the dismissal, relocation or punishment whenever necessary of the civil servants of the Alpes-Maritimes."[14] To his credit, Kahn was having none of this and reminded the section that "we make it a rule in the League never to call for the dismissal of a civil servant." The disappointed section found this to be "a discouraging response since we will therefore have to abandon any hope of purges."[15] At one level it is tempting to dismiss this as an isolated and aberrant example of a section that could not grasp that one of the League's functions was manifestly not to act as a secular and vengeful arm of a sympathetic government of the day. But the section of Nice was in no way atypical, and comparable demands poured in from sections in all parts of France.[16] Moreover, it was working within a political and rhetorical tradition with which virtually everyone in the League was comfortable. If its departmental federation could call for a Committee of Public Safety (here merely echoing the rhetoric of League leaders), the section in Nice can hardly be blamed for seeing itself as a surveillance committee much like the sections of 1793–94. That the sections of those years were defending the revolution (or at least their version of the revolution), rather than the rights of man as theoretically understood by the League, was a proposition that could easily have escaped the section of Nice precisely because the League's leadership rarely troubled to enlighten its members on the point. Likewise, few ever warned of the dangers of substituting Jacobin rhetoric for civil libertarian discourse. In his capacity as secretary general, Kahn knew full well that the League could hardly set up local tribunals purging conservative civil servants. As a militant Socialist, however, he peppered his writings and his letters with expressions of regret concerning the insufficiencies of the purges under the Popular Front. Local sections could be forgiven for missing the nuances.

Freedom of assembly was a comparably difficult problem. In principle, the League fully understood that merely expressing overt contempt for the democratic regime was not, in and of itself, sufficient grounds for denying movements and organizations the right to assemble peacefully. This was the stand they had always loyally, if unenthusiastically, taken with respect to French Communists. But the Popular Front government was always bedevilled by the large formations of the extreme antiparliamentary Right. One of the avowed goals of the Popular Front had been to parry the threat of domestic fascism in the form of the various antiparliamentary leagues. Upon coming to power the Popular Front government promptly outlawed these formations, but others sprung up in their place. One such was the *Parti Populaire Française* (PPF), founded in the summer of 1936 by the embittered ex-Communist Jacques Doriot. The PPF was by most criteria an authentically fascist movement, but it was also a legal political party. Upon learning that the PPF would be holding a meeting in Nice, the local section claimed that it represented a plot against the state and telegraphed Victor Basch demanding that the Ministry of the Interior obtain search warrants and use "armed force" to prevent the meeting from taking place.[17]

The largest and most dangerous of the paramilitary leagues had been the *Croix de Feu*. Dissolved by the Popular Front, it promptly transformed itself into the *Parti Social Français*. Both the League and the government believed, more or less correctly, that the PSF was but the Croix de Feu under a different name.[18] Because the government was, however, unable to prove this in the courts, the PSF was technically a perfectly legal political party and—worse—one that was growing at an exponential rate, claiming several million members by 1937. On March 16 of that year, the PSF held a private meeting in the Clichy neighborhood of Paris. Given that Clichy was a working-class and left-wing stronghold the meeting was deliberately provocative but otherwise perfectly legal. Elements of the Rassemblement Populaire nevertheless organized a counterdemonstration. This led to a violent confrontation with the police that left seven dead and some 300 wounded. Léon Blum, whose government was at this point on its last legs, appealed for calm and noted in passing that however deplorable the PSF might be, it had the same rights to assembly as any other group.

Shortly after the Clichy riots, the Central Committee debated the issue. Jules Prudhommeaux reminded his colleagues that League tradition had always insisted that freedom of assembly applied "even to our adversaries." Given that the PSF had obtained permission from the current Socialist minister of the interior to hold its meeting, he believed that the League might usefully urge its allies in the Rassemblement Populaire to behave more judiciously. Georges Pioch opted for a more pragmatic argument; all of these counterdemonstrations served little purpose save that of giving the PSF free publicity. But their colleagues were unconvinced. Albert Bayet was not impressed by the fact that the PSF meeting had been formally authorized. The critical point was that it ought *not* to have been authorized, "not because it was dangerous in itself but because it is part of a larger whole" by which he apparently meant the PSF's putative plans for overthrowing the regime. "Where," he asked, "has . . . our liberalism led us? We narrowly missed losing our freedom [which] we must now defend using all means." Emile Kahn, after insisting that "we all defend freedom of opinion," was of the belief that it was "the duty of the government" to forbid all meetings of the PSF until, and unless, the courts concluded that it was not an illegal organization. The Committee then unanimously voted a resolution proclaiming that "freedom of assembly . . . must not be confused with the freedom to organize a coup d'etat."[19] In the process the Committee casually assumed that which remained to be—and never was—proven: that the PSF was plotting a coup d'état. Whatever their secret intentions, leaders of the PSF were a good deal more circumspect than, until very recently, their counterparts among the Communists had been. Few in the League would have regarded the flagrantly subversive language of the Communists as grounds for suspending their freedom of assembly. As for Kahn's arguments, they were ones that in any other context he would have effortlessly recognized as being tantamount to demanding a selective reverse legal onus.

The strident—and unreflective—language in this debate probably owed something to the the absence of both Henri Guernut and Victor Basch. Guernut later bluntly reminded everyone that the "counter-demonstration" was, in fact, an explicit challenge to the principle of freedom of assembly. Moreover, a PSF meeting in a working-class neighborhood was no more provocative, and therefore no less legitimate, than a League meeting in a clerical region of France.[20] Basch later attempted to straddle both sides of the debate. He readily acknowledged, making allusion to Blum's declaration, that elements of the

Left ought not to have attempted to disrupt a legal and peaceful meeting. He also noted that the legitimate task of defending the regime devolved upon the government and the courts and not on "the masses." Nonetheless, he dwelt at some length on the legitimate exasperation of the working class in the face of the provocations of the extreme Right. So perhaps the left-wing demonstrators "were wrong but their error is both understandable and pardonable." "Freedom," after all, "is not without its limits and its restrictions." Moreover, the masses could be forgiven for not wanting to leave the preservation of the regime up to the government given the demonstrated failures of governments, in France but also in Germany and Italy, when it came to defending democracy.[21] In short, this tortuous stance represented the mildest possible disavowal of the Clichy demonstrators.

But it was not mild enough for local militants. The president of the section of Clichy belligerently reminded the Central Committee that he had signed the poster calling for a counterdemonstration. He had done so because he did not believe that freedom of association extended to the PSF, which he persisted in seeing as a thinly disguised paramilitary organization that the Ministry of Justice simply refused to deal with. True, Marc Rucard, a notable leaguer, currently headed the ministry, but the various reactionaries in his administration obstructed any efforts to get the party dissolved. He did not appreciate Basch's disavowal of his actions, however qualified, nor the fact that Basch had cited Blum's speech condemning the counterdemonstration. Blum, he pointedly reminded Basch, was the premier, and his speech was a political one designed to calm national sentiments. Basch, by contrast, was not premier but head of the League and therefore ought to have adopted a very different stance.[22] Basch's dilemma was not eased by the fact that at about the same time deputies of the extreme Right proposed a bill in parliament calling for a ban on counterdemonstrations and explicitly evoked the Declaration of the Rights of Man.

The wave of factory occupations by sit-in strikers that accompanied the electoral victory of the Popular Front also posed problems for the League because the occupations were technically illegal.[23] In the euphoric climate of June 1936, no one in the League had been unduly troubled. By 1938, an increasingly embittered Henri Guernut reminded his colleagues that "the League accepted without protest the occupations of the factories which, however, were contrary to the letter and the spirit of the law." In fact, Basch had acknowledged the illegality of the factory occupations but had not found them to be a "serious" violation of the law because they were legitimated by everything the working class had suffered for so long.[24]

This was conventional Socialist rhetoric, not calculated to shock many members of the Central Committee. But if the historic suffering of the working class could trump certain principles, why not others? This was not entirely an abstract issue because the central headquarters soon faced a case of a strike in Toulouse where some of the striking workers had shouted anti-Semitic slogans, notably "Down with the Jewish bosses." The president of the League's section in Toulouse noted that the strike was the result of "an attitude of the employers which is intransigent and at times even revolting." He conceded that the anti-Semitic slogans were "in themselves regrettable" but the circumstances of the strike provided "a more than sufficient excuse." The Executive was properly aghast that a spokesman for the League could excuse such behavior, noting that no matter how "legitimate" the workers grievances were, "making a distinction as to the origins or race of the employers, is to submit to an anti-Semitism condemned by the very traditions of the working class."[25] This was a noble, if somewhat laundered, reading of the history of the working class and anti-Semitism. But, while excusing manifestations of anti-Semitism among the long-suffering working class was certainly more odious than excusing illegal factory occupations, what precisely was the principle that permitted such distinctions?

Among the people who did not grasp the distinction was the president of the section of Toulouse. He was utterly livid at the reproach implicit in the Executive's discussion of the events. His section, he belligerently informed Kahn, would have been prepared to intervene in the affair had both sides been equally wrong. But all of his evidence suggested that the factory owners were the most to blame and this "from the very fact of being Jewish." Jews, he noted, were currently being persecuted by the Right just about everywhere in the world. That France was a unique exception owed everything to the work of the left-wing political parties, including the one currently in power. Yet these same Jews (by which he apparently meant the Jewish bosses) opposed the social legislation of a progressive government and in the process allied themselves with the most openly fascist and clerical forces in France. By virtue of that fact they were "not worthy of being either Jewish or French." It was simply perverse for the League headquarters to confound "refusal to excuse the bad conduct of evil people" with some kind of "complicity with so-called anti-Jewish actions which amounted to next to nothing." He was prepared to let the matter die there but only (and somewhat inconsistently) if the League headquarters agreed to publish a statement to the effect that, because both sides were wrong, there was no reason for the local League to intervene. Failing that he promised to go public with the additional facts he possessed about the conduct of the Jewish bosses which "would do far more harm to Jews, who do not merit it, than a couple of lines in a poster ever did."[26]

The most serious difficulties, however, came over foreign policy. The most pressing issue was that of Spain. On July 18, 1936, the renegade General Francisco Franco attempted a military coup d'état against the democratically elected government of Spain. The coup was only partially successful, leaving Franco in command of about half of Spain and the Republican government in control of the rest. Within days Spain was embroiled in a savage civil war. Because the regular army had largely rallied to Franco, the Republicans were desperately in need of arms. Owing to a commercial treaty with France dating from 1935, for the first ten days the Spanish government was able to purchase war material from her neighbor. At that point Blum and his foreign minister, Yvon Delbos, cut off all further shipments and closed the borders with Spain. At the same time, they persuaded the major powers of Europe to sign a nonintervention pact to ensure that no one would materially aid either side in the civil war. It was an agonizing decision for Blum, although he really had no choice. The intervention of other powers in Spain risked spreading the war to Europe as a whole. Given the polarized climate in France in the summer of 1936, French involvement might lead to civil war at home. And the British government, upon whom France was increasingly dependent, had made it clear that by continuing active support for the Republican cause, France risked diplomatic isolation.

Blum's decision threw both the French Left and the League into disarray. The problem was particularly acute for the League because this was very much *its* government; both Blum and Delbos, after all, had served on the Central Committee. But for the majority, appreciative though it was of Blum's good faith, this was a troubling course of action. The Spanish Republican government was also a Popular Front government, similar in political composition to its counterpart in France. Franco, in its view, was a fascist. Nonintervention implied a degree of moral neutrality there where none could be allowed. Worse, within weeks it became apparent that only Britain and France were seriously abiding by the nonintervention agreement, whereas both Nazi Germany and Fascist Italy were covertly subverting it, sending both war material and troops, disguised implausibly as "volunteers." By October, having seen through the subterfuge, the Soviet Union withdrew from the pact and began direct aid to Spain.

For some months the majority limited itself to veiled criticisms of the government, indignation over German and Italian violation of the nonintervention pact and organization of relief efforts for Spanish refugees. By April 1937, however, Basch had had enough. For too long, he declared "we have stifled our protests because of what was perhaps an excessive degree of loyalty towards a head of government whose action we otherwise approve." Had the frontiers remained open in July, Basch asserted, Franco would long ago have been crushed. Without quite insisting that Blum reverse his decision, Basch demanded a more rigorous surveillance of the nonintervention pact, the immediate withdrawal of all volunteers, and the direct intervention of the League of Nations. This was clearly a case of aggression under Articles 10 and 11 of the League of Nations charter; for those who believed (correctly) that those articles did not apply to civil war, Basch responded that this was a war "sought, prepared and financed by foreign powers." In the (likely) event that such measures prove fruitless, Basch implied that France might well follow the Soviet example and withdraw from the nonintervention pact.[27]

Members of the minority were outraged by language of this kind. The war in Spain, like all wars on the European periphery, threatened to drag the rest of the continent into a terrible conflagration, just as they had in 1914. This was, therefore, manifestly not the moment for partisan cheerleading for one side in the conflict, however sympathetic it might be. League doctrine, if it were to mean anything at all, was quite clear. It was the duty of leaguers to prevent the war from spreading and, if possible, bring it to an end. Had not the League spent twenty years denouncing *bourrage de crane,* the spreading of tendentious rumors designed to stir up war fever? Yet here was the Communist press spreading every tale imaginable about the German role in the Spanish war, including such implausible stories as the alleged disembarkment of German troops in Spanish Morocco. But it seemed not to have occurred to the League leadership to denounce such stories for what they were: transparent attempts to instill anti-German sentiments into the French population.

No one disputed that the war had begun as a military coup. But it soon became a civil war and, discarding a distinction that scant years before had seemed precious, the minority now argued that civil war or no, war was war. The appropriate League response to war, therefore, was not to lobby for conditions that might ensure the victory of one side. Rather, it was to ensure that the war came to an end. Instead of sniping at Blum and harping on the failures of nonintervention, the League ought to have pounced on one of Blum's more useful suggestions: mediation. Surely this was the moment for the League of Nations, in association with Germany, to intervene and persuade both sides to agree to a cease fire and an armistice. It could then organize, on both sides, a plebiscite to determine the future political situation in Spain. In essence this was a new version of a similar arbitration argument made by the minority in 1916. But would this not be tantamount to rewarding the actions of the aggressor, the more so, as the majority would note, in Spain in 1936, unlike World War I, there could not be the slightest doubt as to who the aggressor was? Spokesmen for the minority conceded the point but not its relevance. At best Spain would have to live with a highly decentralized government, and one in which many of its citizens would not feel comfortable. But what were the choices? It was naive to believe that a few arms shipments from France—almost certain to be matched by the fascist powers—would bring Franco to his knees. Franco was comfortably in control of a majority of Spanish territory, and there was no reason to believe that he could easily be dislodged. Both sides were relatively evenly matched; neither side displayed much military brilliance. This was a recipe for a protracted slogging match with utterly predictable consequences. At best the innocent people of Spain would be subject to the unspeakable brutalities of war for years to come; at worst this war would engulf the rest of Europe. There was nothing the League or anyone else could do to reverse what had happened on July 18, 1936. But there was everything they could do to "limit its consequences."[28]

The dispute over Spain was part of a larger debate about the perceived bellicosity of the Popular Front and the majority within the League. The Blum government, its faults notwithstanding, had been, "an amazing bit of luck," a government that clearly desired peace, had made some tentative steps in that direction, and deserved the League's support. Yet all that the majority on the Central Committee seemed capable of delivering were partisan shots from the flank, and this despite the clear desire for peace expressed at the 1936 congress. In order that the issue no longer be equivocated upon, the minority proposed that the agenda of the 1937 congress should concentrate on "peace between the democracies and the fascist states by economic collaboration and disarmament, the necessary preconditions for collective security."[29]

What distressed the minority most was the fact that the apparent capitulation of the League to the forces of war was not, as in the past, the work of the moderates. What seemed to be pushing both the League and the government in a bellicose direction was the insidious influence of the Communists, or at least a desire to keep the Communists in the Popular Front. Having been, until recently, that wing of the League most receptive to the Communists, it required some mental gymnastics for members of the minority now to accuse the leadership of complicity with Moscow. But in 1936 the minority was presented with the perfect issue for an oblique attack on the majority: civil liberties within the Soviet Union, an issue that until recently had preoccupied only the majority.

In 1936 a number of Old Bolsheviks—some of them, like Zinoviev and Bukharin, central architects of the Soviet State in the 1920s—were brought to trial on charges of conspiracy to destroy the Soviet Union. The trials were public, the Western press well represented, and the defendants—all of whom confessed, sometimes in lurid detail—found guilty and executed. Although much of the reporting on the trial in the West was highly uncritical, there was enough uneasiness as to immediately involve the League.

Victor Basch's initial reaction to the results of the first trial was one of "poignant distress." The trial, something right out of Dostoevsky, was replete with irregularities—no defense counsel, no defense witnesses, and inadequate documentation. Basch expressed nothing but "contempt" for "old plotters" like Zinoviev and Kamenev, but conceded that their alleged crimes were utterly implausible. What, he wondered, could the leaders of the Soviet regime be thinking? Just when they most needed the help of the West they seemed to be engaging in practices most likely to turn Western opinion against the Soviet Union. "Any blow to Soviet Russia would appear to us to be the most severe blow to the future of social democracy and we can not help but protest the executions in Moscow." It is very clear from the context that Basch meant that the obvious immoral conduct by the Soviet Union would strengthen the reactionary forces in the West and weaken the cause of democracy.[30] When he proposed a resolution along these lines to the executive committee, its members rejected it on the grounds that "it might create serious rifts with the Popular [Front]."[31] An uncharacteristically accommodating Basch accepted the ruling and settled for the creation of a commission of investigation. In November the commission issued a preliminary report, the work of one of its technical juridical consultants, Marc Rosenmark, a highly distinguished, left-wing but non-Communist Parisian lawyer.

From the outset Rosenmark acknowledged troubling aspects about the trial. Civilian defendants were tried by a military court, no defense counsel was present, and the prosecution called no witnesses. The violent and abusive language of the prosecutor was utterly inappropriate for an officer of the court. The critical issue, however, was the confessions. All sixteen defendants had confessed in open court. There were some inconsistencies in their confessions, which Rosenmark attributed to lapses in memory or slips of the tongue. It was possible that coercion had been exercised before the trial began, but the trial itself was public and open to the foreign press. The defendants had no motive for lying as it was clear that no possibility existed of mitigating the inevitable death sentence if they were found guilty. In short, messy though the trials had been from a rigorous juridical perspective, it seemed unlikely to Rosenmark that innocent men had been convicted.

Most of Rosenmark's report had a detached and analytical quality. His conclusion did not. He wrote:

> It is permitted to think that there are times when a revolution can only be saved by extreme measures and that one should not, at certain times, abandon recourse to exceptional measures. The right to self defence exists for individuals and, *a fortiori*, it exists for nations. To refuse a people the right to deal severely with those who make civil war and with conspirators linked to foreign powers, would be to deny [the historical experience of] the French Revolution.

Granted, most of the time "scrupulous respect for principles and exclusive recourse to civil courts" was an ideal to be cherished. Nonetheless "in times of crisis, of international or external danger, in the presence of terrorist activities, not only should one not blame but one should praise all peoples and regimes that have the courage to establish, if they need to, revolutionary tribunals."[32] This was good Jacobin rhetoric, but it was singularly out of place in a dispassionate assessment of trials. Not only did Rosenmark blissfully take at face value the charges of the Soviet authorities, but he used the classic language of raison d'état more appropriate for an anti-Dreyfusard than for a member of the League.

Selective invocation of the French revolutionary tradition had, of course, always been something of a cottage industry in the League, and others were quick to emulate Rosenmark's rhetorical extravagances. Emile Guerry, a member of the Central Committee, regretted, "platonically" the death sentences. But, he insisted,

> We must carefully restrain ourselves from overtly, or even indirectly, attacking the leaders of the Soviet democracy. Even if their justice was summary, they are entitled to a good deal of understanding from the sons of the French revolution which was, at times and with good reason, a bit quick to judge and somewhat heavy of hand. Let us not forget that a regime that does not defend itself does not deserve to survive.

He urged his fellow members on the Central Committee to understand that "revolutionary periods do not lend themselves to abstract absolutes and that for good or for bad one must be content with relative justice." Rather than passing hasty judgment on "the current leaders of our friendly ally Russia," the League should observe a "cautious reserve and an honest discretion."[33] Nor did the passage of time alter his sentiments. Two years later Guerry thought it appropriate to "recall the multiple executions which took place in France during the Revolution and the threat of a European coalition." He did not see how what the Soviets were allegedly doing was much different and concluded that "there is no reason to concern ourselves with it further."[34]

Not everyone on the Central Committee saw the issue in quite this light. Magdeline Paz had for years contributed articles to the *Cahiers* exposing injustices in various parts of the world: the Sacco and Vanzettti case, the trial of Tom Mooney, and the Kentucky coal wars had been favorite topics. But Paz was closely associated with exiled and dissident Communists like Victor Serge and Boris Souvarine, and she now chose to turn her eyes to Soviet justice. She penned an article assailing the Rosenmark report. It had been written as if the sixteen Moscow defendants had been tried in a Parisian court. The current trials were part of a long series of similar political trials going back to the previous decade. Common to them all were implausible confessions. As early as 1929 former Bolsheviks had confessed to crimes they could not possibly have committed—such as planning a military assault on the Soviet Union under the auspices of the Socialist International! The confessions of Zinoviev et al. were no more plausible, not least because what had struck Rosenmark as minor inconsistencies were in fact major contradictions. The accused had confessed to being places they could not have been and to having met people they could not have met. One of the accused, Goltzman, for example, had confessed to meeting Trotsky's son in the Bristol Hotel in Copenhagen in 1922. Yet the Bristol Hotel had been demolished in 1917! Still, there *was* a Bristol Café. A slip of the tongue, as Rosenmark would have it? Or, as Félicien Challaye would later suggest, the perils of relying on an outdated Baedecker? Piatakov, another defendant, claimed to have flown from Berlin to Oslo in December of 1935 to meet Trotsky. Yet Norwegian authorities confirmed that owing to atmospheric conditions, there had been no international flights into Oslo between the fall of 1935 and the spring of 1936. Others confessed to meeting Trotsky in Paris at times when he was under effective house arrest some distance from the capital. In fact, whenever the alleged conspiratorial activities of the accused took place where they could be verified—outside of the Soviet Union—the charges were transparently false. In short, nothing about the trials ought to have prompted anyone to be sanguine, and a rigorous investigation was obligatory. Her article was passionate, although no more so than others that regularly appeared in the *Cahiers*. Nonetheless, its editor, Emile Kahn, adamantly refused to publish it, and it ultimately appeared in *La Flèche*, the newspaper of a League dissident, Gaston Bergery.[35]

The Rosenmark report, the nonpublication of Paz's rebuttal, and the *Cahiers'* habit of placing news of the Moscow trials under rubrics like: "The Trial of the Trotsky-Zinoviev terrorist centre" outraged members of the minority. Emery reminded everyone that it would be "impossible for the League to remain silent without denying its very ideals." "Naturally, it is not a question of accusing anyone but simply of demanding and obtaining light on the matter." Elie Reynier, president of the federation of the Ardèche was less concerned to avoid accusations, noting that "it is no longer possible to be charitable [*ménager*] with a pseudo-revolution which leads to such crimes."[36] But he also made the point that, having read the Rosenmark report "with a surprise bordering on stupefaction," he had urged Paz to write her rebuttal never dreaming that the *Cahiers,* for which she had so often written, would refuse to publish it.[37] Surely, the minority argued, it went against League tradition to permit only one point of view to appear in its house organ. To be sure, the minority had a long history of griping about not getting enough space in the *Cahiers* but on this issue it was clearly right—it was a major departure from League practices. The best Kahn could muster by way of reply was the lame observation that "a polemical article directed against M. Rosenmark's report would certainly have provoked attacks [*repostes*]."[38]

Although the pages of the *Cahiers* were now closed to them, the minority mounted a spirited campaign in the opposition press against the trials and against the League's majority.[39] With respect to the trials themselves, little was added that had not been said by Paz. But members of the minority made a convincing case that the bulk of the League's leaders simply did not want to find the truth about the Moscow trials lest it weaken the Popular Front and the antifascist alliance with the Soviet Union. George Pioch summed up their case when he declared: "It must not be possible for people one day to say that the great moral force in France refused, allegedly so as not to disrupt the Popular Front, to intervene in an issue which is the Dreyfus Affair a hundred times over."[40]

Did members of the majority in the League really believe in the guilt of the convicted Bolsheviks? Or was it, as the minority charged, a particularly cynical example of "raison d'état"? There is no way of knowing for sure. Certainly many men of goodwill took the Moscow trials at face value at the time. And it must have been galling to receive lessons on the question of civil liberties in the Soviet Union from the likes of Challaye who only recently, they would remember, had declared such questions off limits for the League. At best, Emile Kahn argued, these were the classic reflexes of "jilted lovers," turning violently against a regime they had once so uncritically embraced. But this kind of argument could as easily be turned against the majority, which as Georges Michon would note, "after having displayed an odious severity towards the Russian revolution in its heroic phase, demonstrates today a singular indulgence for a degenerating regime and a party which shows itself in various ways to be fascist."[41]

There was, in fact, a distinctly false note to many of the statements of League leaders on the Moscow trials. Henri Guernut was a good example. No one could accuse Guernut of special tenderness for the Communists; nor was he anything but the very model of juridical rigor. When confronted by the trials, he confessed to having been "profoundly troubled." But a close reading of the transcripts and the fact of confessions in open court suggested to him that the accused were in fact guilty. Of the inconsistencies in their testimony, he said nothing. But there was a time when Guernut, legendary for his gimlet eye for the details, would have pounced on those facts. The death penalty, he admitted, was harsh but then these were, after all, serious crimes. "[T]hey lent a hand to the murder of a people's commissioner [and] plotted and prepared several attempts on Stalin's life." But an earlier Guernut would have acknowledged that it was precisely those charges that were very much in dispute.[42] Similarly, three years earlier, Emile Kahn had permitted André Berthet to publish an outrageous defense of Hitler's Germany in the *Cahiers,* confident that he could effortlessly refute it. Presumably he was less confident about Paz's contribution. As late as January 1938, Kahn was still informing puzzled militants that while the League had certainly protested the form of the trials it "reserved any judgment as to substance" because "the truth was and remains too obscure." It seemed to him, however, that whatever might have been the ambiguities surrounding the first trial, the second trial "established in definitive fashion the guilt of the accused." This being the case, there were reasons for being skeptical about the charges of bias directed against the judges in the first trial. Of course there were those inclined to believe anything that came out of Moscow, just as there were fascists and Trotskyites who "*a priori* suspect and attempt to discredit anything that comes from a regime they detest." He did admit that it would be hard not to believe that the recent convictions of administrators and academics were inspired by "a desire for political reprisals." As for the Paz report, it was "a personal polemic" of the kind "our adversaries pounce on" in an attempt to "harm both the League's reputation and its efforts at recruitment."[43] Assuming that Kahn believed any of what he said about the substance of the trials, there are still disturbing elements in this response. One did not have to be either a Trotskyite or a fascist to detest the current regime in the Soviet Union. "Political reprisals" was not a phrase he would have used to describe the persecution of German Jews. Not only did the League routinely publish internal quarrels but it took some pride in doing so as a "glass house." It had never been a secret that the political Right had long poured over the pages of the *Cahiers* in search of embarrassing revelations. Suppressing things that might hurt the League"s image or its recruitment was a very sudden innovation. In 1938, when the League was still (albeit very half-heartedly) investigating the issue, Kahn was at some pains to insist that he in no way disputed the Soviet Union's right to dismiss civil servants and diplomats who did not agree with the government's policy. "It is," he noted, "most regrettable that the France of the Popular Front did not do the same; the cause of peace would have been better for it."[44] Can he have really meant this? Quite apart from the fact that the League had traditionally (or at least when left-wing governments were not in power) opposed the dismissal of civil servants for purely political reasons, he appears to have forgotten that the Soviet civil servants had not been "dismissed"; they had been executed. Of course Kahn was not calling for Stalinist style purges in France. But, and it is astounding enough, he was comparing the judicial murder of Old Bolsheviks to the dismissal of a prefect.

Even Victor Basch, having, as usual, gotten it right the first time in September 1936, chose, in a significant departure from custom, not to pursue the issue with his usual tenacity. He later argued that neither he nor the League had the time or the resources necessary for the very thorough investigation a case of this complexity would require.[45] There was something to this; the League had many issues before it in 1937. But it is an odd excuse coming from the leader of a League that in 1920 had convoked no fewer that 80 witnesses in an exhaustive inquiry into democratic abuses in the same Soviet Union.

As the anti-Bolshevik socialist William Drabovitch would note, all of this was a far cry from Ferdinand Buisson's classic line to the effect that the League existed "in order to meddle in things that did not concern it." There was, he argued something pathetic about the deferential letters the League periodically submitted to the Soviet embassy. They were not, by contrast, in the habit of writing the German or Italian embassies to inquire whether there was any truth to the rumors about recent and regrettable legislation. The quirky legalism surrounding the Moscow trial was simply bizarre. "What would Leaguers say," he asked, "were there a debate on the Reichstag Fire (where there were *also* 'confessions') and one relied only on the declarations of Goebbels, the

Hitlerian prosecutor and the newspaper [*Der*] *Angriff*?"[46] It is also significant that when a third round of trials were announced in 1938, Georges Gombault quietly acknowledged their speciousness, using very much the arguments
presented the previous year by the minority. These were the views of a high
profile member of the Central Committee, but they were expressed in small
print in the back pages of *La Lumière*.[47] It is hard not to believe that it represented a quiet mea culpa.

The battle between the minority and the majority over the Moscow trials,
Spain, and the orientation of French foreign policy climaxed at the 1937 Congress in Tours. After a prolonged and vituperative debate, the majority prevailed by a vote of 1,088 to 258 with 54 abstentions. The outcome was a
crushing blow for the minority. For the first time in years they had failed to obtain at least a significant minority of the votes. All sides agreed that the thun-
derous applause that traditionally greeted speakers like Emery, Challaye,
Château, and Alexandre was notably missing in 1937. What had gone wrong,
Emery bitterly asked? Why had the same speeches, making the same points,
made by the same people, fallen on deaf ears? His own explanation was that
the militants had become weary and resigned, a trait he believed to be endemic
in any "traditional democracy" where the enthusiasm of the rank and file soon
became victim of the conformism of the leaders.[48] But there were other, and
more compelling, explanations for the defeat of the minority.

In the first place, their ranks were thinner than in previous years. Jean-
Marie Caillaud and André Lesseurre of the federation of the Seine, Gabriel
Cudenet of the Seine-et-Oise, as well as Paul Rivet and Paul Langevin, previously such ardent supporters, were curiously silent in 1937, having quietly rallied to the side of the majority.[49] Cudenet, previously such an ardent pacifist,
was declaring by July 1937 that "the hour has come . . . to affirm the Jacobin
tradition for which defence is its raison d'être"; this was manifestly not the
time to "bow our heads" before Hitler.[50] Although it was perfectly true that
the message of the minority was substantially what it had been in the past, the
circumstances in 1937 conspired to give it a strangely alien hue. In the past, the
minority had always been able to capitalize on the shortcomings of the government of the day—more often than not a conservative one—and the Central
Committee's complicity with it—or at any rate the insufficiency of its protests.
But in 1937 the government in power for the last year had not been that of
Painlevé or Herriot but that of Léon Blum, a government, if ever there was
one, that could be described as the League in power. One could, of course,
and the minority most assuredly did, draw attention to this government's

weaknesses and failures. The undeniable fact remained, however, that this had been, by any standard, the most progressive government in French history.

For most of its history, the minority had been able to tap the emotional wellsprings of a significant number of militants, whether it be over Painlevé and colonial wars, or Herriot and sanctioned slaughterhouse workers. But that year's cause was Spain, and no matter how reasonable the minority's position—and no matter how consistent it was with League principles—it was a certain loser against the mostly platonic resolutions in favor of Republican Spain. Similarly, the minority's stance in favor of the Old Bolsheviks was unimpeachable in terms of League traditions. But in the past it had been the minority that reproached the Central Committee its scruples about the Soviet Union, appealing to the sentiment of more than one delegate for whom such scruples seemed like "bourgeois legalism." Nothing much had changed in that respect in 1937 except that the minority found itself on the other side— a side to which it was not accustomed.

Still there was the cause of peace, about which the minority had not wavered in 20 years. Until recently the cause of peace had been entirely congruent with that other cause so cherished by the League, the struggle against the Right. The fight for peace and against capitalism and clericalism had been the same struggle throughout most of the League's history. By 1937, however—and indeed since the middle of 1935—this had ceased to be the case. The Right, be it capitalist or clerical, acutely alert to changing domestic circumstances in France and all too aware of the potentially revolutionary consequences of a war led by a France with a powerful Communist movement, had quietly abandoned its traditional anti-German reflexes. Albeit for very different reasons, significant segments of the French Right adopted positions that were rather closer to those held by the minority than those held by the majority.[51] It suited the purposes of the pacifist Left to concentrate on people like Henri de Kerillis, right-wing deputy from Neuilly and regular columnist for the militarist *Echo de Paris,* who faithfully persisted in the Germanophic traditions of an earlier Right. But it was no secret that Kerillis was very much an exception on the Right. There were, of course, elements within the Popular Front who shared the pacifist reflexes of the minority—Emile Roche, Anatole de Monzie, and above all Georges Bonnet. But they were right-wing Radicals dedicated to watering down or eliminating the social and economic planks of the Popular Front platform. Without admitting that the struggle for peace and the struggle for social and economic reform were henceforth separate—something few in the minority would have been prepared to concede—the pacifists were caught in a logical dilemma that could only benefit the majority on the Central Committee.

It was a certain sign of their defeat that seven members of the minority promptly resigned from the Central Committee (although not, initially at least, from the League): Challaye, Bergery, Emery, Michon, Paz, Pioch, and Reynier.[52] The resignations shocked the League. Emile Kahn went so far as to ask Georges Pioch, his persistent antagonist, to rejoin the Committee. Pioch refused but continued to attend League congresses.[53] At the meeting of the Central Committee of October 10, 1937, Basch, not altogether convincingly, expressed regret at the departure of Challaye. He had after all been a colleague, albeit a troublesome one, for thirty years and had taken some courageous positions, most notably with respect to the colonial question. His trouble was that he was the most extreme member of the Committee, given to making personal attacks and being consistently and invariably wrong about Germany. Worse, he had a tendency to push League principals "to utopian extremes." Other members of the majority, Bayet, Guernut, Barthelemy, and Joint, agreed. Remaining members of the minority reminded everyone that had Kahn simply published the Paz report and had he not appeared to have rigged the most recent congress, the resignations could have been avoided.[54] A source of some dismay to all sides was the obvious satisfaction the discord in the League was giving to the Right. For the more belligerent members of the majority, notably Collette and Gombault, this was proof that the dissident members were playing the game of reaction; others, notably Casati and Château, disputed this conclusion. Yes, permitting their dissent to make the pages of right-wing newspapers like *Le Matin* was regrettable but no more so than the excoriating criticism of any dissent coming from people like Bayet. More internal democracy, and more distance from the Popular Front and above all the Communists, might avoid a repetition of this regrettable incident.[55]

Once again, at the heart of the dispute was the question of politics and its role in, and impact upon, the League. The old veteran Jacques Hadamard cut to the heart of the matter when he reminded everyone that this was really a dispute about the conduct of French foreign policy. But the proper goal of the League was the defense of the rights of man. The question of peace, although important, "was at best only indirectly linked to the proper goals of the League, if not more or less marginal to it."[56] It was, not surprisingly, the former secretary general, Guernut, who most squarely addressed the issue. There was a moral crisis in the League, he observed, "because some of our colleagues believe that the League is too political."[57] Both men were correct, although these were belated revelations.

Early in December 1937, Guernut called a special meeting of the Central Committee to discuss the League's relations with the Popular Front. He still believed, as he had three years earlier, that joining the Popular Front had contravened Article 15 of the League's statutes. Although stopping short of advocating a formal withdrawal from the Popular Front or limiting itself exclusively to juridical matters, he insisted that the League must strive for a greater degree of critical detachment and try harder to avoid becoming enmeshed in party politics. The *Rapport Moral* at the congress of Tours, he could not help but notice, certainly sounded like a triumphal report on Léon Blum's first government. The banquet of the congress was presided over by Blum, surrounded by all kinds of serving ministers. Blum felt it appropriate to inform the assembled members of a notionally apolitical League about the recent congress of the Socialist party and its reasons for supporting the successor Chautemps government. Significantly, and regrettably, the banquet ended with a rousing chorus of the *Internationale*. None of this suggested any real political independence. Blum and his associates were members of the League, to be sure, but Painlevé and Herriot had been as well, and the League had notoriously never hesitated to condemn their shortcomings.[58] In all of this there was more than a little of the rancor of a former Radical deputy who in 1936 had lost a close and nasty election to the Socialists, something which, to judge by the atypically caustic allusions to ulterior motives, did not escape some of his colleagues.[59] Moreover, he neglected to mention that the League's leadership had been, in fact, extremely reluctant to criticize either Herriot or Painlevé. Nonetheless he had a point. As Ferdinand Corcos acknowledged, this was part of the debate about political as opposed to juridical roles that dated back to the League's foundations. He also noted that at the time of the right-wing threats at the turn of the twentieth century, the League had involved itself in republican demonstrations "without aligning itself on a permanent basis to political organizations" and reserving itself the right "to retreat into its tent." Perhaps the time had come to do this again.

This was not an argument that carried any weight with Basch, Kahn, Gombault, or Grumbach, all of whom subjected Guernut to unusually harsh attacks. Gombault countered Guernut's appeal to principle with an appeal to precedent. At the time of the Affaire des Fiches, he correctly recalled, the League had chosen not to attack "a government against which the forces of reaction had been unleashed." Had Guernut somehow forgotten, Basch belligerently asked, the night of February 6, 1934? As for the ministers who presided over the congress banquet, had they not been leaguers long before they became ministers? (This was true enough but hardly an argument that met Guernut's objections.) What was at issue was not whether the League should be involved in politics, but rather, which politics it should be involved in.

If Hadamard was correct in arguing that the conduct of French foreign policy was not really the business of the League, it made little impact on his colleagues. If anything, by 1938 they were more obsessed than ever with foreign policy, although the emphasis had shifted. By the time of the Czech crisis of September 1938, the cause of peace had lost much of its force within the League. Fairly typical was the declaration of Georges Bourdon as the Munich crisis reached the boiling point.

> Perhaps the [League] was wrong to say too loudly and to repeat too often that it wanted peace. Peace alone is not a goal or even an ideal. The ideal is justice, honor and fraternity. We ought to have said this earlier but we did not. We must say it today. The sadness of our fathers after the defeat of 1871 must have been great but they at least did not have themselves to blame. We cannot say as much.[60]

Prudhommeaux attempted, amid *vive protestations,* to congratulate the Western democracies for trying to solve the ethnic problems of Czechoslovakia. Trying to maintain "the territorial integrity" of Czechoslovakia would be a hopeless task, likely to result in a Spanish-style civil war. A treaty signed with the Czech government in 1926, without the French people having been directly consulted, was a poor excuse for war. "If the Sudeten [Germans] are stupid enough to want to be Germans and to march with a goose step," it was, after all, their business.[61] Few chose to support him. The Central Committee issued a strong condemnation of the Munich accords, and the next few issues of the *Cahiers* were filled with articulate condemnation of the settlement. The agreement was condemned as a betrayal of Czech democracy, a crass capitulation before the forces of fascism, an insult to French national honor, and a grave threat to French national security. There were those within the League who wondered if the Central Committee had not overstepped its mandate by publishing a pro-Czech manifesto during the Munich crisis. This was by now such an old issue that the majority had little trouble proving that this activity was entirely consistent with its statutes, as was a brochure denouncing the conservative deputy, Pierre-Etienne Flandin, for sending a telegram of congratulation to Hitler. Ought it not, in the interests of fairness, have published the report of Lord Runciman that recommended giving most of the Sudetenland to Germany? No, the Central Committee assured everyone. Runciman was a Germanophile, his report was biased and incoherent, and his conclusions did not follow from his evidence.[62] On this point it was in fact entirely correct, although this left unexplained why individual leaguers ought not to have been allowed to judge the document for themselves.

The Central Committee's stand on Munich prompted sharp reactions from the more pacifist sections, notably those in the Rhône and the Ardèche. The federation of the Rhône had been in open revolt since at least 1934. In March 1938, the vice president of the departmental federation announced that the League had become merely "an association in the service of French chauvinism and imperialism."[63] In the wake of the Central Committee's strongly anti-Munichois stance, the Rhône federation held an emergency congress in December at which Emery and League delegate Bayet slugged out their by now entirely predictable differences concerning the Munich agreement. Bayet failed to convince anyone, and the federation decided to give the Central Committee until February of the following year to reverse its stand on foreign policy. Utterly predictably, this did not happen. By March 1939, most of the sections as well as most of the leadership of the Federation decided to go their separate ways. As Emery noted, "there is no longer anything useful to do in the League and we have grown tired of discussing the subject." All that remained was for the various sections that decided to "go autonomous" to choose a new name. Emery suggested either the Pacifist League of the Rights of Man or the François de Pressensé Group.[64] In the last months of the Republic, League headquarters, with the help of André Philip, was still trying to reconstruct its organization in the Rhône.

The reaction of the federation of the Ardèche was even sharper. On October 14, 1938, Elie Reynier and the rest of the executive of the federation sent a brief and abrupt note to Basch announcing that "It is no longer possible to collaborate . . . with a League whose Central Committee is ready to begin yet again, and lightly, the crime of 1914" and they were therefore resigning from the League. In fact, this was a rather more moderate letter than Reynier and some of his colleagues had wanted to send. The original accused the Central Committee of being "linked . . . with the Stalinist warmongers," citing notably Julien Racamond, the token Communist on the Central Committee. Moreover, the Central Committee's stand had led to a recrudescence of anti-Semitism in the land (which the now ex-members would "resist") but that was understandable in light of "the role of Basch, Kahn, Grumbach, Gombault, Kayser, with ministers like Mandel and Zay and Socialists like Blum, Moch, [and] Zyromski ."[65] In about half of the sections in the department, the executive followed Reynier in resigning from the League. Elsewhere the Central Committee's anti-Munichois stance provoked isolated acts of protest, but by and large most sections of the League seemed to have agreed with the position of the leadership.[66]

Dissident notes were still allowed to appear in the *Cahiers*. René Château, the left-wing Radical deputy from the Charente-Maritime and the head of the large departmental federation, pleaded that the Munich accords were "the best solution to the worst dangers." The source of the recent crisis went back to the fundamentally flawed postwar settlement. Given that the Left in general and the League in particular had always criticized that settlement, why, he wondered, were those like himself who consistently still did so, attacked as traitors? There was no reason why France could not do business with Hitler, just as it had done with Mussolini. Nor was there any reason why Hitler, like Mussolini, would not mellow with time; he had, after all, been a very bitter young man when he wrote *Mein Kampf.* A necessary condition for preserving the peace was more, not fewer, negotiations with Hitler, dealing with the redistribution of colonies and natural resources.[67] René Gérin, another pacifist on the Central Committee, made an eloquent case for a "more realistic" approach to dealing with Germany. The French masses had learned by now that "national honor", whatever that might mean, was not worth squandering human lives. All of the currently fashionable slogans about "humiliation" and "shame" were but deceptive rhetoric. "There is no shame," he insisted, "in belonging to a second rate, or twentieth rate, military power." This was no longer Richelieu's Europe, and the ideas of the seventeenth century had run their course. At another level, realism dictated that one realize that there were eighty million Germans and only forty million French. True, France had the colonial Empire and her British ally. But how could members of the League justify involving involuntarily colonized peoples in "a European dust-up"? The notion that Britain had French interests at heart was appealing only to those ignorant of recent history. As things stood, France was but a glorified colony of Great Britain and was it not "as humiliating to see England make and unmake our ministers as to see the Germans involve themselves in French domestic politics"?

As for Hitler, he did not really seem to be a madman. To this point he had limited himself to undoing the perfectly unjust postwar treaties, and he had been "very cautious and methodical in his foreign policy." Heretofore he had restricted his ambitions to German-speaking peoples, and he was unlikely to extend his domination to non-Germans if only because "his own racism forbids it." He might well seek to draw the Czechs, Hungarians, Poles, and Ukrainians into his economic orbit but "if he wished to conquer and govern them, this would be impossible." Even if Hitler did become, as the majority insisted he already had, "crazy," he was unlikely to be able to bring the German people with him. Nor did refusing war mean that the pacifists would be so cowardly as to "accept the oppression of an invader." Were this to happen, one could count on the working class to rise up against their class enemies, in marked contrast "to the conservatives, more disposed than proletarians to ally with an invader who, on social questions, thinks the way they do." The struggle against fascism was as valid as ever, but there were two kinds of antifascism. There was "antifascism for internal use against the Maurras's, the Doriots, the La Rocques, the Flandins and others." And although it was true that they had also worked against war in September 1938, "it was for different reasons than ours." War against external fascism, against Hitler and Mussolini, was just another name for the discredited union sacrée. He was not quite right about the likely reaction of pacifists to "the oppression of an invader," as his own history of collaboration under Vichy would demonstrate. But he was not wrong either in his assessment of the likely reaction of much, if not all, of the French Right to the same German oppressors. All in all it was a carefully argued brief. [68]

But briefs of this kind carried little weight in the League by 1938. The momentum had been shifting since at least the congress of Tours toward a more firm stance on foreign policy. Nothing more clearly demonstrated the dramatic nature of the shift than the more or less simultaneous article by Paul Langevin, the distinguished chemist, pacifist, and spiritual founder of the Popular Front. A scant four years earlier Langevin had been the authoritative opponent of Herriot. Now his tone had radically changed. We must avoid, he now declared "the false solution of weakness which in order to save the peace, amounts to yielding repeatedly to ever greater demands." He and his associates had always worked for peace "but in so acting we did not think or mean that the awareness of danger must mean fleeing danger nor cowardly abandoning a neighbour threatened or sacrificed." Moreover, "if it is true, as I had occasion to say in the past, that even preparation for a defensive war means accepting war, the fact of demonstrating that we are not disposed to retreat indefinitely in the face of threats stemming from our past weaknesses, may become the only means to avoid both servitude and war."[69] Although gracefully done, this represented a substantial retreat from Langevin's previous position. Nor was he alone. Ferdinand Corcos, long an articulate pacifist and member of the minority, became, if anything, more intransigent than Basch and his traditional allies. If Corcos still voted occasionally with the minority, it was because he found the majority to be insufficiently firm!

One reason why the pacifist cause lost ground in the directing circles of the League was the increasingly ambivalent stance of the recently-resigned members of the Central Committee. René Gérin may have wished to keep the cause of peace and the cause of anti-fascism associated.[70] In fact, however, for a number of dissident leaguers the best way to preserve the peace was to debunk the whole threat of fascism. Similarity, while Gérin clung to the distinction between left-wing and right-wing appeasement, in the writings of at least some of the dissident leaguers, that distinction was increasingly blurred. Challaye provided the best example. From September 18 to 26, 1938, Challaye had been in Germany on an exchange visit. In his subsequent account *Huit jours de septembre en Allemagne*,[71] Challaye expressed his open admiration for Nazi German society. Full employment, evident prosperity, magnificent auto routes, and widespread social equality were the most prominent features of the new regime. He granted that the absence of freedom would trouble any Frenchman. But he cited, without comment, the observations of an "intelligent German" who insisted than any French Socialist would feel a greater affinity with Hitler's Germany than with the Weimar Republic.[72] The only thing that troubled Challaye was the question of the Jews; he mentioned anti-Semitic persecutions five times and took pains to stress that this was the one feature of the new Germany with which he had the most difficulty. Yet even Hitler's anti-Semitism had to be put into context. Again he cited the "good German." Surely there were good aristocrats before 1789, but who today would fault the French revolutionary regime for doing away with them? Similarly, in Nazi Germany there were "good Jews who are victims of the legitimate revolt of the Germans against the bad Jews."[73] Using the experience of the French Revolution to justify the Nazi persecution of the Jews was certainly an odious exercise, but arguably not more so than Guerry's entirely analogous effort to justify Stalin's murders.

Still, lest the point escape sceptical French readers, Challaye hastened to cite the recent editorial of his friend, Gaston Bergery, where he had argued that in order to understand Nazi anti-Semitism one would have had to have been in Germany in 1923 and seen the "opulence of the Jewish businessmen" riding around in their luxury automobiles, perfectly indifferent to the starving masses of the population.[74] Nor, Challaye continued, was it necessary to leave France. Any Frenchman wishing to understand German anti-Semitism could "evoke the image of certain recently arrived Jews that one meets in certain French democratic circles."[75] This was a transparent reference to the League and to Salomon Grumbach. Lest any of this (as it likely would) induce read-ers to hatred of Jews, Challaye hastened to remind his audience that there were also good Jews—Spinoza being the most striking example.

This kind of language soon provoked the ire of Bernard Lecache, a former associate of Bergery and the editor of *Le Droit de vivre,* an organ of Jewish de-fense. In response Bergery gamely insisted that he despised anti-Semitism. Still, he thought that its growth in France owed something to the excessive influence of Jews in public and political life. True, Léon Blum was French be-fore he was Jewish, but it was troubling that his entourage consisted of "rela-tives or friends, or friends of relatives, or relatives of friends, the great majority of whom were Jewish." He told the story of an associate who had attempted to obtain some information from the Blum government and who returned an-nouncing that "they sent me from Blumenfeld to Rosenthal, from Rosenthal to Blumenthal, from Blumenthal to Rosenfeld."[76] By the late 1930s this kind of discussion had particularly sinister connotations. Unable to document any significant Jewish overrepresentation either in parliament or in the Blum gov-ernment, the extreme Right, and notably such scurrilous journals as *Gringoire,* had turned their attention to the number of Jews in the administration. Bergery cannot have been unaware of this fact.

Challaye was unfazed by Lecache's charges, so much so that even Bergery declined to publish his response. He had never claimed, Challaye insisted, that all Jews wanted war or that only Jews wanted war. All he had ever asserted was that "a large number of Jews" sought to "use the French army, the British navy, and the Soviet and Czech air forces, to destroy the state that so unjustly persecutes their fellow Jews." Moreover, he was prepared to document the "warlike activity of notorious Jews, many of whom, shirkers in 1914 or per-petual draft dodgers or safely exempt in ministerial offices or newspaper of-fices, would have made war with the bodies of our children." Once again, the reference to Grumbach would have escaped few contemporaries. Nonethe-less Challaye felt compelled to add that people like "the Jew Mandel," prepar-ing the "great massacre" could be found in parliament, the press, and especially in the League. "Jews like Salomon Grumbach, Louis Lévy, Weiskopf (also known as Gombault, also known as Pierre de Clam, also known as Nicholas Paillot, etc.), Paul Levy of *Ecoutes,* Richard Bloch of *Le Soir,* Julien Benda, Emile Kahn, and even the greatest of them, the Léon Blums, the Victor Baschs, have obviously fallen under the influence of their Jewish environment."[77] As always, Challaye was at pains to stress that he had in mind certain Jews, maybe most Jews but not all Jews. Yes, "it could be that we might experience a moral and intellectual repugnance when confronted with certain Jews," but there was always the salutary example of Spinoza.[78] By any standards, this was appalling language and not made less so coming from a man who for thirty years had held a post on the Central Committee of the League.[79]

But Challaye was not unique. His colleague Léon Emery was equally determined to persuade his former comrades that the defense of the rights of man did not necessarily entail hostility to Nazi Germany. What troubled him was that the League's earlier goal of fighting against *both* fascism and war had been subtly perverted. The war/fascism couplet had made sense in 1934 because the fascism in question was *French* fascism, the stalking horse of the authoritarian Right and the forces of capitalism, both of which were also trying to drag France into war. But after 1935 the struggle against fascism had come to focus almost exclusively on foreign, and notably, German fascism. No one was more guilty of this than the League which Emery now snidely referred to as "the conscience of an ossified [*moulée en plâtre*] democracy." Instead of fighting for peace and democracy, the League, "corrupted by politicians," had subordinated "everything to . . . the struggle against Hitlerian Germany" and was prepared "to support the worst forms of domestic reaction in order to be protected from 'fascism' which they invariably tend to locate on the other side of the frontier."[80] In the first place, Frenchmen looking to smite fascism need not look far. One only had to know where to look, and heretofore the League had been looking in the wrong places. The League, like much of the Left, had long been obsessed with the right wing leagues like the Croix de Feu and its successor the PSF. This was utterly naive because "the PSF long ago became a traditional party." "The only clearly fascist party to be found in France" was the Communist party.[81] The mere fact that an ex-Communist like Jacques Doriot could so easily become a fascist leader suggested that little really separated fascism from communism.[82] Both Soviet Communism and German Nazism were a form of "authoritarian socialism."[83] Fascist Germany was every bit as much a revolutionary regime as had been Soviet Russia or Jacobin France. And just as monarchical Europe and, later, bourgeois Europe had had to come to grips with the revolutionary movements of their respective eras, so too democratic Europe needed to comprehend the "revolutionary dynamism" of the new Germany. To dismiss Hitler as "the watch dog of capitalism"[84] was simpleminded. Although capitalists might have supported fascist regimes in their earlier stages, "certain citadels of international finance like London, New York, Zurich and Amsterdam" had in recent years become increasingly antifascist and "the Jews, especially in America, have contributed greatly to that evolution."[85]

Hitler, much like the French PSF had "a very wide popular base."[86] Moreover, this popular base reflected the fact that fascism could generate "an energy" that was superior to those evoked by "democratic ideals."[87] The Nazis
instilled "egalitarian sentiment" into Germans, promoted "public works in
ways that are often ostentatious but not without concrete results," so that "the
material condition of the German people had clearly improved."[88] In essence,
then, Nazi Germany had evolved into a "regime with a popular and principally
working class base."[89] Such opposition as there was came largely from
Catholics, the "old bourgeoisie" and some of the old trade unions whose workers were, ironically, "often the best paid."[90]

Like Challaye, Emery had the most trouble with the persecution of the Jews,
something he found "abominable" and which inspired in him "horror and disgust." But surely this did not make Germany "an outlaw among nations."[91]
"Are we convinced," he asked, "that a Nazi is by definition a monster?"[92] A
France that had revoked the Edict of Nantes, an America that had enslaved
blacks, and Western "democracies" that continued to oppress colonial peoples
were in no position to point fingers. Furthermore, the "persecution of the Jews
[had] an economic and social dimension," because the Jews were "a social class
against which a people has mobilized." This kind of mobilization was a "char-
acteristic trait of revolutions" wholly analogous to the French revolutionary terror or to the Soviet Union's war against the Kulaks. In contrast to the current
French regime which he excoriated as corrupt, decadent, and controlled by the
financial and industrial oligarchies, "fascism is an authoritarian socialism"
whose revolutionary dynamism he repeatedly compared with Jacobin France.[93]
The ugly aspects of the Nazi regime were but the inevitable transitional stage
through which all revolutions must go. With "a fundamental change in the international climate and the balance of power," the less attractive aspects of the
regime would subside.[94] It followed then that peace, not war, was the best way
to deal with Hitler. Some of this extraordinary language can be assigned to the
fact that Emery was by now a very bitter man, having lost his once magic hold
on so many of the League's rank and file and now threatened with more or less
total blindness.[95] Yet the majority of these lines were penned while Emery remained the head of his large section of Lyons, still enjoying the support of his
Lyon colleagues.

The looming threat of war in 1939 tempered but did not end the tensions
within the League. Hitler's annexation of Bohemia and Moravia on March
15, 1939, briefly sobered even Challaye and Emery. Challaye admitted that for
the first time Hitler had conquered people who manifestly did not want to

be part of the Third Reich. The time for "confident and cordial relations with Germany" was now past; "correct" relations were the most one could ask for.[96] Emery denounced the destruction of what was left of Czechoslovakia as an "imperialist crime." But he was also quick to add that there was little resistance to Hitler's coup within Czechoslovakia and general indifference to it among the French popular classes.[97] Challaye's atypically indignant piece seems to have irritated some of his pacifist readers, for he was soon reassuring everyone that Hitler was unlikely to continue his aggressive behavior and that, in any event, his conquest of Czechoslovakia was not morally different from Western imperialism.[98] Nor, he made it clear, were there any valid grounds for France to fight for Poland.[99]

Tensions among the Central Committee diminished in the spring; by March Albert Bayet could triumphantly assert that his colleagues finally agreed upon foreign policy.[100] In fact the agreement was short-lived, and by the early summer, despite Basch's frantic efforts to reconcile everyone, the irreconcilable differences were again manifest.[101] The League's last congress in Mulhouse in 1939 adopted almost unanimously a platform in favor of collective security; the only dissent came from Casati, Château, Planche, and Delaisi who came, as they acknowledged, merely to show the flag.[102] Despite the general unanimity, yet another personal incident marred the Congress, this one involving the pacifist Marc Casati and the arch hawk Salomon Grumbach. Casati interrupted Grumbach by shouting "to Switzerland," a transparent reference to the fact that Grumbach, before 1914 a citizen of German Alsace, had spent the war as a correspondent for the Socialist newspaper *L'Humanité* in Switzerland. In an unprecedented move, the congress, minus four votes, passed a motion condemning Casati's language. Because past attacks against Grumbach had taken the form of veiled allusions to his Jewish ancestry, the League was obliged in the last prewar issue of the *Cahiers* to deny the gleeful (and spiteful) claims of Charles Maurras in the *Action Française* that at long last even the League had adopted anti-Semitism.[103]

While the internal differences among League leaders sharpened, many rank and file were voting with their feet. By 1939 League membership was barely 60 percent of what it had been six years earlier. At one level the decline is puzzling. Membership in parties of the Left, notably the Communists and Socialists, was soaring in the mid-1930s. Given its prominent role in the Rassemblement Populaire and in the Popular Front governments, the League had never been more central to French politics. Reflecting on this paradox, Francis Delaisi wrote Basch in the summer of 1936: "I am troubled, like all of my comrades, to see the membership and the resources of the League decline when simultaneously its prestige is growing."[104] To the degree that people joined the League for the patronage possibilities it could afford, never had there been so many League ministers. In their attempts to explain the loss of members, local leaders of the League suggested a number of factors. All agreed that the economic depression had caused many members to cease paying their dues. But League dues were very modest, and for the unemployed membership was free. Despite much higher dues, the Socialist party attracted tens of thousands of new members. Insofar as the cost of membership explains the decline in effectives, it speaks to a very casual attachment to the League of many of its erstwhile militants.

Some local leaders cited disillusionment with the disappointing results of the Popular Front experience. But the decline in League membership antedated by several years the formation of the Popular Front. More plausible were those who spoke of the increasingly debilitating effects of internal political infighting within sections. Political tensions had always been a feature of the internal life of the League, but they grew more intense in the wake of the Herriot affair and in the later years of the Popular Front. Radicals feuded with Socialists; pacifists feuded with proponents of collective security. The president of a section in the Dordogne that had decided to dissolve itself reported: "The general opinion has been that the League, buffeted by the various divergent tendencies within the parties of the left, at least in our part of the world, is no longer capable of bringing together individuals to discuss issues which are viewed in very different ways." Commenting on this report, the President of the federation of the Dordogne, suggested that the essential problem was that principles that seemed very clear to "those of us who are old Dreyfusard . . . lose their value among the younger generation."[105] He was here alluding to the fact that during the Popular Front years scores of parapolitical organizations sprung up at both the national and local levels. Most were ephemeral, and none had a mandate comparable to that of the League's original charter. But in terms of left-wing political mobilization, long the principal motivation of many local League militants, they appeared to be doing the same things as the League and, by virtue of being newer, were more attractive. The president of the federation of the Seine-Inférieure complained as early as 1935 that "the multiplicity of new groups harms us because [our members] tend to turn eagerly towards the newest of them." "The proper activities" of the League he wrote a few months later, were hampered by "the tendency of our sections to confound their activities with those of the Rassemblement Populaire." and risked "getting lost" in the now fashionable "mass action." "I fear," he concluded, "that Leaguers will gradually cease attending meetings and even cease to belong [to the League.]"[106] The president of the federation of the Deux-Sèvres and the secretary of the federation of the Haute-Saône reported similar findings.[107] Behind such analyses was an oblique recognition that the League had become too political, when not exclusively political. Consequently, what had once united so many leaguers, the defense of the rights of man, became less important than what divided them: conflicting views about left-wing politics. For those whose commitment to the League had always been purely political, the late 1930s offered a host of newer alternatives, less burdened by irritating scruples about being, in theory at least, above politics. Of the many new recruits who flocked to the expanding Socialist and Communist parties, some, in an earlier era might have found a home in the League. Others were almost certainly former League members who, upon at last joining a political party, now considered their former association to be superfluous if not irrelevant.

By 1939 the League had experienced five tumultuous years. To all appearances, its reduced numbers notwithstanding, it remained a formidable organization, far less internally divided than it had been in 1934. But, as the experience of the war and its aftermath would reveal, the League had become a very fragile institution.

EIGHT

Vichy

The collapse of France in 1940 caught the League, like most of the French, by surprise. As late as May 16, when the Battle of France was raging, a confident Emile Kahn told the president of the federation of the Isère that recent developments meant that he would be postponing, but not cancelling, his anticipated propaganda tour in that department.[1] A week later, when the war was on the verge of being lost, the section of Sainte-Claude in the Jura was still trying to find the right balance when dealing with German natives in France. Owing to the dangers of a Fifth column, close surveillance seemed appropriate but only if it involved no "inhuman treatment or attacks on their dignity." At the end of the month, Kahn still found time to thank the section for its thoughtful reflections on the subject.[2] By June, however, it was obvious that a German invasion of Paris was imminent. Kahn dutifully ordered his staff to pack up the League's archives in preparation for departure from the city. He was, however, too late, and when the Germans descended on League headquarters in the middle of June they found the archives conveniently stacked by the front door. With its archives confiscated, its headquarters occupied, and its activities now illegal, the League ceased all operations. By the time the Vichy regime was installed a month later, individual members of the League had already gone their separate ways.

Victor Basch managed to escape from Paris on June 18, first to Brittany, and later, and with some difficulty, to Lyon in the unoccupied zone. Physically ailing, depressed both by the defeat and by the suicide of his son Georges, deprived of his precious library, Basch and his wife Ilona managed to survive a thoroughly miserable existence for the next three and a half years. On January 10, 1944, they were arrested by two agents of the Vichy paramilitary police, the Milice. Both, now in their eighties, were driven to a lonely alley and summarily shot.[3] A similar fate befell Jean Zay and Marx Dormoy, prominent deputies and longtime members of the League. Central Committee member

Odette Renée Bloch was deported to Dachau in 1943 where she perished. The presidents of the federations of the Sarthe and the Hérault; the vice president and the secretary general of the federation of the Charente-Maritime and the secretary of the federation of the Pyrenées-Orientales were shot by the Germans or died in concentration camps.[4]

A significant number of the League leaders made some kind of contribution to the Resistance or the Free French. About thirty of the prewar members of the Central Committee were active, to some degree or other, in the Resistance in metropolitan France (most notably Albert Bayet, Frédéric Joliot-Curie, André Philip, Paul Rivet, Marc Rucart, Etienne Vacquier) or in the external Resistance (Georges Boris, Pierre Cot, Georges Gombault, Jacques Kayser, Marius Moutet). Others, Salomon Grumbach, Elie Reynier, and Paul Langevin were either imprisoned or interned under the Vichy regime.[5] Given the advanced age of most League leaders, it was an honorable record. Given the values professed by the League, their response was not surprising.

What *was* surprising was the number (albeit a rather smaller number) of former League leaders who were actively involved in the collaboration. After the liberation, the League formally purged eleven of its Central Committee members for their roles under the occupation.[6] Two, Maurice Thiolas and Robert Jardillier, did little more than join the great majority of the deputies of the Left who voted full powers for Pétain in 1940. Most of the rest, moving in the entourage of the prewar pacifist and arch collaborator, Marcel Déat, had contributed, for greater or shorter lengths of time, to an assortment of collaborationist journals.[7] At least a further six former members of the Central Committee were active collaborators.[8]

The proportion of the League's leaders in the Resistance as opposed to Vichy (roughly thirty versus about seventeen) is of course an imperfect proxy for the League as a whole because the position taken by the bulk of the militants cannot be known. Still, the prewar minority, roughly 30 to 40 percent of the League, does seem to have continued through the war years. Taken as a group, the League's leaders who rallied to Vichy were at least as likely to have played an important role in the prewar League as those who opted for the Resistance. Collaboration came in all kinds of forms (as of course did resistance) ranging from tepid critiques of the Third Republic to *collaboration à l'outrance.* League collaborators ran the gambit.

What cannot be in dispute is that a significant number of former leaders of the League contributed, with varying degrees of enthusiasm and for longer or shorter periods of time, to collaborationist newspapers like *L'Oeuvre, L'Effort,*

La France Socialiste, Les Nouveaux Temps, Germinal, Aujourd'hui, and *L'Atelier.*
These were newspapers that celebrated the tenth anniversary of Hitler's seizure of power, referred to Adolph Hitler as *Der Fuehrer,* called the allied forces "the Jewish coalition," and cheered the victories of the "European forces" on the Eastern Front. Whatever private reservations the contributors might have had, the association of League members with such newspapers requires an explanation.

At one level it seems incongruous that men who had, short years or even months before been leaders of the self proclaimed "conscience" of the democratic republic, could so easily become defenders of a regime that was in every respect its antithesis. Yet there was a certain perverse logic to their *ralliement* to Vichy, one that was anchored in the prewar obsessions of the League's minority: anticapitalism and pacifism. Given the increasing disillusionment with a regime "corrupted" by the puissances d'argent, a democracy rotted from within by a venal press and parliament, and a government that had twice fallen into the hands of irresponsible warmongers, it was all too easy not to regret in any way the passing of the Third Republic.

The most extreme response by ex-leaguers to the defeat in 1940 was that of Félicien Challaye. In June of 1940 he began writing a novel. Temporarily disenchanted with the policies of the Vichy government, he put the novel aside and did not complete it until the spring of 1945. Entitled *Etrange chemin de la paix,* it was never published.[9] Part pacifist tract, part roman à clef, the novel dwelt at length on the forces responsible for France's descent into war—notably "a very large number of Jews seeking to destroy a regime which had so cruelly persecuted their coreligionists."[10] One man "personally embodied the various tendencies pushing for war: the slimy Jew, Mösse Drecklein." Drecklein, who bore a striking resemblance to Challaye's prewar antagonist within the Central Committee, Salomon Grumbach, was portrayed as being singularly devoid of attractive qualities.

The hero of the novel, a certain Robert Lefort, recalled that he, "some of whose best friends were Jewish, experienced an instinctive repugnance for this Jew, an Alsatian of low birth who became a rich French deputy." Drecklein spoke both French and German, "in both cases with a deplorable accent" and "lived very well off mysterious resources." "Mediocre, vain and loud-mouthed," Drecklein was one of those who pushed France into an unnecessary war "for the Soviets, for the Jews, for the émigrés, for the big French, English and American capitalists." Lefort believed the war to have been a tragic mistake. Germany may have been a totalitarian regime but the interwar policy of France had been so gratuitously hostile as to leave the Germans little choice but to declare war in 1940. Nor had there been any legitimate reason for French bellicosity. Lefort, like the author, had visited Germany in 1938 and had been impressed by the economic prosperity and full employment. "I will not dwell," he commented, "on the persecution of the Jews, of which I do not approve but which I realize it is not without some justification."[11]

Despite periodic (and by now ritualistic) references to Spinoza, Challaye could not contain his visceral hatred for the Jews. In a scene depicting the execution of three prominent members of the war party, one of them, transparently patterned after the prewar conservative and anti-Munichois deputy, Henri de Kerillis, goes to his death with an aristocratic flair. A second, who could only have been Edouard Daladier, accepts his fate with a courageous stoicism. The third, Drecklein, by contrast, "sweating and crying, begs the judge to save his life." He had to be dragged screaming from the courtroom and carried, bound with ropes, to the stake. Throughout, Challaye harped on the malevolent influence of the Jews in French society and insisted that "the great majority of the Jews and virtually all influential Jews have a crushing responsibility for the coming of the abominable war."[12]

Challaye's private ruminations, while jejune, were nonetheless consistent with his public proclamations. He was quite convinced that Marshal Pétain represented a new form of socialism. If the Marshal preferred the word *social* to *socialism*, it was because the latter label was too easily identified with the likes of Salomon Grumbach. But in the various utterances of Pétain, one could easily discern "everything that is socialism—traditional French socialism."[13] Of course, by this time Challaye had discovered an eclectic range of spiritual allies. Charles Maurras, for example, was no longer the virulent anti-Semite, bête noire of the League. The social program of this "friendly southern poet" was, to be sure, weak and his Germanophobia to be regretted. But Challaye was nonetheless "grateful to him for having denounced certain flaws in the previous regime" and for having abandoned his anti-German reflexes in 1939. He also gave Maurice Barrès, another famous anti-Dreyfusard, low marks for his limited grasp of the social question and for his overheated nationalism. But Barrès "was not wrong to insist on the importance of the nation, defined by him as '*la terre et les morts*.'"[14]

Léon Emery responded similarly to Vichy. Exiled to Bordeaux for his prewar pacifist sentiment, he returned to Lyon in 1943 courtesy of the intervention of the Vichy Minister of Education Abel Bonnard. He was soon writing procollaborationist pieces in the Vichy press. The United States, he argued, wanted to ravish, not liberate, France. One side or another would win this war, but French interests dictated that she should side with "the winner who will have the most need of our support and be the most likely to appreciate it, both morally and materially." He had in mind, of course, Nazi Germany, because he believed that "the only route to follow must be that which leads to European collaboration against the Bolshevik danger so foolishly and criminally supported by the egotism of Anglo-American financiers."[15] The "quickest means" of ending the current European crisis, he assured the readers of *L'Atelier,* was "a German victory in Russia."[16] He accepted a post as lecturer in the *Ecole des Cadres* of the *Légion Française des Combatants* in Avelard. As his published lectures, *L'Occident en péril,* indicate, his students were informed that "all that stands between Russia and western imperialism is the German army: we have no hesitation in saying that in the immediate future all our hopes are with that army."[17] As late as May 1944, Emery remained convinced that the defeat of Germany meant a Communist dictatorship and only "Germany offers the example of an advanced socialist society."[18]

Moreover, as his wartime history of the Third Republic[19] clearly demonstrated, he could no longer mask his contempt for the democratic regime. He privately expressed reservations about a work that seemed filled with too much "accumulated personal bitterness."[20] Publicly, however, he acknowledged that *La Troisième République* had been a critical success, its publication something of a literary "event."[21] The book was, in fact, a sustained polemic against the democratic republic, which he portrayed as little more than a cover for the domination of finance capital. His discussion of the Dreyfus affair lasted two paragraphs and ended with the observation that the affair soon degenerated into a sectarian quarrel in which "Jewish money played an excessive role." The principal result of the affair was to provide the pretext for the persecution of the church, with the Freemasons and a "new sacerdotal caste," the Ligue des droits de l'homme, in the lead.[22] The last years of the regime saw the total capitulation of much of the intellectual elite before the forces of international communism, seeking, in conjunction with the "Jewish international," to draw France into a criminal war.

In every way the book was a tract for the times, although apparently insufficiently so for its sponsor Domenique Sordet, a former staff writer for the *Action Française.* In his introduction, Sordet praised Emery for his rigorous critique of the previous regime, noting (correctly) that his account was a good deal more severe than that of the royalist historian, Jacques Bainville. What troubled him, however, was that Emery had "neglected one of the essential factors in the sickness from which France suffers: the maleficent activity of the

Jews."[23] This reproach did not trouble Emery very much. In a good-natured reply, he confessed that one of the reasons why he had failed to deal with "the role of the Jews and Free Masons in the decomposition of the regime" was the fact that he had never had any dealing with either group. "My quasi silence on the issue can be explained then by . . . my ignorance of the facts and of the texts" which might have permitted a more rigorous discussion of the question. "That there is here a major question to be examined, I have no doubt, and I ask no more than to be thoroughly informed of the matter."[24]

The wartime outpourings of Challaye and Emery seem incongruous, coming as they do from former leaders of the League. Still, they were ex-members of the League and their writings were at least consistent with the kind of statements they had made in the last two years of peace. More complex and more subtle is the case of René Château. Château had been the president of the League's largest federation, that of the Charente-Maritime. Member of the Central Committee, he was also the deputy from La Rochelle, a dissident Radical who belonged to *Le Parti Radical Camille Pelletan*, a phantom party created in 1933 by his close friend and fellow leaguer, Gaston Bergery, in an attempt to escape the legendary corruption of the traditional Radical party and to push much harder than did the party of Daladier and Herriot for the cause of peace. Château enthusiastically welcomed the Popular Front government of Léon Blum while expressing reservations both about the provocative role of the Communist party and, in time, Blum's commitment to peace.[25] He was a leading member of the minority, a consistent critic of the League's aggressive stand over Spain, its caution about the Moscow trials, and its generally antimunichois stance. Nonetheless, unlike Emery, Challaye, and Bergery, he stayed in the League and continued to preside over its federation in the Charente-Maritime. As late as the annual congress of the federation in July 1939, Château drafted a motion, approved by Victor Basch, that condemned Hitler's "Prague coup" of March 15, called for resistance to aggression but also for an international conference to resolve peacefully the current problems in central Europe and to work for international disarmament.[26] Nothing whatsoever in his public pronouncements suggested that he was anything other than a confirmed democrat.

The dramatic French collapse of 1940 changed all that, or more accurately, it provided a context in which Château could express sentiments largely suppressed in the waning days of the Republic. In July 1940 he coauthored, along with Gaston Bergery and sixteen other deputies, a declaration (the Bergery declaration) to be read before the meeting of the National Assembly on July 10. Among Château's coauthors were a number of dissident leftists (and former leaguers) such as Marcel Déat and Jean Montigny, but also, and strikingly, a number of deputies from the extreme parliamentary Right, most notably the deputy from the Ardèche, Xavier Vallat. Vallat was a former monarchist and one of the most intransigent opponents of the Popular Front, which Château had once greeted with such enthusiasm. When Léon Blum had presented his government to the Chamber in June 1936, Vallat had disgraced himself by provocatively announcing that, for the first time in its history, the great Gallo-Roman nation of France would be governed by a Jew.[27]

The Bergery declaration began by addressing the causes of the catastrophic defeat France had just suffered. An incoherent French foreign policy, one that failed to be either consistently conciliatory or consistently firm was much like French domestic policy. Too many of the prewar governments were "under the domination of coalitions of financial and economic interests." This too was consistent with prewar minority rhetoric. New, however, was the discovery that "so-called governments of the Left put the state under the domination of a union bureaucracy which represented, unfaithfully into the bargain, only one class in the nation and which was already infiltrated by agents in the pay of foreign powers." This was language far closer to the consistent diatribes of a prewar Xavier Vallat than to anything ever articulated by the prewar dissidents in the League. In an attempt to pave over the traditional divide between Right and Left, the authors stressed that the late Third Republic had betrayed both those who had hit the streets on the night of February 6, 1934, and those who had occupied the factories in June 1936. The former had wanted an end to the corrupt political class but had been forced to settle for the lackluster compromise represented by Gaston Doumergue; the latter had wanted a genuine social revolution only to be given "a Blum Ministry behind which manoeuvred the Duclos and the Martys."[28] In short, no matter who was running the late Third Republic, the authors refused to see anything but "a caricature of democracy and liberty."

Now that France had been crushed, it was critical to ensure a policy that minimized the damage—both moral and economic. This depended upon Germany who could either emulate the French mistakes of 1918 and impose a vengeful peace or seek a harmonious collaboration. It made sense, they insisted, for Germany to opt for the latter course if only because, as they perceptively noted, it would be "impossible to crush permanently a real nation of 40 million inhabitants especially when one has to control some 40 million Slavs . . . in central and eastern Europe." But the only way to ensure such a policy on the part of the victors was to create in France a regime capable and worthy of this collaborationist enterprise.

The requisite "new order" would have to be, "social," "national," and above all "authoritarian." The social part was, of course, easiest for the ex-leaguers. "Nothing would be more serious and more dangerous than to escape from Stalinism only to consolidate the plutocracy." It was equally important to "restore our wounded national pride." The word *national* had not been an important part of the prewar League lexicon; as the authors confessed, "certain among us in the past, with the best of intentions, underestimated the importance of the phenomenon of the nation." Most problematic of all was the idea of authority. French history had alternated between "periods of authority which degenerated into tyranny" and "periods of liberty which degenerated into disorder." "The new order" would have to be "a synthesis of authority and liberty." Nor was this a mere paradox since political liberty was "an empty phrase if it amounts to little more than the liberty to debate before an empty table in a defeated nation." "We fully understand," the authors noted, "that we will lose some of the forms of liberty; we ask the head of the government to preserve the substance."

The authors of the Bergery declaration were perceptively aware that by proposing an alternative to the previous regime that was "both national and social, there will be those who are horrified at the prospect of a more or less docile imitation of national socialism." But this was a quarrel over words. "The rush to a national form of socialism is universal among the major nations, with the notable exception of England. Everywhere else, from the New Deal in the United States to Soviet Stalinism, to say nothing of the totalitarian states of central Europe and the Iberian peninsula, the peoples are finding dramatically different routes to an identical goal."

One can find in this extraordinary document distant echoes of the concerns expressed in the prewar period by dissident members of the League—most notably with respect to foreign policy and to the deficiencies of the parliamentary regime. But few in the League ever spoke with such candor and certainly not Château. By contrast, there is little in the document that would have been out of place in the prewar speeches of Xavier Vallat. What was entirely absent from the document is any reflection whatsoever of the founding principles of the Ligue des droits de l'homme!

Château's adhesion to the authoritarian doctrines expressed in the Bergery declaration was not a momentary aberration. He was, until well into 1943, an articulate defender of the Vichy regime. Everywhere in Europe, new forms of government were emerging, and France must draw the appropriate conclusions. The legitimacy of the Third Republic was based on "the popular vote which the parties corrupted by dividing the community." But a single mass party, like the parti unique, the *Rassemblement National Populaire* (RNP) currently being organized by Marcel Déat, struck him as the best way to re-create the political community "in a form that is at once organic and dynamic." Indeed, in 1940 he had agreed to be one of Pétain's *missi dominici* (the irony of the label, with its obvious monarchist reference, seems to have escaped him entirely) charged with establishing the RNP in four departments.[29]

While persistently denying that Germany was his role model, the pacifist schoolteacher clearly displayed a penchant for repressive and authoritarian regimes. The chief defect of the Third Republic, he once declared, was that it was too "soft," in marked contrast to the First Republic, the only good one, which knew how to execute its enemies. In an article entitled "At the dawn of an authoritarian epoch," Château assured his readers that even after peace arrived France would not go back to the liberal ways of the prewar era. There are times, he opined, when "brutal action is necessary, without worrying about . . . minor scruples, without excessive respect for principles or codes either."[30]

But his support for Vichy was always critical. He was acutely aware that the disappearance of the much despised parliamentary regime did not amount to the triumph of anticapitalism; the legendary *trusts* were very much intact. Moreover, the Catholic Right was once again in the ascendancy. But he, like many dissident leaguers, believed that Vichy, at least as it existed in 1940, was but a transitory stage in the ultimate revolutionary *redressment* of France, a revolutionary upheaval that must await the victory of the Axis forces. In the meantime he, like many of his prewar associates, was content to be the left-wing opposition to Vichy, an opposition rooted not in the values of the prewar regime but in that of the still undefined revolution to come. In essence, men who had once been the "conscience of democracy" chose to become, as it were, the "conscience of the national revolution."

Château peppered his articles in *L'Oeuvre* and *France Socialiste* with attacks on the clerical reactionaries in Vichy circles. The National Revolution, he insisted, was not intended to permit the church to hector honest lay schoolteachers or exercise exclusive control over French youth. Of course, his criticisms were cautious ones; "Neither clericalism nor anti-clericalism" was now his chosen slogan, a phrase that the former Freemason and president of the federation of the Charente-Maritime would never have uttered before the war.[31] A new Europe was in the making, and France had the "unexpected luck" of participating in it.[32] France could not squander this opportunity by clinging to the economic old regime any more than it could afford the political old regime.

It was time to abandon "the good old capitalism of yesteryear" along with "anarchistic liberalism" in order to "build a new state as others have done."[33] The cornerstone of this new state would be a form of socialism. It would certainly not be the materialist socialism of prewar France; rather, France was marching "towards a new, free and strong socialism, just as the Germans, the Russians and others have done."[34] Reference to German National Socialism was of course a sensitive point, and Château was quick to add that not only was German National Socialism not an item for export (a point he had made repeatedly before the war) but "our revolution need not copy the German revolution."[35] Yet he was equally adamant that more loyal Franco-German collaboration was an essential precondition of the new French revolution and was quick to denounce the reactionaries in Vichy who paid only "lip service to collaboration."[36] As late as the summer of 1942, he was still trying to disabuse obdurate French Socialists who somehow still believed that Germany was in the grips of an oppressive and reactionary regime. The National Socialist regime was in fact remarkably progressive; "in a word, a form of socialism. Not quite our style, to be sure" but a socialism nonetheless. Anyone looking for "white terror, frenzied clericalism, reinforced capitalism" should turn not to Germany but to Vichy France![37]

Nor was he entirely pleased with the traditional authoritarianism of Vichy. Vichy wanted to restore authority, and he had no quarrel with this aim. But the idea of authority had changed since the time of the Capetians; it required some popular legitimation. Significantly, he opened the columns of his collaborationist *France Socialiste* to Eugène Frot, the independent Socialist deputy from the Loiret. Château and Frot shared a lot in common; both were members of the League, deputies, pacifists, and Masons. Frot was one of the great enigmas of the late Third Republic. He had been minister of the interior at the time of the Stavisky riots and enjoyed a brief, if undeserved, prestige on the Left for his presumed defense of the Republican regime.[38] He served on the League's Central Committee and distinguished himself at the 1935 congress for his firm, and unpopular, defense of the existing parliamentary regime. In the late 1930s, however, he was in the camp of the extreme pacifists, and with the arrival of the Vichy regime he accepted a post on its National Council. Nonetheless, in 1941–42 he chose to write several articles in defense of the Republic. In the first he argued that there had been too much opportunistic sniping at the Republic and republicans; France was technically still a republic, and whatever new order Pétain had in mind could not be built without the support of republicans. This was not exactly the tone of most of the collaborationist press, and hostile readers belligerently wondered if they might soon expect from Frot a defense of the parliamentary system or even the Masons. Frot promptly responded with a vigorous defence of parliamentary democracy! He granted that the system had its faults, notably ministerial instability, and was often inefficient. But this was no reason to condemn a regime that offered "indisputable advantages" and which corresponded to "the wishes of the great majority of Frenchmen." The Vichy regime was, he conceded, doing its best amid serious obstacles. Nonetheless, he believed that most Frenchmen would like to have their deputy back and see a return to parliamentary control over the passing of laws and decrees. In short, it was, by any standards, a remarkable defense of the democratic republic, the more notable for having been made in a frankly collaborationist newspaper. He ended by provocatively promising the aforementioned defense of the Freemasons, the recently dissolved organization to which he had belonged.[39] He did not get to write that article or any other because he managed to seriously antagonize the more dedicated partisans of the new order. Jean Luchaire's *Nouveaux Temps,* for example, compared Frot's nostalgia for the democratic regime with a dog's penchant for eating its own vomit. Too many of the former members of the League, it complained, still harbored longings for the corrupt old Third Republic.[40] Château hastened to dispute this claim, but even he stressed that the new regime must have some contact with the people.[41]

Others were similarly concerned. Camille Planche, former president of the League's parliamentary group and president of the federation of the Allier certainly now admitted that the famous triad liberty, equality and fraternity, was outdated. Significantly he had been among those who in the 1930s had sought a significant redrafting of the Declaration of the Rights of Man, with a more prominent social orientation. But he too noted that when Marshal Pétain had been voted full powers in the summer of 1940, the form of the republic deliberately had been preserved. In a veiled critique of Pétain, he also noted that the new constitutional arrangements had retained civilian control over the military.[42] He did not dispute that France would need a new constitution, something the Vichy regime was working on at a glacial pace, and he agreed that it would have to be much more authoritarian. But an authoritarian regime was not the same as a dictatorship. He agreed that a one-party state might be desirable, but at the same time some form of "popular consultation" was imperative. Like his prewar associate, Château, Planche's critique of the regime was part of a campaign for the return of Pierre Laval, who, owing to the machinations of extreme right-wing elements in Pétain's entourage, had been dismissed as premier in December 1940. After Laval's return to power in the spring of

1942, Planche was clearly elated and wrote an article entitled: "Long live the republic," a slogan, he contended, that was "no longer a seditious cry"[43] Much as did Château, Planche struggled to reconcile his support, however qualified, for the Vichy regime with his earlier democratic rhetoric. The former president of a major departmental federation of the League seemed unable to grasp the elementary fact that no matter who was in charge at Vichy, Pétain or Laval, France was living under a dictatorship. Nor could he see that platonic appeals for some kind of "popular consultation" meant virtually nothing as long as one simultaneously conceded the principle of the single-party state.

Théodore Ruyssen, a long-standing member of the League's Central Committee, insisted in October 1940 that it might be a mistake to scrap all features of the prewar parliamentary regime. At a minimum the new order would need to grant *some* kind of popular representation. Nonetheless, he too agreed, as he most certainly would not have a few months earlier, that there was a "legitimate reaction against the caricature of democracy which has dishonoured France these last twenty years." "One can justifiably criticize the excessive individualism that characterized the electoral system of . . . the Third Republic." It now seemed evident that families, professional corporations, and "the principal organizations that make up our national life" should be represented in parliament. In fact, of course, these were propositions that he would never have accepted a year before, if only because they were then, as they were in 1940, the traditional stock and trade of the antidemocratic Right.[44]

Although many of their wartime proclamations sound utterly inconsistent with the prewar values of the League, there were also certain logical continuities, most notably with respect to pacifism. At the end of 1940, the Vichy government decided to place France's prewar political and military leadership—Léon Blum, Edouard Daladier, and Maurice Gamelin—on trial at Riom for their prewar diplomatic and military conduct. The avowed purpose of the trial was to definitively discredit both the prewar leaders and also the republican regime itself. The trial turned into a fiasco as the defendants managed to demonstrate that, contra the charges against them, they had in fact made a major effort to rearm France in the late 1930s. Château had written enough prewar articles deploring Blum's arms spending to know how strong Blum's case was. He also perceptively noted that demonstrating, even if it were possible, France's insufficient military preparation in the 1930s proved nothing about Blum or the old Republic. It might have badly bungled one war but, by the same token, it had handled another one rather successfully. But the crime of the Republic was not that it lost one of the two wars it waged; its real sin was to have drawn France, quite unnecessarily, into either of them. If Blum and his associates had anything to answer for, it was not having lost the war, but having been willing to fight it in the first place. Here the blame could be shared with elements of the Catholic Right, from Louis Marin to Henri de Kerillis. Sectarian zeal rather than any desire for justice, he concluded, motivated the Riom affair.[45] On this count he was certainly right although his condemnation of the *Third* Republic for making war seems inconsistent with his open admiration for the *First* Republic. He gave the latter high marks because it had executed a king and guillotined black marketers; somehow he forgot that it had also been exceptionally good at, and rather given to, waging war.

In the years before the war, members of the League's minority had advocated an economically integrated Europe that would also be a socialist one. The most articulate of them, the economist Francis Delaisi, insisted that such a Europe would avoid both the threat of future war and also the social consequences of an irrational and dysfunctional capitalism. During the war he continued to elaborate on this theme, filling the pages of the overtly collaborationist *L'Atelier* with articles about a future integrated socialist Europe.[46] Now, however the new Europe would be modelled on the very successful example of Nazi Germany, a regime Delaisi credited with solving the economic problems that had stymied old-fashioned liberal economies and ensured Germans the highest salaries in Europe. Hitler, one learned, was "always in contact with the people, never separated from them by a bureaucratic barrier . . . which is the greatest danger in a regime of personal power." As a result, "by the judicious application of new methods provided by science and technology, Germany had escaped from the tragic and millenarian rut of the class struggle."

Hitler, however impressive his economic achievements, was no democrat, and Delaisi was uncomfortably aware that this remained an issue for at least some of his prewar comrades in the League. He chose to write a series of open letters to a certain Forestier, a fictitious individual whose profile could only fit Delaisi's prewar ally on the Central Committee, the historian, Georges Michon. What clearly bothered Delaisi was that his old comrade-in-arms was troubled by his overtly collaborationist stance. Why, Delaisi wanted to know? After all, he noted, 'it was not yesterday that I denounced the illusions of the ballot box"; throughout the 1930s, he reminded everyone, "I never ceased to denounce the illusion of the democratic regime." In fact Delaisi had done nothing of the kind in the 1930s, although it is entirely possible that he had privately held the views he so triumphantly now pronounced. The trouble with Michon, he continued, was that although the historian basically agreed with him on most points, Hitler was a major stumbling block for him. "The very name Hitler gets his back up." For some reason Michon found "the persecutions of the Jews, that collective responsibility of a race for the crimes of its leader" to be "a medieval regression." Having read only a few pages of *Mein Kampf,* Michon somehow could not grasp that in order to fight the "military discipline of the Communist party," Hitler would have to employ "an even more brutal military discipline." Nor did he seem to appreciate that Hitler had put six million men back to work, restored social peace in the factories, introduced social insurance, and vastly augmented the leisure of the working class. In a word, Hitler had restored "dignity and honor" which explained why there was so much that was deeply popular about the Hitlerian dictatorship. Michon had no real excuse for such obtuseness because he had entered into the Central Committee of the prewar League to fight the bureaucracy of "the Baschs, the Kahns, the Gombaults and the other Jews *à vrai ou faux nez,*" and in the process he might have learned that "the day of democracy is finished."[47]

One of the most striking features of the collaborationist leaguers was the ease with which they embraced the newly fashionable anti-Semitism of the Vichy period. Even among those who were most outspoken in expressing their reservations about Vichy, not one breathed a word of protest concerning the anti-Semitic legislation adopted in the first weeks of the regime. Indeed, so commonplace was anti-Semitic rhetoric among many of the ex-leaguers as to raise the question of how much was owed to conviction and how much to conformism. André Weil-Curiel ironically noted in 1940 that the Jewish conspiracy that now so obsessed many of his prewar comrades was of very recent date; few had been aware of the Jewish peril short months before. Moreover, his former colleagues, ignorant of his role in the Gaullist resistance but fully aware of his status as Jew, nonetheless continued to receive him warmly.[48] But Weil-Curiel was—or at any rate had been until 1936—a member of the League's pacifist minority. The sins of the Jews, in the eyes of the bitter ex-leaguers, were usually the sins of the warmongers and, in their eyes coming to the same thing, the dominant majority within the League. Obsessed, as always, by the origins of the war, Château complained that France had been dragged into war by the three internationals: capitalist, Bolschevik, and Jewish. "There is," he declared "a tribal atavism which holds these people together, in spite of the distances, from Warsaw to Paris to New York to Jerusalem." Touch a Jew, anywhere, he opined, and Jews the whole world over would rise up to defend him, which explained why after 1933 Jews were determined to drag France into a war over issues that did not concern her. Nowhere was this Jewish bellicosity more prominent than in the League where by August 1939 "Grumbach, Gombault, Moch, Kahn and the rest of the tribe were spreading the flames" that would lead to the tragic conflagration.[49] Armand de Charpentier, a high-profile and long-standing member of the minority took similar issue with the prewar leadership. "Without consulting either the sections or the federations, [the Central Committee] supported the Spanish Communists, the *in camera* judgments in the Soviet Union and the summary executions of Russian generals and senior functionaries who had the temerity not to believe that everything was for the best in 'the Soviet paradise.'" In 1938 the editors of the *Cahiers* somehow thought it appropriate to support the Czech leader Beneš in his campaign "against the legitimate resistance of the Sudetens," in the process forgetting that the League had been created precisely for "the defence . . . of oppressed peoples." Nor was any of this accidental, because the League's leaders sought war exclusively "to meet the desires of the war-mongers and the four Jews who ruled over the Committee."[50] René de la Marmande, another long-standing member of the League, fleshed out the list of Jewish leaders of a "*Ligue . . . enjuivé*" who had dragged France into war: Georges Boris, Cécile Brunschvicg, Léon Blum, Odette Renée Bloch, Suzanne Collette Kahn, and Jean Zay. These leaguers were representatives of "that Jerusalem which will never pardon Hitler's Germany for defending itself against their conquering instincts."[51]

The language adopted under the Vichy regime by members of the prewar minority was in shocking contrast to the presumed values of the League. To be sure, by 1939, many of the leaders of the minority, Emery, Challaye, and Bergery, had effectively abandoned the organization, although others, Delaisi, Château and Planche, did remain on the Central Committee and did attend the last prewar congress.[52] The disillusioned ex-leaguers did not speak with one voice. Some were more outspoken, more embittered, and more persistent in their adherence to the new regime. But all had in common a set of values they had inherited from their years in the League. All were pacifists for whom World War II was both unnecessary and largely the fault of the West. All believed in European economic integration and in the creation of a supranational European state as a means for avoiding future war. All condemned the political sterility and the social immobility of the Third Republic. These were not always unworthy views and, with the exception of pacifism, these were concerns that were shared by many of their contemporaries in the Resistance.[53] So the ideas expressed by dissident leaguers under Vichy had a respectable enough pedigree and clearly reflected their prewar preoccupations.

What is so striking is that they reflected not at all the values that were supposed to have informed the League.

In the end, Château and his comrades found themselves in the impossible situation of abandoning the values of the democratic republic without fully embracing either the traditional conservatism of Vichy or the German-inspired totalitarianism of the more wholehearted collaborators like Marcel Déat. Periodic oblique appeals for more popular representation were ignored in Vichy and scorned by the Parisian *enragés*. Their assorted appeals for some kind of *new* socialism were empty exercises, doomed to fall on deaf ears, either in Vichy France or Hitler's Europe. There was something pathetic about Château's stance on the Milice, the paramilitary force unleashed by Vichy against dissidents in 1943. All the while conceding that the Milice was "indispensable" for the repression of Bolshevism, Château pleaded that it should not be composed exclusively of "reactionaries," ought to distinguish Bolsheviks from Socialists, and might try to recognize that a lot of Communists were but misguided workers.[54] Déat might have fancied himself the "official spokesman of German national socialism," but the fact remained that no less an authority than Joseph Goebbels had assured France that when the war was over she could adopt the social and political regime of her choosing, a republic that would be both "popular and virile."[55] All of this earnest rationalizing earned Château only the contempt of men like Déat and his entourage for whom all this cavilling merely proved that Château and his ilk had never grasped the revolutionary essence of National Socialism and secretly longed for the *ancien regime*. "Having opposed the bellicose enterprise of the Communists in 1938," Déat dismissively observed, "does not mean that one has broken with all of the ideologies of 1936."[56] Shortly before he was forced to abandon his collaborationist journalism, Château plaintively noted that he was being attacked on all sides, both for having publicly abandoned his republican principles and for secretly clinging to them.[57]

More determined, but no less pathetic, was Challaye, who was still writing in the collaborationist press scant days before the liberation of Paris. The ultimate statement of his moral and political bankruptcy came on the death of Philippe Henriot, the prewar deputy from Bordeaux and representative of the extreme Catholic and nationalistic Right. When the dissidents in the League were mobilizing against fascism on February 6, 1934, Henriot was writing a pamphlet praising the right-wing rioters as saviors of France. There was no more vitriolic critic of the Popular Front than Henriot. In 1938 he had adopted a Munichois stance that was close to that of the left-wing pacifists but he, like an important part of the French Right, had forgotten it all by September 1939 when he belligerently called for war against Hitler. Under Vichy he enrolled his son in the SS and by 1944 became minister of propaganda.[58] His murder by the Resistance in early July 1944 elicited considerable indignation from the left-wing collaborationist press. (An outrage that was notoriously lacking at the time of the murder of Victor Basch and his wife six months earlier.) Later in July, on the thirtieth anniversary of the assassination of Jean Jaurès, Challaye, in an otherwise moving piece on the death of the great socialist leader, wrote: "The hatred of Germany which has always caused the French people such harm was at the root of the assassination of Jaurès and of the recent murder of another great orator serving the same cause: Philippe Henriot."[59]

The liberation did not alter Challaye's views. He was, astonishingly, acquitted of the charges of collaboration, largely owing to the intervention of his prewar ally, Michel Alexandre. A Jew, interned under Vichy, Alexandre nonetheless testified that Challaye was one of the finest examples of a pacifist tradition dating from the days of Jaurès. In the 1950s Challaye continued to insist that he was a philo-Semite who deeply admired Jews such as (and always) Spinoza. In the same breath he continued to vituperate, in very much the same terms as he had done before 1939, against the Jews who had pushed Europe into war. He remained, as always, a passionate advocate for Franco-German reconciliation, all of which explains his friendship with Paul Rassinier, one of the first of the Holocaust deniers who regularly contributed to Challaye's journal *La Voie de la Paix*.[60]

At one level, the spectacle of high-profile members of the League rallying to the Vichy regime seems nearly incomprehensible. The League was a civil liberties organization, founded to defend an innocent Jew and was the self-proclaimed conscience of democracy. The Vichy regime represented the destruction (or more accurately the suicide) of democratic France; one of its first measures included savagely discriminatory measures against Jews. Yet, almost from the beginning the League had been more than a civil liberties organization; it was, ritualistic demurrals notwithstanding, an important formation of the French Left. And the Vichy government was not, at least in its early years, so very inimical to the Left (or at least some fraction thereof). Marshal Pétain retained many of the social values of a man born in 1856, but in the prewar years he was in no way identified with the political Right; as late as 1936 Léon Blum proclaimed him to be the most republican general in France. Pierre Laval, a former Socialist (and leaguer) had moved rightward in the 1930s, but in 1940 he was hardly a politician of the traditional Right. That very fact explains why he was ousted from power for a year and a half by the extreme-right wing elements in Marshal Pétain's entourage, for whom neither his foreign policy (collaboration with Germany) nor his domestic policy (Laval was indifferent to the clerical dreams of the extreme Right) were tolerable. For those very reasons, some members of the League were inclined to consider him as something of a savior. They were less happy with his successors, Pierre-Etienne Flandin and Admiral Darlan, yet neither of these were representatives of the classic extreme Right. Flandin was center-right; his appeasement stance at the time of Munich would not have troubled many in the League. Darlan is often portrayed as an apolitical technocrat but he entered politics in 1936 as the protegé of Léon Blum, a friendship he attempted to repay in the summer of 1940 by his efforts to spirit Blum out of France.[61] The chief ideologue of the National Revolution was Marcel Déat, a former leaguer and until 1939 distinctly a politician of the Left, albeit a dissident one.

Moreover, it was not so very difficult for many in the League to reconcile themselves to the policies of the Vichy government. The very concept of "collaboration" with Nazi Germany now seems utterly abhorrent. This was less obvious in 1940. After all, members of the prewar minority, faithful to their belief that economic rivalries were the root cause of war, had long argued that only closer economic integration with Germany could ensure European peace. What they got under Vichy was more like ruthless German exploitation of French economic resources, but at least until 1943 it was possible to view this as a wartime expedient to be rectified when peace was restored. Vichy may have been the negation of democracy, but the democratic regime it replaced was a bourgeois liberal democracy for which many in the League had frequently expressed their contempt. The slogans about "a rotten and corrupted regime" under the arcane domination of the "trusts" and the "puissances d'argent" may have been lazy rhetoric for most members of the League, but for some they were not. Conditioned by years of facile rhetoric denouncing the democratic regime, there were those in the League (and on the Left in general) who did not regret its passing. Nor should this be very surprising because some elements in the League had declared well before 1940 that they *would not* regret its passing. To be sure, they were a good deal clearer about what they despised about the Third Republic than about what should replace it. The various dreams of a new regime, both somehow more authoritarian but also more socially progressive were, in retrospect, pathetically naive. But a prewar League given to tedious theoretical disquisitions on the dictatorship of the proletariat did little to instill a greater sense of realism in its members.

Nor was Vichy's anti-Semitism the "line in the sand" one might have expected. Few, with the possible exception of Challaye, were visceral anti-Semites, still less racial ones. But by the late 1930s Jews—or some Jews (Basch, Kahn, Gombault, Grumbach, and Blum)—had come to symbolize "war mongering." Gentile partisans of resistance to Germany, like Jules Moch, became, as it were, honorary Jews. Pacifists like Michel Alexandre or (so they believed) André Weil-Curiel effectively became honorary gentiles. Seen in this light, Vichy's anti-Semitic legislation was not so much an overt violation of the League's principles with respect to racial discrimination as an affirmation of what for many was a more important principle: unconditional opposition to war.

In short, the Vichy regime represented an overt violation of everything the founders of the League in 1898 believed to be its principles. By contrast, there was much in the Vichy experience that was not inconsistent with what many by the 1930s thought the League ought to stand for.

Epilogue

What does the distressing stance of some members of the League during the Vichy regime say about the history of the League itself? One answer might be: nothing. These individuals, however shocking their behavior, were a distinct minority within the League and, strictly speaking, a minority within the prewar minority. An organization as large of the League would inevitably attract a few rogues, and their presence, however regrettable, says nothing important about the League itself. Yet, although the League certainly did attract rogue elements, these men were not the kind of leaguer who might have been casually associated with the organization for its electoral utility—as might have been true, say, for Marcel Déat or Pierre Laval. They had been members of its Central Committee, presidents of important departmental federations, frequently wrote in the *Cahiers,* and were outspoken at League congresses. Emery might have represented a minority within the prewar League, but it was not such a small minority as that, witness the fact that he carried fully 40 percent of the delegates at its 1935 congress. They were in fact some of the most high-profile members of the association.

It is also possible to suggest that however central these men may have been to the life of the League they nonetheless were individuals who never internalized its principles, were in it for the "wrong" reasons, and simply did not belong in the same company as a Victor Basch. At one level this is incontestably true. But the issue is more complex than that. The man with the single most appalling record under Vichy and into the postwar years, Challaye, was also in many ways an incontestably excellent leaguer. His stance on the Painlevé affair and the Moscow trials was far more principled than that of his fellow Central Committee members. His arguments against French colonization today read as far closer to League principles than those of his principal antagonist Maurice Viollette. It was Challaye who in 1924 wanted to keep League sections from involving themselves in the elections; ten years later it was he who insisted that the League publish the names of all of its parliamentarians, just at the moment, in the wake of the Stavisky scandal, when that list could prove most embarrassing. Of course he was largely motivated by his suspicion of and hostility to the dominant role being played in the League by politicians. But this was entirely consistent with League principles—if not League practice. In retrospect it is easy enough to suggest that Challaye's protest about Grumbach's presence in Louis Barthou's foreign ministry was motivated largely by his dislike of Jews in general and Grumbach in particular. Yet he was surely not wrong to insist that long-standing League principles dictated a greater detachment from the corridors of power, especially when it involved a government that the League so vocally detested. Challaye's attacks on the Soviet Union at the time of the Moscow trials involved some personal contradictions and were driven by ulterior motives. But with respect to both form and substance, he was not wrong and closer to the League's oft-stated values than were his colleagues in the majority. Not least of the ironies of Félicien Challaye is that his stance on Algerian independence in the 1950s and 1960s was far more progressive than that of his fellow veterans on the Central Committee, Paul Rivet, Albert Bayet, and Maurice Viollette—all by any other standard far more honorable men, but, at the time, stubborn defenders of *L'Algerie française.*[1]

Perhaps Elie Reynier best exemplifies the many contradictions within the League. It is hard to imagine a more contemptible letter than the one Reynier chose to write upon resigning from the League. It was right out of Challaye's more despicable writings. But he, too, much like Challaye, was a model leaguer. However dubious his reasons for resigning from the League in 1938, it is hard to dispute that his earlier resignation from the League over the affaire des fiches was utterly principled. In the interwar years he, more than any other federal president, exposed the League's hypocrisy on the question of women's suffrage and pounded home the message that his sections ought to cease doing things that were not part of the League's mandate. And however close he may have been to Challaye in 1938, his conduct under Vichy was above reproach, and he returned with distinction to the League in the postwar years.

It might also be argued that what some leaguers said and did under Vichy speaks more to the momentary disorientation of men literally stunned by the defeat than it does to their basic League commitment. This might explain the momentary aberrations of Théodore Ruyssen. And certainly one can find almost nothing in Château's prewar writings that prefigure his virulent, although typically circumscribed, attacks on the democratic republic. More often than not, though, Challaye, Bergery, and Emery being the clearest examples, their Vichy stance was but a continuation—albeit an accelerated one—of their prewar position. To be sure, views held in the late 1930s were an imperfect predictor of post-1940 attitudes. Although he agreed upon just about everything with his prewar comrade, Georges Michon could not follow Francis Delaisi into collaboration.

The apparent paradox of individuals being both principled leaguers and savagely anti-Semitic and pro-Nazi collaborators can, to some degree, be resolved if one abandons the comfortable assumption that the Revolution (and by extension, the counterrevolution) is a "bloc" or that Vichy can be effectively summarized as "the revenge of the anti-Dreyfusards." As Simon Epstein has recently brilliantly demonstrated, the Dreyfusard tradition, of which the League chose to be the living embodiment, was a good deal more complex. One could be both an anti-Semite and a Dreyfusard. Colonel Picquart personally had little use for Jews; he risked his career for Alfred Dreyfus simply because he thought him to be innocent. The subsequent political evolution of Dreyfusards defied prediction. There is no political evolution, no matter how tortuous, that one could not assign to at least one Dreyfusard. In 1898 Georges Valois was an anarchist, a philo-Semite, and a Dreyfusard. By 1906 he had joined the Action Française and become a virulent anti-Semite. In 1925 he founded the ephemeral but explicitly fascist *Faisceau*. By the 1930s he was back on the fringes of the Left (and indeed on the fringes of the League!). He fought in the Resistance and died in Bergen-Belsen.[2] Others took different routes and, as Epstein clearly shows, many of them played a leading role in the Vichy regime.

The French Left (much like the French Right) was a complex and confusing phenomenon, drawing on different and conflicting traditions, guided by ambiguous signposts. The French Revolution, with its notion of "fraternity" could inform integral pacifists, just as the Jacobin tradition could justify Republican ultrapatriotism. Partisans of liberal democracy could cite the First Republic but so too could, and did, those who sought a more authoritarian regime. The French revolutionary tradition could be of equal comfort to anti-Semites and to philo-Semites.

But the League ought to have been spared these confusions. It was not—or was not supposed to have been—merely another formation of the Left. Its guiding principle was not the various and conflicting traditions of the French Left but the Declaration of the Rights of Man. The Declaration is a remarkably lucid document. And the League founded in 1898 did not choose that document at random. It provided the League with a clear doctrine as to what it could and should do. Granted, the Declaration was not without its shortcomings. It was of no help at all on the vexed question of war and peace and not much more useful with respect to the best way to organize society and the economy. But those were—and remain—essentially political questions. What the Declaration did contain was more than enough to be getting on with. So although the range of issues it could address would have been restricted, had the League stuck exclusively to the Declaration it might have achieved a great deal more than it did. The list is long. Armed only with the Declaration, the League could have championed the cause of women's suffrage, it would have denounced the affaire des fiches for the scandal it was, it would have challenged the discriminatory legislation against religious congregations, and it would have championed the cause of a free press and not permitted itself to embrace the patent self-interest of left-wing newspapers nor to subscribe to the demagogic rhetoric about the state's need to restrict free expression. Its position on the Moscow trials would have made no difference to the outcome, but it would have been an honorable one and not a disgraceful one. It would not have permitted so many of its members to treat the League as a patronage machine, thus rendering more plausible its entirely admirable call for a less corrupt Republic. Absent patronage, the League might have been less willing to permit politicians to use it as an electoral springboard and to be less enamored of the number of cabinet ministers upon whose help it could call.

Of course the League would have paid a price for this. A League of this kind would not have had 180,000 members. Nor so many ministers in any given cabinet. It is possible, although not certain, that this might have hampered its activity in the one thing it incontestably did so well—the defense of victims of injustice. But this is not obvious either. A smaller League would have had fewer resources but would not have had to squander its time and energy on the multitude of inappropriate cases with which it was deluged. Fewer League ministers might have produced fewer positive outcomes in the case of questions of injustice—although this point is not certain either. On the other hand, had the League not seemed like just another left-wing pressure group, its interventions might have been taken more seriously, even by conservative ministers. And certainly, had there been fewer League ministers, so much of the League's energies would not have been taken up with debates about their political conduct. Liberated from the need to debate the ratification of the interallied accords, proposed changes in the electoral laws, the merits of compulsory automobile insurance, the internal regulations of the Rassemblement Populaire, the origins of World War I, the conduct of French foreign policy in the late 1930s—all issues over which it could exercise little influence—the League would have been free to concentrate its energies on those issues upon which it could have some effect. Its interventions would have been that much more effective because of the accrued moral authority of being something other than an "intergroup" of the Left.

The League did not choose this route, a fact that dissidents in the first decade of the twentieth century deplored and that League leaders in the late 1930s increasingly regretted. Its reasons for so doing are entirely understandable but also perfectly regrettable. What went wrong? To some degree the League was victim of the entirely ambiguous legacy of the Dreyfus affair. At one level, this was just the case of one army officer wrongly and illegally convicted of a crime he did not commit. Charles Péguy was not altogether wrong in arguing that the successful outcome of the case did not authorize the winners to launch attacks on the army and the church. But the League could counter that the Dreyfus affair brought to light other problems in French society, notably the presence of reactionary elements in the army and the church whose *ralliement* to the democratic Republic was, at best, half-hearted. Moreover, if Captain Dreyfus was a victim of injustice, were the many members of the French working class not also condemned by an economic system to a life of misery? If the illegal imprisonment of one innocent man were a crime, what about the death of literally millions of equally innocent men in utterly unnecessary wars? There was a compelling logic at work here, so compelling that the League seems not to have noticed—or only late in the game and inconsistently—that this same logic stood in an uncomfortable relationship with their mission of defending the rights of individuals. If defense of the democratic regime became paramount, issues like the voting rights of women, freedom of association, or freedom of the press might have to be sacrificed. If issues of war and peace became paramount, the victims of Hitler or Stalin (depending upon where one stood on that issue) would have to be ignored.

Moreover, by virtue of becoming the League's constant reference point, the Dreyfus affair effectively blinded League leaders to the sectarian nature of their conduct. Almost by definition, the League founded to defend Captain Dreyfus was above politics and therefore above reproach. It glorified and exaggerated its role in the affair.[3] But it was also highly selective in what it appropriated from the history of the affair. Clemenceau and Picquart had played a decisive role in the liberation of Dreyfus but were not leaguers and thus subject to consistent attacks. Painlevé and Herriot, far less central to the liberation of Dreyfus, were League members and therefore, at least in the eyes of League leaders, above reproach.

Nothing whatsoever distinguishes Emile Guerry's defense of Stalin from Félicien Challaye's defense of Hitler (unless one takes into account the fact that the victims of Stalin in 1936–37 were far more numerous than the victims of Hitler in 1938.) Both evoked the killings in the French Revolution as a justification. At some point someone in the League ought to have pointed out that judicial murders—whether committed by Jacobins, Stalin, or Hitler—were all overt violations of the rights of man, did not justify one another, and ought to be condemned out of hand. No one did. Victor Basch took great pleasure in citing Article 35 of the Jacobin Declaration of the Rights of Man, to the effect that when the government violates the liberties of the people, insurrection was a duty. But so, too, did Colonel Charles des Isnards of the virulently antiparliamentary Jeunesses Patriotes. At some point, someone ought to have pointed out that in a democratic regime the ballot box, and not the street, was the appropriate vehicle for protest. But no one ever did—unless one counts Basch's rather lame retractions in 1935. That Basch was a convinced democrat is beyond dispute, as is the fact that he took his rhetoric far less seriously than did other more authoritarian elements in the League. The point, though, is that it was often the same rhetoric. What the Vichy experience so strikingly reveals is the degree to which people who fundamentally shared little in common could have for so long remained in the same organization by virtue of sharing the same demagogic discourse.

World War II very nearly destroyed the League. Its archives had been seized by the Germans and disappeared for over half a century. Its headquarters had been devastated, and its office equipment stolen. Death, natural or otherwise, took much of its prewar leadership as too did the collaborationist activities of many prominent leaguers. Until the 1950s, the League was always on the verge of bankruptcy, headed off (just barely) by some important donations, an interest-free loan by the CGT, and by renting out part of its building. Whereas the prewar League had more than forty permanent employees, in 1960 it had only four.[4] Of course they now had far less work to do. In 1929 (a fairly typical year), the League received over 17,000 letters and dealt with more than 6,000 cases of injustice; in 1963 the relevant figures were 1,136 and 126, respectively.[5] The *Cahiers,* greatly reduced in size, now appeared only at irregular intervals. But the critical problem faced by the League (and the source of its financial woes) was its inability either to attract new members or to persuade more than a tiny fraction of its prewar members to renew their interest in the League. In 1950 the League would, rather sadly, hold up the federation of the Marne as an exemplar because its membership stood at 44 percent of its prewar total.[6] But the Marne was a very exceptional case. The federation of the Charente-Maritime, the largest in the prewar years, virtually ceased to exist after 1945. At the initiative of the Freemasons (who had been its founders at the beginning of the century) it was slowly reestablished in the early 1950s. But it never came close to its prewar size. In 1936 this Federation had some 8,000 members in 103 sections. In 1960 it had only 200 members in 4 sections. By the 1950s the League had succeeded in reestablishing about a fifth of its prewar sections, but they were now much smaller. Overall membership in an organization that had once counted 180,000 adherents, was probably no higher than 7,000 in 1950 and 10,000 fourteen years later.[7] In short, twenty years after the end of World War II, the League had far fewer members than it had enjoyed in 1900, two years after its foundation.

What explains the precipitous decline of the League? World War II and the Occupation were certainly factors, although they mostly accelerated a decline evident in the late 1930s. But the war does not explain everything. The Socialist party was every bit as divided in the late 1930s as was the League (and for the same reasons); it was even more compromised under Vichy. Yet it emerged in 1945 with an additional 100,000 members.[8] But there was always something artificial about the League's huge membership. For much of its history its militants often treated the League as a comfortable (and inexpensive) political club. Faced with the social and political crises of the mid-1930s, unprecedented numbers of Frenchmen were politically mobilized. The Socialist party increased fivefold; the Communists tenfold. But at precisely this moment, League membership began to decline. Some of those who left, Radicals for the most part, believed that the League had fallen into the hands of the Socialists and Communists; many Socialists did not see the point in simultaneously belonging to two organizations that seemed to be doing roughly the same things. To the degree that the League's activity seemed increasingly to involve the conduct of French foreign policy, those who felt strongly about the matter found what was now the largest political party a more useful vehicle for their activity. After 1945, Radicalism, the political home of so many of the original leaguers, quickly lost its political influence. The dominant party on the left became the Communists. League membership was open to Communists, and some did enter the League (Madeleine Rebérioux being the obvious example). But few postwar Communists, unlike Radicals and Socialists, would have had the experience of joint membership in the League.

Nor was the Dreyfusard tradition, the great rallying cry (albeit to a decreasing degree) of the prewar League as effective after the war. By the 1950s there were relatively few French who had directly experienced the "affaire." League president Daniel Meyer's 1960 feud with the editors of *Le Petit Labrousse* over its minor misrepresentation of the League's role in the affair had a quaintly antiquarian quality to it, which would not have been the case in, say, 1924.[9] A far more immediate memory was that of the Occupation, which the League could not really exploit. It could, and did, stress the role in the Resistance of some of its leaders, but this was an issue upon which it could hardly linger without exposing the overt collaboration of others. The clerical menace that had fueled League discourse for decades was an increasingly marginal issue by the 1950s. Pacifism, a potent theme after the great carnage of 1914–18, had far more ambivalent connotations in the post-World War II period, associated as it was with appeasement and collaboration.

What is striking is the extreme bitterness and disillusionment of many pre-war militants. Lucien Cancouët was atypical of many League leaders in that he came from a very poor working-class background and was an autodidact, something he never let anyone forget. Nonetheless, he was an active member of the section of the fourteenth arrondissement for twenty years and president for at least seven.[10] Militant pacifist, he intervened no fewer than fifty times at League congresses in the 1930s.[11] After the war, all he cared to remember about the League was that it "never detached itself from politics and was at times an electoral springboard for ambitious politicians." The League was "as feeble and almost as sectarian as were the [political] parties." He listed his League activities as one of the "errors" in his life. "The League absorbed a good part of my activities and I wasted my time there."[12]

Finally, the League had been the quintessential example of the political culture of the Third Republic. The section, whatever else it represented, offered rural and small-town Frenchmen an opportunity for sociability. Every couple of months one could gather with a group of like-minded friends and talk politics. The issues they kicked around were often local ones, but it was comforting to know that there were people in Paris who would take note. Citizens of a tiny village could discuss the larger national political issues, debate the exact terms of a motion that would ultimately be published by the *Cahiers,* and leave with the feeling that they had some input into the conduct of national affairs. Every once in a while one might expect some more or less important Parisian to address the section on some major question, leaving everyone with the feeling, or at least the illusion, of being part of a broader and more important political community. Once a year, section members could hop on a bus to the departmental capital to attend a federal congress, where they might rub shoulders with the inevitably present deputies and perhaps get to exchange a few words with a Basch, a Guernut, or a Kahn. For keener section members there was almost always a case of injustice to which they could devote their energies.

All of this counted for less in the increasingly urban world of the 1950s. A talented orator coming from Paris had once offered a rare escape from rural isolation. Now it meant leaving the house to hear a discourse one could pick up any night of the week on television. A greatly expanded social service sector reduced both the need and the opportunities for the informal social work activity of the League. The difficulties of civil servants, once the object of much of the League's action, were now taken in hand by the increasingly professional labor unions.[13]

To what extent can the League's uneven record in its first fifty years be attributed to factors unique to France? Was there something uniquely *French* about the League's history? The question addresses itself to those who believe that the French intellectual tradition is significantly bereft of the values of the Whig tradition or Anglo-Saxon liberalism. One way to answer it would be to briefly compare the League to its nearest counterpart, the ACLU.

At its foundation in 1920 the ACLU was directly inspired by the League. But in critical respects it has always been a very different organization, operating in a dramatically different context. Although, like the League, the ACLU has always been on the Left, it is, and always has been, far less immersed in day-to-day politics than its French counterpart. Sitting members of Congress or of the Cabinet have never played a preponderant role on the ACLU's directing organs. Leaders of the House and Senate Democrats, to say nothing of Cabinet members of Democratic administration, are rarely if ever high-profile leaders of the ACLU. It is hard to imagine being able to draw together a congressional ACLU caucus large enough to include the majority of congressional Democrats. Whatever the personal political preferences of ACLU members, the organization enjoys a far greater detachment from electoral politics.

Directly related is the fact that the ACLU is, in proportionate terms, a far smaller organization than the League. Forty years after its foundation the ACLU had only 45,000 members. Today it has fewer than 300,000 members. Taking into account the huge population difference between France and the United States, a comparably sized League would have had at most 40,000 members at its peak rather than 180,000. The ACLU is smaller, at least in part, because few Americans join it in the hopes of belonging to a powerful patronage machine, finding a convenient surrogate for active membership in the Democratic Party, or escaping from small-town isolation.

Finally, the respective political cultures differ. There is no real French equivalent to the Federalist Papers, just as there is no American equivalent of the Jacobin tradition. The slogan: "the republic in danger" has no resonance in

American life. Americans do worry at times about the erosion of civil liberties, but few take seriously the proposition that the democratic regime may collapse. But then Americans have lived since the foundation of the Republic under the same political regime and more or less the same Constitution. Crassly opportunist though the cry of "republic in danger" might have been in the early twentieth century, the French were haunted, in ways Americans were not, by the fact that two previous republics had been overthrown by two different Bonapartes and that for over eighty years no regime survived for two decades. The temptation to invoke political expediency to justify selective application of civil libertarian principles was correspondingly greater in the League.

Nonetheless, there are instructive parallels between the two organizations. The ACLU was no less blind to the realities of the Soviet Union in the 1930s than its French counterpart.[14] During World War II, stunned by the Nazi-Soviet pact, the ACLU faltered on the rights of American Communists, and summarily expelled Elizabeth Gurley Flynn from its ranks for no better reason than her political opinions.[15] It took a very equivocal stance on the unconstitutional internment of Japanese Americans.[16] In the 1940s and early 1950s, a period one historian of the ACLU has dubbed "The Era of Expediency,"[17] the ACLU's position on the McCarthyite witch hunts was at best ambivalent. While doing everything to distance itself from Communism, the ACLU did condemn, correctly, the House Un-American Activities Committee as "the chief threat to civil liberties."[18] At the same time, however, the ACLU, or more accurately some branches thereof, were prepared to cooperate with both the House Un-American Activities Committee and the FBI, in the latter case passing on information about Communists in their ranks.[19]

In critical respects, however, the best test of the ACLU's dedication to principles came in the spring of 1977. In that year, Frank Collins, leader of the National Socialist Party of America, a frankly neo-Nazi party, announced its plans to organize a march in Skokie, Illinois, a suburb of Chicago. Collins did not choose that suburb at random; it was predominantly Jewish and was home to a substantial number of survivors of the Holocaust. Local authorities promptly banned the march. At the request of Collins, the ACLU actively defended his party's constitutional right to free assembly. The decision prompted outrage within the ACLU and a wave of very public resignations.[20] The protests were both understandable (given the significant Jewish membership in the ACLU) and somewhat puzzling. After all, the ACLU's stance on Skokie was hardly without precedent. In the 1960s the ACLU had routinely defended the civil liberties of American Nazis. Its then leader, George Lincoln Rockwell, rarely went anywhere without a list of local ACLU sections upon whom he could count to defend him from the persistent obstruction of local authorities. Moreover, in those years the ACLU took considerable pride in its defense of Rockwell because it reinforced its claim to be disinterested protectors of civil liberties for everyone, including the most offensive. So what had changed by 1977? The answer would appear to be that the composition of the ACLU had undergone some important modifications. From 45,000 members in 1960, it had expanded to 275,000 in 1977. Most of the newcomers had joined the ACLU in the wake of the civil rights struggles in the South and the draft resistance battles of the early 1970s. Many of the new members joined as left-wing activists rather than civil libertarians. On those issues, civil liberties and progressive politics more or less coincided; on Skokie, by contrast, they did not.[21] In this respect the ACLU was not different than the League; in both cases a significant influx of new members spoke to the changing political climate rather than to an increased dedication to human rights.

The Skokie case would in time become part of the legend of the ACLU.[22] In some respects it functioned much like the officers of Lâon did for the League. American critics of the ACLU contend that Skokie was a token action intended to "counter arguments that the organization was obsessed with helping criminals and leftists."[23] The League's critics in France said similar things about its defense of the officers of Laôn, but they had a better case. Not only was Pressensé's defense of the officers motivated by tactical political calculations, but the conduct of the officers was innocuous compared to that of Frank Collins and his followers. What both the ACLU and the League had in common was the certainty that any attempt to apply their principles evenhandedly would come under assault from the Left—including a Left within their ranks. In 1976 at Camp Pendleton, California, a group of black marines attacked white marines who allegedly belonged to the Ku Klux Klan. In the subsequent investigation, both groups were treated in ways that violated their constitutional rights. The local chapter of the ACLU chose to defend both groups despite the strenuous objection of the parent Southern California board and the usually allied National Lawyer's Guild who found it guilty of "poisonous evenhandedness."[24] The charge of poisonous evenhandedness is reminiscent of the charge of "false liberalism" so often levied by charter members of the League.

In essence, then, the same tensions between left-wing (or "progressive") politics and civil libertarian principles were present within both the ACLU and the League. On this issue, it might be argued that the League in its first forty years suffers by comparison with the ACLU in its last forty. But they were different years. In the 1930s, 1940s, and early 1950s the record of the ACLU was not dramatically different from that of the League.

Both the League and its American counterpart would prove, at times, incapable of abiding by the liberal principles to which they subscribed. It is important to acknowledge, however, that those very liberal principles are notoriously demanding, precisely because there is no guarantee that they will yield a desirable (or "progressive") outcome. Most liberals take it as an article of faith that in the long run they will. But it *is* an article of "faith," and the long run is a very long time. "Liberty with all its risks" is an easy slogan in the abstract, but in concrete terms the risks can at times seem overwhelming. The enduring image of the League is not, therefore, only the various ways in which it failed to live up to its mandate. Equally worth remembering is the little schoolteacher who rode a bus for 600 miles to passionately plead the cause of an innocent man.

Notes

INTRODUCTION

1. ACLU membership figures must be used with caution as the ACLU distinguishes between "members" and "memberships" and inflates the former on the grounds that the partners of card-carrying members often share their commitment to the organization.

2. Henri Sée, *Histoire de la ligue des droits de l'homme, 1893–1926* (Paris, 1927).

3. Wendy Ellen Perry, "Remembering Dreyfus: The Ligue des Droits de l'Homme and the Making of the Modern French Human Rights Movement" (Ph.D. diss., University of North Carolina, 1998), 326.

4. Françoise Basch, *Victor Basch: De l'affaire Dreyfus au crime de la Milice* (Paris, 1994).

5. See most notably the fine collection of articles in the special edition of *Le Mouvement Social* (no. 183, April–June, 1998) devoted to the League.

6. See in particular, Sylvie Claveau, "L'Autre dans les Cahiers des Droits de l'Homme, 1920–1940. Une sélection universaliste de l'altérité à La Ligue des Droits de l'homme et du Citoyen en France" (Ph.D. thesis, McGill University, 2000).

7. Madeleine Rebérioux, "Politique et société dans l'histoire de la Ligue des droits de l'homme," *Le Mouvement Social* (no. 183, April–June 1998), 16.

8. Ibid., 22.

9. Ibid., 6.

CHAPTER I

1. The best source for the early years of the League is Henri Sée, *Histoire;* additional useful information (including some corrections) can be found in the account of Emile Kahn, then secretary general, in *La Lumière,* June 10, 17, 24; July 1, 1938. Important also is Perry, "Remembering Dreyfus," chapter 1.

2. The name originally proposed had been the *Ligue pour la defence des droits des citoyens.* Sée, *Histoire,* 10.

3. On the early activity of the League, see Mathias Morhardt, *L'Oeuvre de la ligue des droits de l'homme, 1898–1910* (Paris, 1911), 98–101.

4. To be discussed in some detail in the next chapter.

5. In the early 1930s, the Radical party had somewhere between 70,000 and 100,000 members, the SFIO closer to 50,000, and the Communist Party more like 20,000. All such figures, unlike those of the League, are suspect and likely to be on the high side. Because membership in the traditional parties of the Right was always both small and notional, it is just possible that in 1933 the League had more members than all French political parties combined.

6. Perry, "Remembering Dreyfus." 256.

7. These figures can be found in Archives de la Ligue des Droits de l'Homme (hereafter ALDH), carton 26.

8. Pierre Arches, "La Ligue des droits de l'homme et du citoyen à Parthenay et dans les Deux-Sèvres (1935–1936)," *Bulletin de la société historique et scientifique des Deux-Sèvres* 2e series, tome X, no. 2–3, 1977, 376. The author also suggests (378) that in the department as a whole, the percentage of women was likely slightly below 3 percent.

9. Nothing in the decade suggested serious progress in female representation. In 1923, women were 0.5 percent of the section presidents; in 1925, the comparable figure was 0.23 percent; in 1927, 0.47 percent; and in 1929, 0.48 percent. This information is derived from the *Annuaire officiel de la ligue des droits de l'homme* found in the *Cahiers,* 1923, pp. i–xi (supplement to issue of August 26, 1923); 1925, 387–99; 1927, 219–34; 1929, 343–60.

10. By far the best prosopographical study of the League's leadership is the pioneering work of Perry, "Remembering Dreyfus": See also, Claveau, "L'Autre," 108–59 and Jean and Monica Charlot, "Un Rassemblement des Intellectuels: La Ligue des Droits de l'Homme," *Revue Française de Science Politique,* vol. 9, no. 4, December 1959) 995–1028.

11. *Annexe au Bulletin no 44 de la section mâconnaise de la ligue des droits de l'homme,* 1910.

12. The list can be found in ALDH 150.

13. Arches, "La Ligue," 367.

14. On the average, one president of a section out of three gave no socioprofessional identification. In 1923, teachers represented 15.8 percent of the presidents of sections and civil servants 14.8 percent. Local politicians accounted for 23.8 percent, local businessmen for 32.3 percent, and members of the liberal professions for 10.9 percent. In 1925, the relevant percentages for those three categories were teachers 20.5 percent, civil servants 11.4 percent, local politicians 19.06 percent, businessmen 33.8 percent, and liberal professions 12.1 percent. In 1925, teachers were 19.8 percent, civil servants 11.8 percent, politicians 23.7 percent, businessmen 31.9 percent, and liberal professions 10.0 percent; in 1929, teachers represented 21.3 percent, civil servants 14.0 percent, politicians 20.6 percent, business 33.0 percent, and liberal professions 8.0 percent. For sources, see note 9.

15. Claveau, "L'Autre," 110–20. Representation of members of the liberal professions exceeded by a factor of fifty-three their representation in the population at large; teachers and civil servants were overrepresented by a factor of at least two; peasants and workers were underrepresented by a factor of four. Claveau's analysis is exceptionally rigorous but does not disaggregate the various levels of League leadership. From her data, however, it is clear that nearly 55 percent of the cadres of the League were drawn from the liberal professions, teachers, or civil servants.

16. *Congrès national de 1931* (Paris, 1931) 70, 129; *Congrès national de 1932* (Paris, 1933), 44, 93.

17. For a recent and perceptive discussion of the role of Jews, Protestants, and Freemasons in the founding of the democratic republic see Philip Nord, *The Republican Moment* (Cambridge, MA, 1995), chapters 1, 4, and 5.

18. Perry, "Remembering Dreyfus," 263–66. Her definition is elastic in that she includes people "identified to some degree with Protestantism" and "known to have identified with Judaism." A more rigorous reading of her evidence reduces the percentages of Protestants and Jews to, respectively, just under 15 percent and just under 11 percent.

19. Historians of the Masonry have disputed this point. Pierre Chevallier, *Histoire de la franc-maçonnerie française* (Paris, 1975) vol. III, 36–37, contends that two presidents, Ludovic Trarieux and Ferdinand Buisson, as well as the first secretary general, Mathias Morhardt, were Masons. But he, like contemporary right-wing critics of the League, assumes, incorrectly, that every League leader who ever addressed the meetings of a Masonic lodge was necessarily a Mason.

20. On the critical role of the Masons in the foundation of the League in the Charente-Maritime as well as its reestablishment there after World War II, see Claudy Valin, *La Ligue des droits de l'homme en Charente-Maritime* (Saint-Jean d'Angely, 1988) 55, 229.

21. Whereas the League was cautious about its links with freemasonry, the Masons could be less discreet. For some examples, see Pierre Pitois, *Les Buts politiques de la ligue des droits de l'homme* (Paris, 1935), 17.

22. *Congrès national de 1925* (Paris, 1925) 124.

23. Perry, "Remembering Dreyfus," 26–66. A handful of nonparliamentarians on the Central Committee also appear to have been Masons. The most important were Albert Bayet, Charles Richet, and Dr. Sicard de Plauzoles.

24. Because the Masons were a secret society and because the issue of their political influence was a highly partisan one, establishing which public figures were or were not Masons has always been a difficult exercise. The names mentioned are taken from the partisan but relatively cautious account of Saint-Pastour, *La Franc-Maçonnerie au parlement* (Paris, 1970.)

25. *Congrès national de 1927* (Paris, 1927), 7. See also *Cahiers,* 1928, 619.

26. *Congrès national de 1935* (Paris, 1935), 298.

27. Edmund Bernus, *Pages Libres,* February 27, 1909. As late as the 1930s, League dues, ten francs a year, were less than one-fifth of those charged by the Socialist party and one-sixth of those levied by the General Confederation of Labor.

28. *Les Droits de l'homme* (Mayenne), May 1930.

29. *Les Droits de l'homme* (Calvados), January, February 1929.

30. *Bulletin de la section mâconnaise,* November 1905.

31. Bernus, *Pages Libres* February 27, 1909.

32. *Les Droits de l'homme* (Meurthe-et-Moselle), January 1934.

33. *Le Ligueur* (Marseilles), June–July 1934.

34. *Cahiers,* 1928, p. 354. The rabbit question appears to have loomed large in that department, as Guernut would be dwelling on it a decade later. *La Tribune de l'Aisne,* September 24, 1934.

35. *La Flèche,* October 6, 1934.

36. Some sections made a fetish of French revolutionary (or at least Jacobin) symbolism. *L'Equité* (a bulletin of a number of Parisian sections) dated its issues both by the modern calendar but also by the French revolutionary one. The issue of January 1, 1932 was therefore also dated 11 Frimaire An 141.

37. The number of nonresident members, twelve in 1926, was increased to eighteen in 1934. There were forty resident members.

38. Complaints about windy orators, personal feuds, and the generally chaotic nature of many congresses were a staple of the League's local bulletins. For example, *Bulletin trimestriel de la Fédération de Seine-et-Marne,* March 1930; *La Ligue des droits de l'homme* (Ardennes), third trimester, 1927, September 15, 1928.

39. *Congrès national de 1937* (Paris, 1937), 353.

40. *Congrès national de 1925* (Paris, 1925), 122–43.

41. In 1935 and 1936, 12 percent of the delegates were women. More typical were the years 1924, 1925, 1932, 1933, and 1937 when, respectively, 7 percent, 6 percent, 8 percent, 6 percent, and 9 percent of the delegates were women. At most congresses, between one-half and one-third of the women present (63 percent in 1932, 44 percent in 1933, and 42 percent in 1925) had the same last name as a male delegate. Of course, this does not prove they were the wives of the men in question, that they were not delegates in their own right, or that it was not the men who were present in a spousal capacity.

42. The frequent references to "applause from the left" in the stenographic record of the League's 1926 congress suggests that at least some of the time delegates of the minority sat as a group on the left side of congressional meeting halls.

43. The federation of the Seine was the largest in the League and was often perceived as a unified left-wing stronghold. In fact, there was always a great deal of dissension within the federation, and at any given time nearly half of its seventy-five sections were in a state of open dissent. The section of Monnaie-Odéon shared the sixth arrondissement of Paris with the far more moderate but significantly less active section of St. Germain. See Antoine Weexsteen, "La fédération de la Seine de la ligue des droits de l'homme, 1926–1939" (Mémoire de maîtrise d'histoire, Université de Paris 1, 1993, 11, 35–38; Antoine Weexsteen, "La fédération de la Seine de la Ligue des droits de l'homme dans les années 1930," *Le Mouvement Social,* no. 183, April–June 1998, 139–66.

44. See, for example, *Bulletin official de la section de Monnaie-Odéon,* January 1928, in ALDH, 158 for a running battle with the federation of the Charente-Inférieure. See also, *Notre Action: Bulletin mensuel de la fédération de l'Aisne,* March 1929, June 1931.

45. *Bulletin officiel de la Ligue des droits de l'homme* (hereafter, *B.O*), 1908, 1010–1039; 1104– 1111.

46. For Duplantier's attacks on Pressensé see *Bulletin de la section maçonnaise,* August 8, 1908. The source of these political tensions is discussed in the next chapter.

47. *B.O.,* 1910, 673–712; Morhardt's actual fine was something like 1,200 francs plus costs. For his critics, see *Les droits de l'homme* (a newspaper under the control of League dissidents) 6, June 11; 2, July 29; August 6, 1911.

48. Anyone reading the police reports in AN (Archives Nationales) F7 13086-13089 cannot help but be struck by the futility of the exercise. Hundreds of agents produced thousands of reports, all detailing the utterly predictable speeches of League members. By virtue of not relying on the equally accurate press reports, the Ministry created more work for agents whose task was to find out who people like Cahn or Caillaux were and to determine if they were not, in fact, the same as Kahn or Caillaud.

49. The exchange involved Félicien Challaye and Salomon Grumbach and almost certainly involved the increasingly anti-Semitic anger of the former. Alas, it cannot be found in the League's existing archives.

50. By the mid-1930s, and owing entirely to its internal problems, the League did become somewhat (but only somewhat) less transparent. It ceased publishing the names of its politicians who belonged to the League (who were often an embarrassment) and, on occasion, dissenting views.

51. Perry, "Remembering Dreyfus," 76.

52. To be discussed in Chapter 7 in the context of the Moscow trials.

53. The responses of sections to the questions of the month can be found in ALDH, 185–90.

54. For example, in one 1910 issue of the *Bulletin officiel,* no fewer than ninety-three sections submitted nearly identically worded resolutions concerning the recent execution of a Spanish freethinker. There were nearly as many similar resolutions in the next issue. *B.O.* 1910, 49–60, 135. Upon receipt of identical resolutions from different sections, all attacking the Central Committee, League leaders often suspected that they were being subjected to a carefully orchestrated letter-writing campaign. See, for example, Secretary General Emile Kahn to Serol, October 21, 1938 in ALDH 146.

CHAPTER 2

1. Buisson had been misled by his fellow Radical, Léon Bourgeois, recently appointed minister of the interior. Bourgeois had, quite dishonestly, assured Buisson that there was conclusive evidence of Dreyfus's guilt. The best source for the earliest days of the League is a series of articles written by the secretary general after 1932, Emile Kahn. Kahn, a young history student at the time of the foundation of the League was witness to all its earliest history. In 1938 he wrote a series of articles in *La Lumière* (June 10, 17, 24; July 1, 8, 1938) celebrating the fortieth anniversary of the League and, incidentally correcting the minor errors to be found in both Henri Sée, *Histoire* and Jean Psichari, *B.O.* 1904, 887 ff.

2. As the League's more adroit dialecticians would not fail to note, the Declaration, as lucid and concise as it was, *did* permit a degree of interpretative "wiggle room." Article 10 qualified its assertion of freedom of opinion with the words "provided such expression does not trouble the lawful order." Article 17, while insisting on the sacredness of private property, did concede that citizens could be deprived of it when (and only when) to do so was in the obvious public interest, provided there was a fair indemnity.

3. By way of example, both Alphonse Aulard and Charles Seignobos were founding members of the League.

4. For an example of the initial agonizing in Socialist circles see *Les droits de l'homme de la ligue Stephanoise,* 30 July 1899. Here local Socialist Dreyfusards and League members struggled against local Guesdistes who argued that the Dreyfus affair was an internal matter of the bourgeoisie, and socialists ought to let "the Jews and the Jesuits fight it out among themselves." The newspaper countered that "even though he is both rich and Jewish" Dreyfus was a worthy cause simply because he "suffers unjustly." Moreover, it argued, this affair opened the door to a much wider range of reforms including disarmament, international arbitration, and the suppression of permanent armies.

5. See, for example, *Congrès national de 1931* (Paris, 1931), 41; *Congrès national de 1936* (Paris, 1936), 36.

6. *Nouvel Age,* January 17; April 13–20; May 30, 1935.

7. *Congrès national de 1935* (Paris, 1935) 207.

8. *La ligue* (Saône-et-Loire), November 1933.

9. The prime movers of the idea of a new declaration were Jean Maristan, vice president of the section of Marseille, and Gustave Rodrigues, author of a tract entitled *La droit de vie* (*unique solution du problème social* (Paris, 1934). Of course they disagreed with one another as well as with the Central Committee. For some of the feuds associated with the new declaration see Maristan to Kahn, January 30, February 28, March 17, April 22, May 20, 1936. ALDH, 138.

10. The 200 families were technically the 200 largest stockholders in the private Banque de France until 1936. More generally they were the symbol of the financial oligarchy. De Wendel, a major steel magnate, headed the powerful steel trust, the *Comité des Forges.*

11. *Congrès national de 1936* (Paris, 1936), 237–275.

12. Any precise statement of the political allegiances of early League leaders is difficult, owing both to the vagueness of French political labels and the fact that a number of early leaders were more or less apolitical. By Wendy Perry's meticulous calculations, of the twenty-eight early leaders whose political affiliations are more or less certain, seventeen (or 60 percent) were centre-gauche, five Radical, and six Socialist. Perry, "Remembering Dreyfus," 27.

13. Strictly speaking, by the end of the first decade of the twentieth century, the term *modéré* was reserved for those on the far Right.

14. French law made it difficult to form national political parties until the adoption in 1901 of the law on associations.

15. *Bulletin de la section Maconnaise,* February, May 1906; June 1907; October 1908; June 1909. A courageous minority in this section, led by a local Protestant minister, attempted to dispute Teissier's doctrine of the sanctity of private property, which he considered to be tantamount to "theft." In this section he was fighting an uphill battle, and for his pains he came close to being expelled by the section. April, June, August, 1906; March, 1907.

16. The emergence of the Communist party did not for long rid the SFIO of its ultrarevolutionary wing. Some of the more overtly revolutionary elements in the SFIO could not stomach the kind of discipline demanded of the Communists, abhorred what passed for Socialism in the Soviet Union, and concluded, by the 1930s at least, that Soviet-style communism was uninterested in, if not hostile to, revolution in the West.

17. Just what those circumstances were was a matter of arcane debate. World War I appeared to fit the bill, although not all socialists agreed that this was in any way an appropriate occasion. In 1924, the Socialist leader, Léon Blum, declared that Socialists would not enter governments until they were the largest party in parliament and thus in a position to dominate the government. This did not happen until 1936.

18. For a thorough, albeit partisan, discussion of the Affaire des fiches, see François Vindé, *L'Affaire des fiches* (Paris, 1989).

19. See his letter, *BO,* 1904, 1578.

20. Ibid., 1905, 9–10.

21. The best summary of his career is Remi Fabre, "Francis de Pressensé," *Le mouvement social* (April–June, 1998, no. 183.), 61–92.

22. *B.O.,* January 16, 1905, 11–12, 18. The reference to "the party of forgers" is to the anti-Dreyfusards who had forged some of the evidence against Captain Dreyfus.

23. The army certainly did harbor some deeply Catholic and secretly royalist officers but they were no more numerous than ambitiously republican ones. In any event, most officers, at least until 1940, if not the mid-1950s, kept their political preferences to themselves.

24. *B.O.,* 1905, 88–89.

25. Ibid., 1905, 198.

26. Ibid., 1905, 273.

27. Célestin Bouglé, *Le Bilan des ligues* (Bordeaux, 1903) 24.

28. *B.O.,* 1903, 775.

29. Ibid., 1903, 777–779.

30. Ibid., 1903, 780–783.

31. Ibid., 1909, 214.

32. Fabre, "Francis de Pressensé," 82–86.

33. *Bulletin de la section Maçonnaise,* August, October 1908. Here, as elsewhere, Radicals rarely shared even the fairly tepid anticolonialism of the Socialists. It also did not help that the Protestant schools in Madagascar had been primarily the work of Anglican clergy.

34. *B.O.,* 1907, 351–84, 677–89, 704–25, 783–95, 819–39, 841–76; 1908, 1197–1204, 1335–60. See in particular, H. S. Jones, "Civil Rights for Civil Servants? The ligue des droits de l'homme and the Problem of Trade Unionism in the French Public Service, 1905–1914," *Historical Journal,* vol. 31, no. 4, 1988, 899–920.

35. *B.O.,* 1909, 632–33.

36. Ibid., 1910, 720.

37. Perry, "Remembering Dreyfus," 97.

38. *B.O.*, 1911, 69–78.

39. Ibid., 1909, 646, 712, 745, 1236.

40. Ibid., 1909, 1089.

41. Ibid., 1910, 1266.

42. Ibid., 1909, 812.

43. Because the League was both highly political and transparent, hardly a year went by without commentators detecting a "crisis." Only in the years before World War I and World War II, however, did the crises translate into a decline in membership.

44. *Les droits de l'homme,* 20 November 1910. This newspaper was the political organ of a dissident member of the League, Paul Hyacinthe Loyson.

45. Ibid., January 8, 1911.

46. Ibid., December 18, 1910.

47. Ibid., June 11, 1911.

48. *B.O.*, 1911, 121.

49. *Congrès national de 1927,* 40–54.

50. *Notre action* (Bulletin mensuel de la Fédération de l'Aisne), December, 1930.

51. *Cahiers,* 1920, 16, 8.

52. *Cahiers,* 1920, 14–15.

53. See, for example, the debate surrounding the disruption of a meeting at Collombes in May 1927 and agonizing about whether in the future League members could even share a podium with a Communist. *Cahiers,* 1927, 346.

54. *Cahiers,* 1930, 326. Despite the pleadings of Challaye and others, on this occasion the Central Committee did issue a condemnation of the systematic terror in the Soviet Union.

55. *Congress national de 1936* (Paris, 1936), 444–48.

56. Serge Berstein, Histoire du parti radical, (Paris, 1980), vol. I, 246–47; Daniel Bardonnet, Evolution de la structure du parti radical (Paris, 1960), 245; Jean et Monica Charlot, "Un Rassemblement," 1002.

57. Basch informed one delegate at the 1934 congress that 160,000 of the 180,000 League members were Radicals. *La ligue d'Orléans,* June 1934.

58. Claveau, "L'Autre," 136–42. As the author notes, the political affiliations can be established for just over 50 percent of her sample, and Radicals were less inclined to stress their political affiliation than were Socialists. By including unsuccessful candidates for the Central Committee, more often than not from the militant left-wing minority, her analysis almost certainly exaggerates the importance of the Socialists.

59. The five revolutions were those of 1789, 1792, 1830, 1840, and 1870.

60. *Congrès national de 1927,* 195–242.

61. *Congrès national de 1934* (Paris, 1934), 50. Basch's antagonists within the League repeatedly threw that line back in his face, especially when he attempted, with good reason, to expose the demagoguery of much of the organizations's left-wing minority. See for example, Emery in *La Flèche,* 3 November 1934.

62. *Les droits de l'homme* (Calvados), May-June, 1934.

63. *Bulletin mensuel de la ligue des droits de l'homme* (Vincennes), February 1934.

64. *Congrés national de 1933* (Paris, 1933), 316. Chabrun was suffering from a mortal illness at the time and had also been defeated in the 1932 elections, all of which might explain his splenetic discourse.

65. To cite but the most obvious example, in 1937 the Senate would bring down Léon Blum's Popular Front government.

66. *Cahiers*, 1934, 539.

67. Ibid., 1935, 285.

68. *Congrès national de 1935 (Paris, 1935)*, 146–69; 275–82.

69. *Cahiers*, 1924, 334.

70. For the debate see *Cahiers*, 1929, 470 ff. Blum, who almost never attended its meetings, nonetheless resigned from the Central Committee shortly thereafter. Indeed, it would appear that he quit the League altogether because four years later Emile Kahn was surprised to learn from the president of Blum's section that he had not been a member since 1929. Montel to Kahn February 1, 1933; Kahn to Montel, January 30, February 30, 1933 in ALDH 22. Blum is not listed as one of the League's deputies in February 1934. He certainly did belong to the League in 1937 and probably had since 1935.

71. *Cahiers*, 1927, 88.

72. Ibid., 1931, 675, 461.

73. *Ligue des droits de l'homme* (Drôme), October 1929.

74. *Congrès national de 1927* (Paris, 1927), 167.

75. *Cahiers*, 1931, 460.

76. See, among many examples, the interrogation of Steeg in 1927, *Cahiers*, 1927, 107, also, 309.

77. *Cahiers*, 1927, 256; also 235, 254.

78. Ibid., 1931, 761.

CHAPTER 3

1. *Congrès national de 1927*, 37.

2. *B.O.*, 1902, 161–62.

3. Ibid., 1902, 408.

4. Ibid., 1902, 465.

5. Ibid., 1902, 435.

6. Ibid., 1904, 540.

7. Ibid., 1904, 542. To be sure, the real objects of Moutet's complaints were Radical-dominated sections that were systematically excluding his fellow Socialists.

8. Ibid., 1904, 541.

9. Ibid., 1906, 423, 611, 744, 764, 776, 787, 795–96.

10. *Congrès national de 1925*, 225–28.

11. *Cahiers*, 1928, 228.

12. *Les droits de l'homme* (Charente-Maritime), July 1928.

13. Claudy Valin, *La ligue des droits de l'homme en Charente-Maritime*, 179.

14. *Cahiers*, 1938, 50–52.

15. These numbers are from the calculations of Emile Kahn on February 7, 1934, in ALDH, 22. They are higher by thirty-three deputies than the (admittedly incomplete) list published in the *Cahiers* (1933, 45 ff.) but lower (by forty deputies) than the initial calculations by Kahn in May 1933 (in ALDH, 23.) During the same period, the number of senators dropped from seventy-one to sixty-seven. In 1933, the League claimed that it had in excess of 240 deputies in parliament (*Congrès national de 1933,* 170.) The 1934 figures do not include a number of deputies then under suspicion for their role in the Stavisky affair but at that time still members of the League.

16. When Pierre Laval entered Paul Painlevé's 1925 government, the League was proud to list him as being one of thirteen League ministers in the cabinet. *Cahiers,* 1925, 231. When Gaston Doumergue was elected president in 1924, the League reminded everyone that he had been a member since the organization's foundation, and a member of the Central Committee in 1905, a post he relinquished the next year upon becoming minister of colonies. *Cahiers,* 1924, 408. In the 1920s, Edouard Daladier was a member of the section of Carpentras and later of Orange in the Vaucluse. He would have appeared to have dropped his membership in the early 1930s. President of the section of Charpentras to Kahn, February 2, 1934, in ALDH, 23.

17. Classic examples of this genre of polemics are T. Ferlé, *La ligue des droits de l'homme* (Paris, 1936) and Pierre Pitois *Les buts politiques.*

18. For typical examples of the resentment and suspicion of the rank and file directed against the deputies in their midst, see *Ligue des droits de l'homme* (Indre-et-Loire), December 1, 1931; *La Ligue* (Saône-et-Loire), April 4.

19. *Notre Action (Bulletin mensuel de la fédération de l'Aisne)* November 1929, March 1930, March 1931, January 1932. Owing to illness, Lengrand had to withdraw his candidacy.

20. Henri Sée, *Histoire.* 124.

21. See the bitter debates at the League's annual congresses of 1930 and 1931. The most savage indictment of Guernut, *le politician,* was prepared by the federation of the Seine on January 2, 1931, in ALDH 7. The charges against Guernut were almost certainly unfounded. It was not parliamentary camaraderie but a different conception of the League's role that separated him from the more militant elements. Still, he did become, briefly, minister of national education early in 1936.

22. There were always tensions between Basch and Guernut. Guernut was troubled by Basch's tendency to take uncompromising positions (Guernut to Bouglé, December 16, 1918 in ALDH 4). For his part Basch freely admitted that he, the first nonparliamentary president of the League, felt at times overshadowed by Guernut and his very prominent role in the Chamber of Deputies. See his observations in *Congrès nationale de 1931,* 168–70. Although Kahn was not a deputy, he was an unsuccessful Socialist candidate in 1928 and 1932.

23. *Cahiers,* 1924, 63.

24. Ibid., 1928, 354.

25. Ibid., 1928, 778; 1929, 38.

26. Henri Guernut gave the classic formulation in 1934: "I am accountable for my parliamentary votes to my electors first, to my party second and to the League, not at all." *Congrès national de 1934,* 147.

27. *Congrès national de 1935,* 269, 409–14, 423.

28. A good example is T. Ferlé, *La Ligue.* The author's point, backed up by endless papal declarations, was that the Declaration of the Rights of Man (to say nothing of the League of the same name) was utterly contrary to Roman Catholic doctrine. Yet he knew his League history well, correcting a number of errors in Henri Sée's account. But, his documentation of League parliamentary strength, although based on Ligue sources, was misleading to the degree that he assumed that any deputy that ever belonged to the League remained a member. As a result, his figures for the number of deputies who belonged to the League in the 1930s is somewhat higher than the number who actually belonged to the parliamentary group in those years.

29. *Cahiers,* 1924, 408.

30. Ibid., 1925, 231.

31. Ibid., 1924, 222.

32. The League's central committee did not possess a complete file on League membership. It knew how many members it had as soon as local sections paid their dues. But because many sections were delinquent in sending in their actual membership lists, Kahn often could not easily verify the claims of certain deputies to be members of the League.

33. *Congrès national de 1932* (Paris, 1933), 157–69.

34. The various lists concocted in 1933 and 1934 can be found in ALDH 22 and 23, as can the various efforts to convince prospective members to join the League.

35. By far the best study of the Stavisky affair is Paul Jankowski, *Cette vilaine affaire Stavisky* (Paris, 2000).

36. They included Gaston Bonnaure, deputy from Paris: Joseph Garat, deputy from the Basses-Pyrénées; Albert Dalimier, deputy from the Seine-et-Oise; André Hesse, deputy from the Charente-Maritime; Louis Proust, deputy from the Indre-et-Loire; Auguste Puis, senator from the Tarn-et-Garonne; René Renoult, senator from the Var; and Gaston Hulin, deputy from the Vienne.

37. Bonnaure and Garat.

38. Kahn to Guernut, February 7, 1934, in ALDH, 22.

39. Daniel Bardonnet, *Evolution,* 251–55. The actual name of the organization was the *Comité républicain du commerce, de l'industrie et de l'agriculture.* It got its more common name from the Radical senator from the Seine who was its first president.

40. *Ligue des droits de l'homme* (Indre-et-Loire), January 1, 1933. Proust insisted that he had never attacked Kayser for his Jewishness But he did say that what motivated Kayser were "his origins which incline him naturally towards internationalism." He also described the Socialist party as "the French, 'French' here being only a geographical expression, section of the worker's international."

41. *Ligue des droits de l'homme* (Indre et Loire), December 1, 1932; January 1, 1933; February 1, April 1, May 1, 1934; July 1, 1936; May, 1, 1937; January 1, June, 1, 1938.

42. Claudy Valin, *La ligue des droits de l'homme en Charente-Maritime*, 159–60

43. Kahn to Pouchaudon (president of the section of Corbeil) September 17, 1934; Pouchaudon to Kahn, September 17, 1934 in ALDH 37.

44. *Congrès national de 1935*, 379.

45. *Congrès national de 1936*, 13, 477–86.

46. Guernut to Basch, May 23, 1935 in ALDH 22.

47. *Cahiers*, 1935, 266, 318, 368, 593. Of course local sections still demanded to know who the League deputies were. But now the executive could respond, with visible relief, that the parliamentary group no longer existed. *Cahiers*, 1935, 634. It seems not to have occurred to anyone that, parliamentary group or no, the executive still had a good idea of which deputies belonged to the League.

48. Letters to federal presidents, May 27, October 5, 1936, in ALDH, 23. Here as always the League did not have a central record of all its members because the sections very often did not send in a list of names.

49. Thiolas to Kahn, March 30, April 14, 1937; Kahn to Thiolas, April 1, 1937 in ALDH, 23.

50. *Congrès national de 1935*, 271.

51. *Ligue des droits de l'homme* (Drôme), July–September 1928.

52. *Congrès national de 1927*, 346–62; *Congrès national de 1928*, 294–362; *Congrès National de 1929*, 64–75, 125, 140, 413.

53. The League would cease to do so a few years later when the left-wing Popular Front was in power and also opted to use decree laws.

54. For the details of the case, and some of the acid correspondence it produced, see ALDH, 37, and *Cahiers*, 1934, 483 ff.

55. *Cahiers*, 1934, 526–39.

56. *Le Démocrate*, August 4, 1934.

57. *Cahiers*, 1934, 546.

58. *Congrès national de 1934*, 127–55; 227–59. Not all of the appeals to Basch were entirely gracious. Lucien Cancouët, accurately for once, called Basch "a spoiled child." 257.

59. *Cahiers*, 1934, 544.

60. Ibid., 1934, 180, 442.

61. *Congrès national de 1926* (Paris, 1927), 57, 90.

62. *Démocrate du Jura*, May 5, September 8, 29, November 24, 1934; February 23, March 30, 1935.

63. The most articulate statements of the anti-Herriot case can be found in *La Flèche*, 14, July 28, August 4, September 22 and 29, October 6, 1934; see also the arguments of the president of the federation of the Ardèche, the arch pacifist, Elie Reynier, in *Ligue des droits de l'homme* (Drôme) , July 1934.

64. *Congrès national de 1936*, 36; *Nouvel Age*, 8, November 29, December 13, 1934; *La Flèche*, December 8, 1934. For Weber's wartime record see Jean Maitron et al., eds., *Dictionnaire biographique de movement ouvrier en France* (Paris, 1993) vol. 43, 351–2.

65. *Cahiers*, 1936, 512ff; 520ff.

66. Ibid., 1935, 299–301; 314–15.

67. *Congrès national de 1935,* 437–53.

68. Kahn to Maurice Milhaud, August 3, 1934 in ALDH 8.

69. Richet to Basch, May 11, 1934 in ALDH 153. Richet had actually resigned once before, from 1909 until 1913 in protest over Pressensé's politics, Perry, "Remembering Dreyfus," 841–42.

70. Raynal to Basch, May 20, 1934, ALDH, 153. There are several dozen similar letters in this carton.

71. *Le Démocrate,* 2 June 1934.

72. *Cahiers,* 1937, 391; report of January 1, 1937, in ALDH, 26. The relevant figures for April 1938 were 127,000 and for April 1939 just under 112,000, see *Cahiers,* 1938, 360 and 1939, 396.

73. *Congrès national de 1936,* 439–40.

74. Ibid., 489.

CHAPTER 4

1. *Congrès national de 1934,* 148.

2. *Congrès national de 1928,* 236.

3. *Congrès national de 1924,* 206.

4. The point did escape some local sections who, as late as the 1920s, were still informing their members that at their monthly meetings "les dames sont admises." For example, *Bulletin mensuel de la section de Boulogne-sur-Mer,* March 1922. Ironically, the same issue contained a careful discussion of the fact that "homme" in the League's title really meant "le genre humain." As late as 1932, Mme B. Lop, one of the three women on the twenty-two-person central committee of the League's very large section in Marseille, complained that most women were still misled by the associations name and did not realize that the League was open to them. *Le Ligueur* (Marseilles), November–December 1932. Certainly the hosts of League congresses assumed that the women present were wives of male delegates and were careful to organize various diversions for them on the explicitly stated grounds that they were unlikely to share their husbands' enthusiasm for the sessions of the congress. See, for example, the welcoming address at the 1930 congress of Biarritz, *Congrès national de 1931,* 9; or the prospectus for the 1933 departmental congress in the Gironde, *Ligue des droits de l'homme* (Gironde), February 1933.

5. A superb recent study of women and the League is Claire Lescoffit, "Les Femmes, les féminismes et la ligue des droits de l'homme entre 1919 et 1940, (Mémoire de maîtrise d'histoire, Université d'Evry Val-d'Essone, 2005). The best sources for the women's suffrage movement in France are Steven C. Hause with Anne R. Kenney, *Women's Suffrage and Social Politics in the French Third Republic* (Princeton, 1984) and Paul Smith, *Feminism and the Third Republic: Women's Political and Civil Rights in France, 1918–1945* (Oxford, 1996). A spirited recent synthesis of the subject is Albert et Nicole du Roy, *Citoyennes. Il y a 50 ans, le vote des femmes* (Paris, 1994) See also C. Sowerwine, *Sisters or Citizens? Women and Socialism in France since 1876* (Cambridge, 1982); J. F. Macmillan, *Housewife or Harlot, the Place of Women in French*

Society, 1870–1940 (Brighton, 1981); Siân Reynolds, "Marianne's Citizens? Women, the Republic and Universal Suffrage in France" in S. Reynolds, ed., *Women, State and Revolution: Essays in Gender and Power in Europe since 1789* (Brighton, 1986); Siân Reynolds, "Women and the Popular Front in France: The Case of Three Women Ministers," *French History* 8, no. 2 (1994): 196–224; Paul Smith, "Political Parties, Parliament and Women's Suffrage in France, 1919–1939," *French History*, 11, no. 3 (1997): 338–58; Karen Offen "Women, Citizenship and Suffrage," in William B. Cohen, ed., *The Transformation of Modern France* (Boston, 1997), 125–41.

6. *B.O.*, 1909, 991–95. Women could therefore vote at the municipal arrondissement and departmental level. To the surprise of Vérone, a male delegate added an amendment calling for women's *eligibility* for the Chamber and the Senate. It passed despite the insistence of then President Francis de Pressensé that if one were going to call for eligibility in national elections then one might as well, as he personally preferred, grant them the right to vote at that level as well.

7. The issue of eligibility at the national level was discretely dropped in 1914.

8. *Congrès national de 1924*, 208–9.

9. The point did not escape Maria Vérone who noted a few years later that the whole idea of vote by stages, an acceptable expedient in 1909, was now hopelessly out of date. *Le droit des femmes*, March 1929.

10. *Congrès national de 1928*, 85–87.

11. *La ligue d'Orléans*, November 1926.

12. *Le droit des femmes*, June 1936.

13. *La ligue des droits de l'homme* (Drôme), July 1932. Of course, by 1932, granting of limited municipal voting rights to women would still leave France tied for last place with fascist Italy!

14. *Cahiers*, 1924, 473.

15. *Les droits de l'homme* (Meurthe-et-Moselle), February 1933.

16. Ibid., March 1935.

17. *Les droits de l'homme* (Charente-Maritime), December 1927.

18. Ibid, November 1932.

19. *Les droits de l'homme* (Meurthe-et-Moselle), March 1935.

20. *La ligue française des droits de l'homme* (Gueret), May 1929.

21. Cited in *Le droit des femmes*, July–August 1934.

22. Elie Réynier, pugnacious pacifist and hard-nosed boss of the federation of the Ardèche once, but only once, made a withering assault on the opponents of women's suffrage within the League. *Ligue des droits de l'homme* (Drôme), April 1925 (The Federation of the Ardèche shared editorial space with the bulletin of the neighboring department.)

23. *Les droits de l'homme* (Morbihan), 1927 (reporting on the decisions made at the departmental congress of May 22, 1927).

24. Guernut to Bouglé, August 11, 1926, in ALDH, 4.

25. *Congrès national de 1923* (Paris, 1924), 50.

26. Deszerots to Guernut, June 14, 1932, in ALDH, 143.

27. Rouvier to *Commission Feministe*, January 31, 1929, in ALDH, 9.

28. It is probably not accidental that within two months of this debate the League opted to dissolve its parliamentary group. *Cahiers,* 1935, 594.

29. *Cahiers,* 1935, 348–52.

30. There were, of course, many reasons for dissolving the parliamentary group: the embarrassing Stavisky revelations, the incessant attacks on the voting records of deputies; but Guernut made it clear when informing Basch that he was quitting as president of the group that the last straw had been the attitude of his female colleagues. Guernut to Basch, May 23, 1935, in ALDH, 22.

31. *Congrès national de 1935,* 89.

32. *Le ligeur artésien* (Pas-de-Calais), March–April, May, June, 1937.

33. *Espoir,* July 1944.

34. *Le ligueur artésien* (Pas de Calais), January–February 1945.

35. *Les droits de l'homme* (Charente-Maritime), July 1928.

36. Fernando Corcos, *La paix? Oui, si les femmes voulaient* (Paris, 1929). In the same vein see also his *Les femmes en guerre* (Paris, 1927) and *La paix ordonnée par les mères* (Paris, 1934).

37. Fernand Crocos, *La paix ordonnée par les mères* (Paris, 1934) p. 12.

38. Corcos to Guernut, February 12, 1927 in ALDH 7.

39. *Les droits de l'homme* (Charente-Maritime), May 1937. The resolutions respectively of the sections of Jonzac, St. Fort-sur-St. Dizant, and Néré.

40. *Ligue des droits de l'homme* (Drôme—which shared space with the Ardèche), April 1925.

41. Prior to 1901 all French associations with more than twenty members (with the exception of labor unions after 1884) were governed by an 1834 law that required them to obtain formal permission from the government. When the law was liberalized for labor unions in 1884, many republicans had been reluctant to extend the law to all associations lest this entail freedom of association for the religious congregations. See, H. Jones, *The French State in Question* (Cambridge, 1993, 71).

42. *Cahiers,* 1928, 675–85; 699–705.

43. Ibid., 1926, 302.

44. Etienne Antonelli in *Cahiers,* 1927, 484.

45. Ibid., 1927, 363–67; A similar analysis was made by Léon Thomas of the Draguignon Section, Ibid., 1925, 368–69.

46. Ibid., 1928, 673–75.

47. Ibid., 1928, 688.

48. Ibid., 1928, 701.

49. Ibid., 1928, 105–8.

50. The issue of the congregations was to have been the subject of a session at the League's 1928 congress in Toulouse. As so often happened at League congresses, time ran out and the session had to be cancelled. No one in the League seemed unduly disturbed that the session had been cancelled because everyone fully expected Title III to be resoundingly upheld.

51. William D. Irvine, *The Boulanger Affair Reconsidered* (New York, 1989), 64–66.

52. *Cahiers,* 1929, 228.

53. For the extended debate see Ibid., 1929, 227 ff. and 303 ff.

54. *L'Ami du peuple,* March 9, 1929; Pierre Albert et al., ed. *Histoire générale de la presse française,* vol. 3 (Paris, 1972) 541, 569. Hennessey was appointed ambassador to Switzerland in 1924 and was three times minister of agriculture in the late 1920s.

55. *L'Ami du peuple,* March 5, 1929; *Lumière,* March 16, 1929.

56. *Congrès national de 1933,* 401–2.

57. Guernut to Basch, July 13, 1929, in ALDH, 4.

58. Albert, *Histoire générale . . . ,* vol. 3, 498, 505, 563.

59. But other contributors from the League, notably Georges Pioch and Georges Demartial, continued to defend Dubarry until the newspaper folded shortly thereafter.

60. Morhardt to Basch, December 6, 1935, in ALDH, 146.

61. For their exchange see *La Volonté,* April 26; May 7, 8.

62. *Bulletin trimestriel de la Fédération de la Seine-et-Marne,* second trimester, 1937.

63. *Cahiers,* 1937, 153–4.

64. *Le Républicain de La Rochelle,* February 19, 1937.

65. *Cahiers,* 1937, 752.

66. Ibid., 1938, 322.

67. Ibid., 1937, 336.

68. Ibid., 1938, 446.

69. Ibid., 1938, 446–8.

CHAPTER 5

1. *Ligue des droits de l'homme* (Federation of the Drôme) August-October, 1927.

2. Note to staff by Kahn, January 6, 1933, in ALDH, 27.

3. Azais to Kahn, November 8, 1937; Feugas to Basch October 26, 1937, in ALDH, 26.

4. *Ligue des droits de l'homme* (Indre-et-Loire), November 1, 1932.

5. *Les droits de l'homme* (Charente-Maritime) April–May 1935.

6. For some examples see *Le Ligueur* (Marseilles), November–December 1932; *Ligue des droits de l'homme* (Gironde), May 1937; *Les droits de l'homme* (Eure-et-Loire), June 1936; *Ligue des droits de l'homme* (Drôme) March 1937; *Le ligueur* (Algeria) June 1934.

7. See the sharp exchange on the point at the League's 1932 congress. *Congrès national de 1932,* 44, 117.

8. The distribution of tobacco products was, and is, a government monopoly, and the right to sell tobacco was then restricted to a limited category of citizens having some claim to government generosity.

9. Chavreau to Kahn, June 8, July 4, 1936; Kahn to Chavreau, July 21, 1936; Tocherie to Kahn, November 21, December 12, 21, 1936; Kahn to Tocherie, December 7, 30, 1936, in ALDH, 575.

10. Section of Talmoniers-Amecourt to Morhardt, December 2, 1909; P. Sotton to Kahn, November 14, 1936; Kahn to Sotton, November 16, 1936, all in ALDH, 152.

11. Kahn to section of Urepel, February 5, 1936; section to Kahn, April 10, 1936, in ALDH, 153. Ybarnegaray was at the time the vice president of the Croix de Feu.

12. Agranier to Kahn, March 26, 1938, in ALDH, 138.

13. Kahn to Masson, president of the section of Mulhouse, June 17, 1937. ALDH, 153.

14. P. Sotton to Kahn, October 7, 1938, in ALDH, 152.

15. Kahn to secretary general of Federation of the Charente Maritime, March 2, 1938; April 15, 1938; Guericau, president of the section of Saint Georges-des Coteaux to Basch, February 6, 1938. ALDH, 139.

16. President of the section of Reccy-sur-Ourel to president of the federation of the Cote d'Or, October 14, 1930; ALDH, 140.

17. Kahn to Minville, president of the federation of the Landes, February 29, 1940. ALDH, 146.

18. Maudet, president of the federation of the Charente-Inférieure to Kahn, September 24, 1936. ALDH, 139.

19. Meron to Kahn, February 14, 1936, in ALDH, 657.

20. Kahn to Contou, July 29, 1937; 6, 19 August 6, 19, 1937; Basch to minister of education, August 31, 1937, in ALDH 565. His appeal was unsuccessful.

21. President of the section of Montlieu to Basch, July 13, 1937, in ALDH, 565.

22. Kahn to Meillet, May 8, 1939, in ALDH, 570.

23. Kahn to Texier, October 12, 1937, in ALDH, 655.

24. Morin to Guernut, October 21, 1918; Guernut to Morin, December 20, 1918; Buisson to minister of commerce. January 17, 1919, in ALDH, 575.

25. Kahn to Hassani Said, December 22, 1936, in ALDH, 564.

26. Hardy to Kahn, May 14, 1937, in ALDH, 564.

27. George Grimmer to Walter, president of the section of Saverne, April 20, 1935, in ALDH, 565. English in the original.

28. Damalix to Basch, August 6, 1937; Kahn to Damalix, August 24, 1937, in ALDH, 565.

29. President of the section of Chateaubriand to Bash, March 29, 1938; Kahn to president, April 21, 1938, in ALDH, 563.

30. Kahn to president of the section of Saverne, April 12, 1938, in ALDH, 565.

31. Signature illegible to Kahn , July 2, 1938; Kahn's negative response, July 5, 1938, in ALDH, 563.

32. *Cahiers,* 1937, 214.

33. President of the section of Lourdes to Basch, April 24, 1937, in ALDH 565; Comut to Kahn, June 15, 1936, in ALDH, 568.

34. Kahn to Basch, October 22, 1936, in ALDH, 568.

35. Kahn to Contou, July 29, 1937; August 6, 1937; Basch to minister of education, August 31, 1937. ALDH, 565. The minister turned them down.

36. Marx Dormoy, minister of the interior and long-time leaguer to Basch, November 17, 1936.

37. Basch to minister of finance, December 2, 1939. ALDH, 568.

38. Clerget to Kahn, May 17, 1935; March, 23; April, 29, 1936, in ALDH, 656.

39. Signature obscure to Guernut, June, 14, 1920, in ALDH, 647.

40. Eric Agrikolianski, "Ligue des droits de l'homme: Un engagement associatif entre morale et politique" in Claire Andrieu, Gilles Le Béquec and Danielle Tartakowski, eds, *Association et champ politique* (Paris: 2001), 550.

41. Report of the juridical experts, December 18, 1936, in ALDH, 151.

42. The huge Hannion dossier is in ALDH, 457. Note in particular, Kahn to Gaston Charles, February 1, 1936, and Philippe Lamour, briefly one of Hannion's lawyers to Kahn, February 11, 1936.

43. The entire file is in ALDH, 457. See in particular, section of Cauderon to Kahn, December, 15, 1933; Kahn to Texier (president of the federation of the Gironde, February 3, 1934; Texier to Kahn, January 15, 1934; Kahn to Texier, December 23, 1837; Texier to Kahn , December, 20, 1937.

44. Cases like this in 1918 prompted particularly acrimonious debates within the Central Committee. See Chapter 6.

45. It was, for example, none other than Caillaux, then the dominant force in the Senate, who brought down Léon Blum's Popular Front government in June 1927. On Caillaux see Jean Denis Bredin *Joseph Caillaux* (Paris, 1980).

46. For a classic example see B. Maupas, *Le fusillé* (Paris, 1994). See also Nicolas Offenstadt, *Les fusillés de la Grande Guerre et la mémoire collective: 1914–1999* (Paris, 1999) and André Bach, *Fusillés pour l'example: 1914–1915* (Paris, 2003).

47. Becherend to Buisson, July 18, 1918; Buisson to Poincaré , October 8, 1918; secretary general of the presidency to Buisson, April 14, 1919, in ALDH, 496.

48. Buisson to minister of war, October 20, 1917; April, 19, June 11, 1918; minister of war to Buisson, October 25, 1918, in ALDH, 195.

49. Maurice Bena to Buisson, April 7, 1918; Buisson to minister of war, June 8, 1918; minister of war to Buisson, August 19, 1918, in ALDH, 496.

50. The entire (and extremely complex) Mancini file is in ALDH, 461.

51. Bosser to Kahn, July 30, 1934; January 28, 1935; president of the section of Champigny to Kahn, November 20, 1933, in ALDH, 464; *La ligue (organe de la section to Champigny),* April 1935, in ALDH, 156.

52. The most recent among the many books of the Seznec affair are Denis Langlois, *L'Affaire Seznec* (Paris, 1992) and Denis Seznec, *Nous les Seznec* (Paris, 1992). See also, Victor Hervé, *Justice pour Seznec* (Tréguier, 1933); *Congrès national de 1932,* 130. *Congrès national de 1934,* 191–205; *Congrès national de 1935,* 129–38.

53. *Le Monde,* June 30–July 1, 1996.

CHAPTER 6

1. George Pioch was a good example. His brief stint as a superpatriot would periodically embarrass him during the interwar years when he became an integral pacifist.

2. Tempestuous resignations were not unusual within the Central Committee, although Basch was particularly prone to them. However, it was Buisson, stung by the criticisms of Basch, who initially resigned on October 31, 1918. The Committee persuaded him to withdraw his resignation, at which point Basch resigned. Buis-

son in turn persuaded Basch to withdraw his resignation several months later. At issue in all of this was, as Basch made clear, conflicting conceptions of the League— was it to be a purely juridical organization or, as he preferred, also a politically combative one? *B.O.* 1919, 304–21.

3. *La guerre de 1914 et le droit* (Paris, 1915). *Droit* in French conveys the meaning of both *law* and *right*.

4. *La guerre*, 3.

5. Ibid., 37.

6. Ibid., 41.

7. Ibid., 64, 52, 79.

8. Ibid., 91–97.

9. Ibid., 54–64.

10. Ibid., 80–81.

11. Ibid., 105.

12. Emmanuel Nacquet, "La Société d'etudes documentaires et critiques sur la guerre. Ou la naissance d'une minorité au sein de la Ligue des droits de l'homme," *Materiaux, pour l'histoire de notre temps* (Jan.–March, 1993), 6–10. See also Naquet, "Entre justice et patrie: la Ligue des droits de l'homme et la Grande Guerre," *Le Mouvement Social* (April–June 1998, no. 183), 93–110. See also the reports from agents of the Ministry of the Interior in *Archives Nationales,* F7 13086.

13. *Congrès national de 1916* (Paris: 1917), 45–141.

14. Séverine was the pseudonym adopted by Caroline Rémy in the 1890s when she had been an anarchist journalist.

15. *Congrès national de 1916.* 103, 141. See also the similar debates at the 1917 congress in *B.O.* 1918, 317–76.

16. For typical examples of this debate as well as the vitriol it generated, see the exchange between Emile Kahn and Oscar Bloch, *B.O.,* 1919, 12, 399; or between Victor Basch and George Pioch, *Journal du Peuple,* January 7, 9, 1919. (Pioch was not yet a member of the League but carried on in public as if he were.)

17. *Journal du Peuple,* January 2, 1919.

18. *B.O.* 1919, pp. 30–60.

19. *La Victoire,* January 6, 8, 1919.

20. *Journal du Peuple,* January 2, 3, 15, 1919.

21. *Congrès national de 1935,* 455.

22. Mathias Morhardt, *Les Origines de la guerre* (Paris, 1921), 9ff. *Cahiers,* 1921, 34–36.

23. Challaye, four times wounded during World War I, was a relative late-comer to the question of war origins but was the most effective spokesman for the minority in the interwar years.

24. *Cahiers,* 1928, 630.

25. Ibid., 1921, 27578; 1925, 251.

26. Ibid., 1932, 401.

27. The French would not complete the publication of their diplomatic documents until after World War II.

28. *Cahiers,* 1921, 40–41.

29. *Congrès national de 1923* (Paris, 1924), p. 106. Rucard began his career in the League as founder and secretary general of the federation of the Loiret. He later became the President of the federation of the Vosges, which department he represented in parliament from 1928 to 1940.

30. *Cahiers,* May 5, 1920.

31. Ibid., January 25, 1922.

32. Ibid., 1921, 519.

33. Ibid., January 25, 1922; May 25, 1925.

34. *Congrès national de 1923,* 93.

35. Morhardt, *Origines,* 23.

36. *Cahiers,* 1931, 663.

37. Ibid., 1925, 511.

38. Ibid., 1932, 339 ff, 443 ff; 1933, 15. The spokesmen for the minority thought it suspiciously late in the day to be discovering some "misunderstanding" about the significance of Article 231. The fact that the Renouvin–Bloch thesis first appeared in *Le Temps,* a conservative newspaper with close ties to the business community (and referred to by the left as *le journal du comité des forges*) did not greatly enhance its credibility in minority circles.

39. In the spring of 1930, Challaye made a public speech attacking the abuses of colonial rule in Indo-China. For the reaction of the Right, the government, and League leaders, see ALDH 5, in particular Guernut to Alexandre June 1, 1930; Guernut to Challaye, June 4, 1930 and Challaye to Guernut, June 10, 1930.

40. *Congrès national de 1925* (Paris, 1925), 388–89.

41. *Congrès national de 1930* (Paris, 1930), 94, 99.

42. For example, the responses of the sections of Tarascon (January 30, 1930) and Oued-el-Alleug (March 30, 1930) in ALDH 167. The section of Tarascon did note that "the native is very simple, it is understood that he is a large child." But it added that "his heart is in the right place, to a degree that many do not appreciate."

43. Section of Batna, January 23, 1930; Section of Antony, March 19, 1930, in ALDH, 167.

44. By far the best source for the many divergent currents in French interwar pacifism is Norman Ingram, *The Politics of Dissent* (Oxford, 1991.)

45. *Congrès national de 1935,* 57.

46. *Notre Temps,* July 16, 1933; *Populaire de Nantes,* 15 August, 1936. Jean Luchaire was editor of *Notre Temps,* a left-wing newspaper explicitly speaking for the younger political generation. Many members of the League regularly contributed to it.

47. Some of the clearest discussions of the differences appeared in *La Volonté* in 1933. See in particular February 19, 1933; March 1, 26, 1933; April 2, 26, 1933; May 7, 8 , 14, 1933.

48. *Notre Temps,* April 30, 1933.

49. *La Volonté,* May 7, 1933.

50. *Cahiers,* 1935, 319ff.

51. Ibid., 1934, 79–80. Emphasis in the original.

52. See the electoral statements of minority candidates for the Central Committee, Lucien Cancouët, René Martel, and Marthe Williams, ibid., 1934, 168, 176, and 179.

53. *Libres Propos,* May 25, 1934.

54. *Cahiers,* 1933, 680–83.

55. Ibid., 1933, 683–86. Challaye would later complain that he had been forced, owing to space limitations, to excise sections in which he expressed his indignation with Hitler's domestic policy. That Emile Kahn, editor of the *Cahiers,* permitted the articles of Berthet and Challaye to appear at all testified, as he himself did not fail to observe, to his liberalism. He did permit himself equal space for a rebuttal but even that was remarkably temperate. Ibid., 1934, 32–33)

56. Ibid., 1934, 32.

57. Ibid., 1933, 729.

58. *Les droits de l'homme* (Meurthe-et-Moselle), January, February, March 1934.

59. *Equité,* November 1, 1933, cited in *Cahiers* 1934, 286.

60. *Université Républicaine,* February 1935. The piece was published, with some "reservations," in the *Libres Opinions* section of the bulletin. *Université Républicaine,* published since March 1934 out of League headquarters, folded shortly after this issue appeared.

61. *Nouvel Age,* December 13, 1935. "I am fond of Jews," he wrote, "some of whom are my best friends. But I am horrified by those who hide their Jewishness behind Christian names." He went on to congratulate his favorite antagonist on the Committee, Salomon Grumbach for at least not calling himself Gontran du Ruisseau. "Bach," in German and "ruisseau," in French, both mean "stream" or "brook." The Jewish question invariably brought out, at best, Challaye's sophomoric side.

62. *Ligue des droits de l'homme* (Indre-et-Loire), July 1, 1930.

63. See the debate in the *Cahiers,* 1933, 327–29.

64. Ibid., 1934, 176.

65. See the campaign platform of Parisian *minoritaire,* Marthe Williams, Ibid., 1934, 179.

66. Ibid., 1934, 180.

67. Ibid., 1934, 717, 739.

68. *Nouvel Age,* May 30, 1935.

69. *La Ligue* (Saône-et-Loire), November 1933.

70. *Nouvel Age,* June 20, 1935.

71. *Libre Propos,* March 31, 1935.

CHAPTER 7

1. In due course the Rassemblement Populaire became known as the *Front Populaire.* Strictly speaking the term Popular Front was used to describe the government coalition Léon Blum formed in July 1936, whereas Rassemblement Populaire was reserved for the extra-parliamentary organizations that supported it.

2. René Belin, cited in Georges Lefranc, *Histoire du Front Populaire* (Paris, 1965), 88.

3. For example, Françoise Basch, *Victor Basch: De l'affaire Dreyfus au crime de la Milice* (Paris, 1994), chapter VII.

4. In time, nearly a hundred organizations would adhere to the Rassemblement Populaire. The most important ones, however, were the political parties: Communists, Socialists, Radicals, and the various formations of independent socialists; the labor unions: the Communist CGTU and the Socialist CGT (which would soon unite); the League; and pacifist organizations like Le *Mouvement d'Amersdam-Pleyel,* and the *Comité de Vigilance des Intellectuels anti-fascistes.*

5. *La Flèche,* September 14, 1935.

6. Emery to Kahn, December 25, 1935; the economist Roger Picard also shared Emery's scepticism, Picard to Kahn, December 22, 1935, in ALDH, 3.

7. Emery to Kahn, December 25, 1935, in ALDH, 3.

8. *La Flèche,* July 20, 1935.

9. *Congrès national de 1936,* 489.

10. Given that the League never knew for sure how many of its parliamentarians were leaguers and that its last tentative list dated from February 1934, it cannot be stated precisely how many members of Blum's first government were members of the League. But of the thirty-four deputies and senators who sat in his cabinet, at least twenty-nine were known to have been League members at the beginning of 1934. One more, Edouard Daladier, belonged to the League until the early 1930s.

11. *Congrès national de 1923,* 117.

12. Irwin Wall, "Socialists and Bureaucrats: The Blum Government and the French Administration," *International Review of Social History,* no. 19, pt. 3 (1974), 325–46.

13. *La Lumière,* February 6, 1937.

14. *Le Ligueur (organe mensuel de la Federation de la Ligue des droits de l'homme des Alpes Maritimes)* May, June, July 1936.

15. Ibid., November 1936.

16. *Bulletin trimestiel de la Fédération de la Seine-et-Marne,* 2nd trimester, 1937; *Les droits de l'homme* (Charente-Maritime), May 1937; *Ligue des droits de l'homme* (Gironde), May, November 1937; *Les droits de l'homme* (Meurthe-et-Moselle), June, November 1936; the resolution of the section of Mulhouse in *Congrès national de 1936,* 138.

17. *Le Ligueur,* October 1936.

18. It was an article of faith among the contemporary Left that both the Croix de Feu and the PSF were fascist organizations. Most subsequent scholars have insisted that both organizations represented, at most, an authoritarian conservatism and that the PSF had begun to accept the democratic regime. For a dissenting view, see Robert Soucy, *French Fascism: The Second Wave* (New Haven, 1995) and William D. Irvine, "Fascism in France: The Strange Case of the Croix de Feu," *Journal of Modern History,* 63 (1991) 271–95.

19. *Cahiers,* 1937, pp. 410–11.

20. *La Tribune de l'Aisne,* March 26, April 2, 1937.

21. *Cahiers,* 1937, 201–03.

22. Maxime Fol, president of the section of Clichy to the Central Committee, April 15, 1937, in ALDH, 156.

23. The League's (entirely understandable) failure to protest the factory occupations prompted some resignations. For example, E. Delbos to Kahn, July 8, 1936. Kahn would note that complaints of this kind never managed to document any "infringements on individual liberty." Kahn to Delbos, August 11, 1936, both in ALDH, 24.

24. *Cahiers,* 1938, 50–56.

25. Ibid., 1938, 434.

26. J. Azais to Kahn, July 18, 23, 1937, ALDH, 144.

27. *Cahiers,* 1937, 208–9.

28. The best statement of the case is Emery in *L'Ecole libératrice,* June 12, 1937. The appeal by the minority for mediation in Spain can be found in *Feuilles libres de la quinzaine,* February 25, 1937. See also May 10 and 25, 1937.

29. *Feuilles libres de la quinzaine,* January 25, 1937; Emery's disappointment at the foreign policy of the Popular Front and above all its dramatic increase in armament expenditure was all the greater because, as he would later note, the formation of the Blum government in 1936 had been "one of the great hopes of my lifetime." *Congrés national de 1937,* 109.

30. *Populaire de Nantes,* September 2, 1936.

31. *Cahiers,* 1936, 755.

32. Ibid., 1936, 750.

33. Ibid., 1936, 762.

34. Ibid., 1938, 433.

35. *La Flèche,* December 16, 1936.

36. *Cahiers,* 1936, 755–56.

37. Ibid., 1937, 89.

38. Ibid., 1937, 249.

39. The most able expression of their case is Félicien Challaye, *La crise de la ligue des droits de l'homme* (Paris, 1937). *La Flèche,* July 24, 31, November 13, 1937; *Ecole Libératrice,* February 20, 1937, and *Feuilles libres de la Quinzaine,* 25 May 25, June 10, 1937.

40. *Cahiers,* 1937, 454.

41. *Feuilles libres de la quinzaine,* June 10, 1937.

42. *La Tribune de l'Aisne,* February 12, 1937.

43. Kahn to Kenette, president of the section of Chenerailles, January 7, 1938, in ALDH, 143. This letter has all of the hallmarks of one of his stock letters but is the only one preserved in the archives.

44. *Cahiers,* 1938, 126.

45. *Congrès national de 1937,* 168–74.

46. W. Drabovitch, *Les intellectuels Français et le Bolchévisme* (Paris, 1938), 19, 44–52.

47. *La Lumière,* March 11, 1938. Gombault still emphasized that his critique of Soviet justice was in no way an attack on the Popular Front or on the Communist

party. He simply asserted that the Franco-Soviet alliance would be much easier were Stalin to stop this kind of activity.

48. *Feuilles libres de la quinzaine,* September 25, 1937. Also see Gombault in *La Lumière* July 23, 1937.

49. Weexsteen "Fédération de la Seine," 99ff.

50. *Le Républicain de La Rochelle,* July 9, 1937.

51. Charles A Micaud, *The French Right and Nazi Germany* (Durham, NC, 1943) and William D. Irvine, *French Conservatism in Crisis* (Baton Rouge, 1979) chapter VI. Significantly, by 1939 the extreme right-wing deputy from Paris, Georges Scapini, was now writing in *La Flèche,* e.g., February 24, 1939.

52. For the text of Emery's letter of resignation see *La Flèche,* November 13, 1937.

53. Ibid., July 14, 1937; July 21, 1938.

54. *Cahiers,* 1938, 11–13.

55. Ibid., 1938, 24–30.

56. Ibid., 1938, 27.

57. Ibid., 1938, 31.

58. Ibid., 1938, 50–52.

59. See *La Tribune de l'Aisne,* May 7, 1936. Guernut and his supporters alleged that the SFIO had won because they had gained the support of the extreme Right who could not forgive his proposal in late 1935 to dissolve Leagues like the Croix de Feu.

60. *Cahiers,* 1938, 597.

61. Ibid., 1938, 597–98.

62. Ibid., 1938, 696–99.

63. Jean Fontaine to Kahn, March 28, 1938, ALDH, 3.

64. Emery to Sellier, March 16, 1939; Emery to all sections of the federation of the Rhône, January 12, 1939, in ALDH, 153.

65. Reynier et al. to Basch, October 14, 1938; Reynier to Kahn (no date, but presumably shortly after the last letter) in ALDH, 133. Although Reynier was a Protestant, he seemed unaware that Jean Zay had also been raised a Protestant (although his paternal grandparents were Jewish) and that Jules Moch was in fact a particularly devout Protestant. Georges Mandel, a conservative but anti-German deputy, was never a member of the League, nor was Zyromski.

66. *Cahiers,* 1939, 390–94.

67. Ibid., 1938, 616.

68. Ibid., 1939, 83–86.

69. Ibid., 1939, 79.

70. A point he made in *Le Barrage,* January 19, 1939.

71. *Huit jours de septembre en Allemagne* (Paris, 1938).

72. *Huit jours,* 227.

73. Ibid.

74. *La Flèche,* September 2, 1938. Although it hardly mitigates Bergery's responsibility, his article had been part of an attack on the recently introduced anti-Semitic legislation in Italy. Italians, Bergery had argued, did not have the justification of either the Germans or the French for persecuting Jews.

75. *Huit jours*, 227–29. Oddly, historians of French pacifism, aware though they invariably are of *Huit jours*, make little of Challaye's comments about Jews. Christien Jelen (*Hitler ou Staline. Le prix de la paix*, Paris, 1988, 194–96) is excoriating in his critique of French pacifists but says almost nothing about the overt anti-Semitism in *Huit jours*. Michel Dreyfus ("Pacifistes et humanistes dans les années trentes," *Revue d'histoire moderne et contemporaine*, 35, 1988) believes that the discussion of Jews in *Huit jours* is simply an attack on Nazi anti-Semitism and in that specific context concludes of Challaye that "his honesty, his sincerety and his courage cannot be doubted." 465. Neither author seems aware that *Huit jours* was the basis for Challaye's virulently anti-Semitic novel, *L'Etrange chemin de la paix*, written under the Vichy regime and to be discussed in Chapter 8.

76. *La Flèche*, September 2, November 11, 1938.

77. *La Patrie humaine*, October, 28, 1938.

78. Ibid., December 23, 1938.

79. It should be noted that even some of Challaye's pacifist allies were made uncomfortable by this kind of language. Louis Regaro in *Le Barrage*, the vehicle for classic integral pacifism, protested a "philo-German" approach that came perilously close to being "philo-Hitlerian." In general he deplored the "obvious collusion with the forces of reaction." March 16, April 20, 1939. Note, however, that Léon Emery was quick to come to his colleague Challaye's defense, March 30, 1939.

80. *Feuilles libres de la quinzaine*, January 10, July 10, 1938.

81. Ibid., October 15, 1938.

82. Ibid., May 25, 1938.

83. Ibid., December 31, 1938.

84. Ibid., June 10, 1938, February 15, 1939.

85. Ibid., 15 June 1939.

86. Ibid., 10 June 1938, 15 June 1939.

87. Ibid., March 25, 1938.

88. Ibid., February 15, 1939.

89. Ibid., July 15, 1939.

90. Ibid., February 15, 1939.

91. Ibid., November 30, 1938, February 15, 1939.

92. Ibid., September 10, 1938.

93. Ibid., December 31, 1938.

94. Ibid., September 10, 1938.

95. Emery was a gifted touch typist. This plus the loyal assistance of his wife explains why he continued to be a prolific writer.

96. *La Patrie humaine*, March 24, 1939.

97. *Feuilles libres de la quinzaine*, March 31, 1939.

98. *La Patrie humaine*, May 5, 1939.

99. *La Flèche*, May 5, 1939.

100. *La Lumière*, March 10, 1939.

101. See, for example, the meeting of the Central Committee of June 8, 1939, *Cahiers*, 1939, 445ff.

102. See Delaisi's account of the congress in *La Flèche,* July 28, 1939. Ever since the Prague coup, he noted, "nonresisters" were more or less absent from the League, although he believed that there were still those who believed that something could be achieved by granting Germany "free access to raw materials." Not, he admitted, that the current Central Committee was prepared to even consider the possibility.

103. *Cahiers,* August 1, 1939, 459, 484; *Action Française,* July 20, 1939, where it quipped "Now there is anti-Semitism in the League of the rights of man. My God, what is the world coming to."

104. Delaisi to Basch, June 16, 1936, in ALDH, 39.

105. G. Roques to Kahn, December 11, 1938, in ALDH, 143.

106. Dubois to Kahn, October 29, 1935; 23 March 1936, in ALDH, 159.

107. Federal-president of the Deux-Sèvres to Kahn, February 3, 1937, in ALDH, 143; secretary of the federation of the Haute-Saône to Kahn, November 12, 1935, in ALDH, 154.

CHAPTER 8

1. Kahn to Esmonin, May 16, 1940, in ALDH, 146.

2. Section of Sainte-Claude to Kahn, May 22, 1940; Kahn to section of Sainte-Claude, May 31, 1940, in ALDH, 146.

3. Françoise Basch, *Victor Basch,* chapter 8.

4. *Cahiers des droits de l'homme,* May 1945.

5. For the best discussion of the role of individual leaders during the Vichy regime see Perry, "Remembering Dreyfus," Appendix.

6. Marc Casati, Francis Delaisi, René Gérin, Paul Perrin, Jean Piot, Théodore Ruyssen, René Château, René Gounin, Camille Planche, Maurice Thiolas, and Robert Jardillier.

7. It is not known what, exactly Marc Casati did during the Occupation, and his expulsion might have been attributable largely to his provocative role at the League's last prewar congress.

8. Marcel Bidegarry, Georges Dumoulin, Georges Pioch, Challaye, Emery, and Bergery.

9. A typewritten copy was deposited in the *Bibliothèque Nationale* in 1952.

10. *Etrange chemin,* 115.

11. Ibid., 7, 15–16. The subject of Jews, or at any rate Grumbach, invariably exposed a vulgar side of the otherwise erudite and gentle Challaye. "Drecklein" of course translates as "little shit."

12. Ibid., 74

13. *Aujourd'hui,* October 23, 1940.

14. *Germinal,* May 5, 1944.

15. *L'Effort,* September 30, October 12, 1943.

16. *L'Atelier,* August 29, 1942.

17. Léon Emery, *L'Occident en péril* (Lyon, 1943), 31.

18. *Germinal,* May 5, 1944.

19. *La Troisième République* (Paris, 1943).

20. Léon Emery to Henry Chéron, October 9, 1943, cited in Léon Emery, *Correspondance I* (Carpentras, 1982), 427.

21. *Germinal*, May 26, 1944.

22. Emery, *Troisième République*, 73.

23. Ibid., 13–14.

24. Ibid., 208–9.

25. See, for example, his articles in *Le Républicain de la Rochelle*, September 5, 1936; October 17, 1936; February 5, 1938.

26. Ibid., July 8, 1939.

27. In addition to the eighteen coauthors, the Bergery declaration received the written endorsement of fifty-one other deputies. Of these, forty-one came from the political Right and twenty-eight from the Left and center-left. For the text of the Bergery declaration, see Jacques de Launay, ed. *Le Dossier de Vichy* (Paris, 1967), 263–67; 291–99.

28. Both notorious Communists.

29. *L'Oeuvre*, February 13, 1941; *France Socialiste*, September 26–27, 1942.

30. *France Socialiste*, February 2, 21, 1942.

31. *L'Oeuvre*, May 8, 1941.

32. *France Socialiste*, January 3–4, 1942.

33. *L'Oeuvre*, January 22, March 4, 1941.

34. Ibid., March 4, 1941.

35. Ibid., September 5, 1941.

36. Ibid., January 22, 1941.

37. *France Socialiste*, July 27, 1942.

38. Frot claimed in the subsequent investigation that he had not in fact ordered police to fire on the rioters. Moreover, it soon became apparent that he had been one of Daladier's ministers who had most strongly urged him to resign, despite his parliamentary majority, faced with violence from the street. Dark rumors—which continue to this day—linked Frot with a murky plot to seize semidictatorial power in France.

39. *France Socialiste*, December 23, 1941; February 10, 1942.

40. *Les Nouveaux Temps*, February 12, 13, 1942.

41. *France Socialiste*, February 13, 1942.

42. He was correct in the narrowest sense. One of the few constraints on Pétain's power was that he could not declare war without convoking and obtaining the consent of parliament.

43. *France Socialiste*, January 20, March 26, July 27, 1942.

44. *L'Effort*, September, 9, 1940. Ruyssen continued to write in *L'Effort*, a frankly collaborationist newspaper, but his articles soon lost their political color and were restricted to technical issues like the problems of European economic and monetary union. See, for example, *L'Effort*, November 6, December 4, 1941.

45. *France Socialiste*, February 21, March 13, 1942. Strictly speaking, Louis Marin, leader of the Catholic conservative Republican Federation had not been much of an advocate for war in the late 1930s, but the point escaped contemporaries—and

subsequent historians—owing to his earlier Germanophobic intransigence. Keril-lis, by contrast, had stood out as one of the few conservative partisans of a strong stand against Germany.

46. *L'Atelier,* July 19, September 13, 20, 27, October 11, 25, November 1, 15, 29, 1941.

47. Ibid., June 26, July 13, 17, 31, August 21, September 4, 18, 1943.

48. André Weil Curiel, *Le Temps de la Honte,* vol. 2 (Paris: 1946), 65–83.

49. *France Socialiste,* August 29–30, September 1, 1942.

50. *Les Nouveaux Temps,* February 11, 1942. Charpentier did not need to spell out the names of the "four Jews" since many of the readers of this left-wing collabora-tionist journal would know that he meant Grumbach, Gombault, Kahn, and Basch.

51. *Les Nouveaux Temps,* 19, 29 July 19, 29, August 28, November 4, 25, 1941. Sig-nificantly, they adopted the Right's very elastic definition of who was a Jew. Jules Moch and Jean Zay were on everyone's list despite the fact that both were Protes-tant, the former a particularly devout one. Jean Zay, however, did have Jewish pater-nal grandparents.

52. *La Flèche,* 28 July 28, 1939.

53. On the degree to which both Vichy and the Resistance shared a common de-sire for a fundamental restructuring of both France and Europe, see Andrew Shen-non, *Rethinking France: plans for renewal* (Oxford, 1989).

54. *France Socialiste,* February 24, March 17, 1943.

55. *France Socialiste,* March 15, 16, 1943.

56. *L'Oeuvre,* March 4, 14, 17, 22, 1943.

57. *France Socialiste,* April 12, 1943.

58. On Henriot's career, see William D. Irvine, *French Conservatism in Crisis* (Baton Rouge, 1979), 201–02, 222–23.

59. *Germinal,* July 28, 1944.

60. On Challaye's postwar career, see Simon Epstein, *Les dreyfusards sous l'Oc-cupation* (Paris, 2001), 30–33.

61. Ibid., chapter 6.

EPILOGUE

1. Epstein, *Les Dreyfusards,* 313.

2. Ibid., 268–69.

3. It is significant that as solid a historian as Jean-Denis Bredin, *L'Affaire* (Paris, 1989), does not mention the activity of the League.

4. *Cahiers,* March-April 1960.

5. Ibid., January-February 1963.

6. Ibid., May 1950.

7. Valin, *La Ligue des droits de l'Homme en Charente-Maritime,* 237, 290; The fig-ure for 1950 is derived from the League's financial statement and dividing total re-ceived in dues by the then fee of 200 francs. *Cahiers,* May 1950.

8. On the experience of the SFIO during and immediately after World War II, see Maurice Sadoun, *Les Socialistes sous l'occupation* (Paris, 1982.) Over half of its pre-

war senators and deputies were excluded from the party with the liberation. There were just under 340,000 party members in 1945.

9. *Cahiers,* January–February 1960.

10. In his memoirs Cancouët claims to have presided over the section for twenty years (Lucien Cancouët, "Mémoires inédit" unpublished typescript in the *Institut d'histoire social,* p. 382). Weexsteen claims that he was president of the section only from 1931–37 ("Fédération de la Seine," 116).

11. Weexsteen, "Fédération de la Seine," 131. In this respect he was the most vocal (of a very vocal federation) after President Jean-Maire Caillaud and the loquacious Georges Pioch.

12. Cancouët, "Mémoires," 382–88. His bitterness undoubtedly reflects the fact that he was excluded for life from union activities for a few low-level contacts with the occupying authorities during Vichy. The judgment was later reversed.

13. *Cahiers,* October–November, 1961.

14. William A. Donohue, *The Politics of the American Civil Liberties Union* (New Brunswick, NJ, 1985), 132–39.

15. Aryeh Neier, *Defending My Enemy* (New York, 1979), 72.

16. Donohue, *Politics,* 158–59; Samuel Walker, *In Defense of American Liberties: A History of the ACLU* (Carbondale, 1999), 136–49.

17. Donohue, *Politics,* 138.

18. Ibid., 164.

19. Ibid., 175–88; Walker, *In Defense,* 193. There remains some dispute to this day as to how widespread such practices were; see Neier, *Defending,* 73.

20. The resignations, impressive in absolute numbers, represented only about 15 percent of the membership. Neier, *Defending,* 79.

21. Ibid., 77–78.

22. Witness the obvious, and justified, pride with which Neier, past president of the ACLU, treats the episode.

23. William H. McIlhany, *The ACLU on Trial* (Arlington, 1976), 155.

24. Neier, *Defending,* 87.

Bibliography

Archival Sources

The most useful archival source for the study of the League is its remaining archives, conserved since 2002 at the *Bibliothèque de documentation internationale contemporaine*. The archives are very uneven; there is virtually nothing concerning the pre-1914 period and very little concerning the internal life of the League before the early 1930s. But at least for the latter period there is very rich documentation concerning the life and activities of the League's sections and federations (notably cartons 132–84). Issues arising out of wartime justice are amply documented (cartons 195–237, 496–546) as are issues of peacetime justice (cartons 457–95)

The reports to the Ministry of the Interior F7 13086-13089 in the Archives Nationales contain some useful information on the League, notably for the period 1916–18.

Published Primary Sources

Indispensable are the League's house organs, *Le Bulletin officiel de la Ligue des droits de l'homme* (1902–20) and *Les Cahiers des droits de l'homme* (1920–39). Both contain a wealth of (very candid) information about all aspects of the internal life of the League. The *Bulletin* usually published a stenographic record of the League's annual congresses; in 1916 and after 1921 they were published as separate volumes.

The local press of the League's many sections and federations provides considerable insight into how the League operated at the grassroots level. Consulted were:

Bulletin de la section mâconnaise
Bulletin de la fédération de la Nièvre
Bulletin mensuel de la section de Boulogne-sur-Mer
Bulletin mensuel de la section de Vincennes
Bulletin trimestriel de la fédération de la Seine-et-Marne
Les Droits de l'homme, Bulletin de la fédération des Ardennes
Les Droits de l'homme, Organe mensuel de la fédération du Calvados
Les Droits de l'homme, Bulletin mensuel de la fédération de la Charente-Inférieure
Les Droits de l'homme, Bulletin trimestriel de la fédération de l'Eure-et-Loire
Les Droits de l'homme, Bulletin de la fédération de l'Isère
Les Droits de l'homme, Organe fédéral de la Mayenne
Les Droits de l'homme, Organe mensuel de la fédération de la Meurthe-et-Moselle
Les Droits de l'homme, Bulletin de la fédération du Morbihan

Les Droits de l'homme, Bulletin de la fédération du Puy-de-Dome
Les Droits de l'homme, Bulletin de la Ligue Stéphanoise
L'Equité
Germinal, Bulletin official de la fédération de l'Allier
La Ligue, Bulletin trimestriel de la fédération de Saône-et-Loire
La Ligue, Organe officiel de la section de Saintes
La Ligue de Caen
La Ligue française, Bulletin trimestriel de la section de Gueret
La Ligue d'Orléans
La Ligue des droits de l'homme, Bulletin de la fédération d'Indre-et-Loire
Ligue des droits de l'homme, Bulletin de la fédération de la Drôme
Ligue des droits de l'homme, Bulletin trimestriel de la fédération de la Gironde
Notre Action, Bulletin mensuel de la fédération de l'Aisne

Secondary Sources

Until recently there has been relatively little scholarly work on the League. A welcome exception is the special issue of *Le Mouvement Social* (no. 183, April–June 1998) dedicated to the League that offers a glimpse into the future contributions of a younger generation of French scholars. In a class by itself, and an indispensable reference work, is the doctoral dissertation of Wendy Ellen Perry ("Remembering Dreyfus: the Ligue des Droits de l'Homme and the Making of the Modern French Human Rights Movement, University of North Carolina at Chapel Hill, 1998). Not only is the thesis itself a pioneering work on the League leadership but appended to it is an exhaustive biographical dictionary of all 204 members of the League's central committee from 1898 until 1945. Another important contribution is the doctoral dissertation of Cyvie Claveau ("L'Autre dans les Cahiers des Droits de l'homme, 1920–1940: Une sélection universaliste de l'altérité à La Ligue des Droits de l'homme et du Citoyen en France, McGill University, 2000). It contains a spirited and well-documented critique of the League's leadership and its inability to relate to "the other," as well as a rigorous analysis of the sociology and political leanings of the League's leadership cadres. Antoine Weexsteen provides a thorough, if conventional, account of the League's powerful federation of the Seine ("La fédération de la Seine de la Ligue des droits de l'homme, 1926–1939," mémoire de maîtrise d'histoire, Université de Paris, 1993). Claire Lescoffit has recently produced an important study of women and the League ("Les Femmes, les feminisms et la ligue des droits de l'homme entre 1914 et 1940." Mémoire de maitrise d'histoire, Université d"evry Val-'Essonne, 2005).

Index